CREDIT AND COLLECTIONS

CREDIT AND COLLECTIONS
A Practical Guide

RICK STEPHAN HAYES

CBI Publishing Company, Inc.
51 Sleeper Street
Boston, Massachusetts   02210

Library of Congress Cataloging in Publication Data

Hayes, Rick Stephan, 1946 –
   Credit and collections : a practical guide.

   Includes bibliographical references and index.
   1. Credit. 2. Credit management. 3. Collecting of accounts. I. Title.
HF5566.H38   658.8'8   77-20141
ISBN 0-8436-0753-X

Printed in the United States of America

Printing *(last digit):* 9 8 7 6 5 4 3 2

Contents

List of Figures

List of Tables

List of Sample Letters

Acknowledgments

I would like to thank Juanice Cartwright Hayes, Charles Edward Hayes, and Nancy Raffaelli Richards for helping me through another book.

I would also like to thank the people who helped me get this book to its final states: Nico Van den Heuvel — illustrations; Kathlene McGrory — initial editing; Kathy Rogers — typing; Bill Boggs — second appendix; and Mike Hamilton — my former editor, who gave me the idea for the book.

I would also like to thank Don Wallace, Nelson Saulter, and Roland Faucher of Security Pacific Bank, and Robert Modell of Wells Fargo Bank, all of whom gave me tremendous assistance.

Introduction:
The Aim Is
Understanding

This is a book about credit and collections, translated from the hypothetical to the real. It is dedicated to making the understanding of credit and collections not only easy, but enjoyable.

Unfortunately, most written material on credit and collections tends to look like the U.S. Tax Code. You know what it says, but what does it mean? Since a degree is not necessary to *give* credit, why should you need one to *read* about credit?

Where possible, this book shows graphic illustrations of complex procedures and systems. The flow charts and graphs take you through all the steps of a credit and collection procedure without losing track of the initial procedures or missing the end product.

This book does not profess to be a legal book or a complete treatise on the legal issues discussed.

This book is primarily concerned with *commercial credit* — credit between businesses — not retail or *consumer* credit. The first chapter briefly discusses retail and consumer credit because everyone should be aware of it, but this book is basically for *business-to-business* credit.

Chapter 2 discusses how to set up and implement a credit policy, including department organization, customer classification, and lines of credit.

Credit information services like Dun and Bradstreet and how to use them are discussed in Chapter 3. The credit manager usually has to report the status of his department to management, so I have included in Chapter 4 what information is required, how to calculate the ratios, and how to report (including a sample report).

Chapters 5 and 6 are a detailed analysis (nonfinancial and financial) of a customer to determine creditworthiness. Appendix A includes a program for a programmable calculator that makes doing the complex credit ratios of Chapter 6 as easy as pressing a button.

Credit letters are an everyday part of collection procedures. Chapter 7 shows the credit manager how to use letters that are psychologically effective.

Chapters 8 and 9 cover the problems of slow-paying and delinquent customers from the first collection letter to declared bankruptcy. Since legal remedies like bankruptcy are sometimes of the utmost importance to credit managers, great care was taken to make these chapters readable. So that the credit manager can avoid unnecessary hassles, Chapter 10 is devoted to the methods used to avoid legal entanglements.

The business world today is no longer concerned with sales only in the United States. More and more American businesses of every size are selling their products abroad. Chapter 11 explains international credit and collections, again using flow charts to simplify complex shipping and financing arrangements.

The use of computers for business in general, and credit and collections in particular, is growing at an astonishing pace. The principal reason for this is that the price of computers today is dropping as fast as the prices of calculators fell a few years ago. For the first time in history a business can buy a $10,000 computer that has the same power a million dollar computer had just ten years ago. Computers can perform a good part of the day-to-day clerical functions, leaving the credit manager and assistant time to do more creative analysis work and to concentrate on major areas within the department. Chapter 12 discusses these new computers as well as good manual systems for credit departments. Continuing in this vein, Appendix B shows a full-scale computer program used for credit and collections that you can put into your computer and start using tomorrow with no programming knowledge.

CREDIT AND COLLECTIONS

1

Credit: The Art of Letting Other People Use Your Money

It might strike you as odd to think that extending credit to people who buy your merchandise is comparable to loaning them your money. But, in fact, that is what you are doing. When you sell merchandise to a customer, you have already laid out a sizable amount of money on that merchandise, whether you bought it or manufactured it. Therefore, the people to whom you extend credit are using your money. It is similar to a loan with interest, the loan in your case being the money you paid for the merchandise, and the interest in the loan being the profit you tack on to your cost of goods when you sell them.

Put in this perspective, the key question in considering your customer's request for merchandise is, "Should I loan my money to this company for 30 plus days?" Merchandise is money so why not look at it that way.

Of course, all business is a gamble and loaning or investing money is one of the biggest risks in business. How much you want to risk will determine whether your collection policies are liberal or conservative. Learning to minimize the risk of extending credit is the main purpose of this book.

Before we get into credit techniques and policies, it is important to review several things: credit in our world in general (business and personal); some of the terms used in the art of credit extension; the underlying basis of credit; and how people (you, your employees, and your customers) fit into the mix.

THE CREDIT YOU GET PERSONALLY

Types of Personal Credit

There are three types of personal credit: service credit, retail (merchandise) credit, and loan credit.

We have all encountered service credit. This is the credit we get from dentists, doctors, attorneys, and other professionals. If the professional is someone with whom we have an ongoing relationship, they will usually bill us for their services.

Retail credit falls into three categories: installment plan, regular charge account, and revolving charge. With a regular charge account, you charge the merchandise and pay within 20 to 30 days after you are billed. With a revolving charge, the charge is not paid in full within this period but is converted into what amounts to a long-term loan that is paid back in monthly installments.

Charge customers, according to the transcripts of the 1967 Bank Credit Card Conference at Loyola University, Chicago, represent 60 percent of a department store's sales volume. Their average purchases are of a higher dollar amount and are more frequent than the cash customers'. The major advantage of charge cards to customers is that it allows *float* time. They may buy a Christmas present on December 15, for example, be billed on January 1, but have until January 20 to pay the charge.

Installment plans resemble revolving charges in that the charge can be paid off over a certain period of time. Installment plans are different, however, in that they require a down payment and the merchandise is secured by a legal instrument (a note). Installment plans involve the purchase of one item to be paid for over a long period in equal installments.

Personal loans differ from other consumer credit in two ways. Cash is advanced instead of goods, and credit is extended by banks, consumer finance companies, credit unions, and savings and loan companies. Rather than retail goods or services, personal loans are usually for purchases of expensive items such as homes, home improvements, motor vehicles, and furniture.

Criteria for Extending Credit

Personal resources and employment are the best criteria for granting credit, but there are also other, more subtle criteria that people may look at in a credit extension position.

Wealth and accumulated resources are the prime factors in determining the basis for credit. The feeling is that people of substance pay promptly and also buy in large volume. The extent of a person's wealth, as represented by real estate, stocks, bonds, and profits from business, is an indicator of capital position and ability to pay. Wages, salary, or regular remuneration indicate capacity as well as ability to repay the person extending credit.

Earned income has a high rating in considering a credit application. Income from investments or from a successful business is well rated, while income of an irregular nature is considered undesirable. Outgo and expenses of home operation are considered at all times. In addition, earned income of a family is considered together with prior pay habits, size of family, and whether or not the wage earner is living within his or her income.

Occupation is important because certain classes of occupations are better risks than others. Length of employment and the likelihood of its permanence are also used in determining the risk. A seasonal worker with a high salary when employed is not considered as good a credit risk as a worker who is employed 52 weeks a year with a lower income.

Home ownership is considered a mark of stability and permanence. The applicant who rents is not likely to have the same desirable credit standing as the home owner. People owning small- or medium-priced homes without heavy mortages are usually considered good credit risks.

The length of time in which the applicant has lived at one address is considered. The person who has lived for several years at the same place is considered a better prospect for credit than the one who has moved several times during a short period of time.

Table 1.1 illustrates the estimated loss a retailer can expect on an account allowed to remain unpaid over a specific period of time.

TABLE 1.1
Estimated Loss on Unpaid Loans

Length of Time Account Allowed to Remain Unpaid	Percentage Loss That Can Be Expected
3 months	10
4 months	14
5 months	19
6 months	37
1 year	58
2 years	74
3 years	83
5 years	Usually 100

J. Gordon Dakans, *Retail Credit Manual* (National Retail Dry Goods Association, New York, 1950).

Laws for the Consumer

One recent consumer law is the Fair Credit Billing Act of 1975. This act is designed to protect the consumer against unfair billing practices of people who extend retail credit for the purchase of goods. This act does not apply to consumer loans or any business credit. The rights afforded by this act include:

1. If a consumer sends a written complaint to a retailer about merchandise or billing, the merchant must acknowledge the letter within 30 days and settle it within 90 days. The merchant loses all credit claims up to $50 if he does not meet these deadlines.
2. Merchants charging goods to the wrong account (yours), receipt of shoddy merchandise from the merchant, and claims that merchandise was not repaired properly are all considered legitimate claims against the merchants, and must be acted on in the period of time discussed above.
3. No interest charges on late payments may be made by the merchant and no consumer account can be closed for nonpayment during the dispute period.

4. Banks cannot take charges out of customers' regular bank accounts if there is a dispute about the charge bill, even for parts of the monthly statement not being questioned.
5. Interestingly enough, the same law allows merchants to grant up to a 5 percent discount to people who pay cash and choose not to use credit.

The Fair Credit Report Act of 1971 (Title VI of the Consumer Credit Protection Act) is designed to protect consumers, who are applying for credit, from improper distribution or statement of consumer credit information and from unfair treatment when buying on consumer credit. This act does not apply to business credit, only to consumer credit. The act gives consumers the following rights:

1. You have the right to be told the name and address of the consumer reporting agency responsible for preparing a consumer report that was used to deny you credit, employment, or insurance, or that determined the cost of your insurance or credit.
2. You have the right to obtain this information free of charge when you have been denied insurance, employment, or credit within 30 days of your interview.
3. You have the right to be told the nature, substance, and sources of the information collected about you by a consumer reporting agency. The law does not require that the source of investigative reports or medical reports be revealed.
4. You have the right to be told who has received a consumer report on you within the past six months (within two years for an employment report).
5. In most cases, you have the right to have incomplete or incorrect information reinvestigated and, if the information is inaccurate, to have the information removed from the file.
6. The agency must notify all those you name, who have previously received the incorrect or incomplete information, and see that negative information is deleted.
7. You may have a consumer report withheld from anyone who under the law, does not have a legitimate business need for the consumer information.
8. You have the right to sue a company for damages if that company willfully or neglectfully violates the law.
9. Most adverse information about you cannot be reported after seven years (except bankruptcy, 14 years).

You *do not* have a right under the law to request a report on yourself from a consumer reporting agency; to receive a copy of the agency's report or to handle your file physically; to have federal agencies intervene on your behalf.

There are other consumer laws, especially in the various states, but we will not go into them in this book. If you would like to know more about the consumer laws, you can contact your state's bureau of consumer affairs.

Determining the Maximum Amount a Consumer Can Borrow

Before I end this section on personal credit, it might be interesting to note how banks determine the maximum amount a consumer can borrow from them.

There are very few criteria for determining the maximum that can be borrowed. A rule of thumb that a banker gave me is that monthly payments on fixed debt (not including rent) should not exceed 40 percent of your total monthly income. The maximum unsecured loan (no collateral) that a bank will extend to you is up to one month's gross salary, or not more than 15 percent of your total annual income.

Another measure banks use for determining whether or not you can pay them back is how much your discretionary income is. Discretionary income is your total income minus your fixed obligations (such as rent, food, or loan repayment).

THE CREDIT YOUR BUSINESS USES

A business basically has two types of credit, merchandise (or trade) credit and commercial credit (loans and bonds). Trade credit and how to control and extend it is what this book is about. Credit and collection techniques that apply to you when you extend credit also apply to your suppliers when they extend credit to you. We will not discuss this here except to comment on the remarkable growth of trade credit in the past couple of decades.

Total corporate trade notes and accounts receivable grew 449.5 percent between 1951 and 1973. As you can see by Figure 1.1, net working capital grew at 197 percent and inventories grew at 272 percent in the same period.

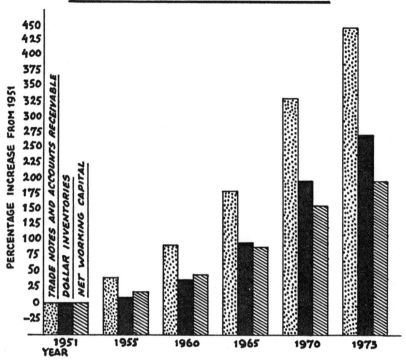

FIGURE 1.1
Growth of Trade Receivables, Inventories, and Net
Working Capital

Different industries follow different credit policies and extend credit as a percentage of total sales in different amounts. In the wholesale trade, for instance, companies who sell oil refinery and pipeline equipment and companies who sell printing and writing paper have the most extensive sales on credit. These industries sell fully 97.7 percent of their goods on credit. On the other hand, wholesalers of beer, wine, and distilled spirits only do about 51 percent of their sales on credit. The percentage of goods sold or credit depends on the particular industry. If you want to find out how much of the sales of your industry are on credit, check with the U.S. Department of Commerce for the latest data.

The other sources of credit available to a business are lenders such as banks, commercial finance companies, and the government. These sources provide loans on equipment, property, accounts receivable, inventories, working capital and unsecured loans. Loans will not be covered in this book; however, I would suggest that you consult my book *Business Loans: A Guide To Money Sources And How To Approach Them Successfully* (CBI Publishing Company, Inc. Boston, MA, 1977).

THE THREE C'S OF CREDIT

Credit managers have the "Three C's" (3 C's) to guide them in their everyday business. A discussion of the 3 C's should appear in every book ever printed on credit, collection, or lending. The 3 C's are: Character, Capacity, and Capital. These words and what they symbolize to credit agents are very important. All borrowers (individual or business) or users of credit are judged by their character, their capacity for running their business and paying back the extender of credit (bank or supplier), and the capital they have invested in their business or will use to pay the creditor.

Character

Character is one of the most important determinants of whether a customer pays a supplier or a borrower pays a bank. However, as Miller and Relkin said: "character defies definition from a theological or philosophical point of view, and is even more difficult to nail down in a business and economic sense."[1] Don Wallace, vice president in the urban credit department of Security Pacific Bank, described character simply as "the way an individual loan officer [credit manager] perceives the customers desire to repay the loan [pay the supplier]. Character is the honest inclination and willingness to pay. If the borrower is obliged he will make every effort to pay." The *Dun and Bradstreet Handbook of Credit and Collections* describes character as

[1]Donald F. Miller and Donald B. Relkin, *Improving Credit Practice.* (American Management Association, 1971).

follows: "Character refers to the sincerity with which a customer undertakes a trade obligation and the determination he will have to see that obligation through."[2]

Take your pick. Sincerity seems to be the key word. Everyone judges character differently. Perhaps it is just that gut feeling you get with experience that the guys who are running the company are the type of people who pay up.

Capacity

Capacity is more objectively measured than character. Capacity is the ability of a company and its management to make good on their commitments. Some companies will really try to pay, but if they do not have the financial and managerial ability to pay, it does not do the credit manager much good. Capacity can be judged by purely objective factors that can be taken from the company's financial statements, your appraisal of their management, and information from credit reporting agencies.

Capital

Capital must be viewed relatively. Adequate capital in one situation will not be adequate in another. A strong company that is growing slowly may have plenty of capital (money) but the same company if it is growing by 50 percent to 200 percent a year might (and probably does) have inadequate working capital. As Miller and Relkin puts it, "Adequacy [of capital] is dependent upon the magnitude of the objectives of the owners."[3] The capital a company has is the financial resources it has at the time it places the order and until the time it pays for it.

Other C's

Three other C's that are sometimes mentioned along with the above 3 C's of credit are coverage, collateral, and conditions. Coverage is the

---

[2]Harold T. Redding and Cuyon H. Knight III, *The Dun and Bradstreet Handbook of Credit and Collections.* (New York: Thomas Y. Crowell, Co., 1974).

[3]Miller and Relkin, *Improving Credit Practice*, p. 316.

insurance a company carries to compensate them for losses. If there is ever a fire at your customer's business that burns up all the inventory you have shipped, you will probably have a hard time collecting even if the company is covered with insurance, because your loss has to be proven. If the company is not covered, you will have an *extremely* difficult time recovering your money. Adequate insurance coverage is a sign of good management policy, and is an important factor in determining whether credit will be extended. A credit agent should think at least twice before extending credit to a customer without insurance.

Collateral includes financial and other resources, such as cash, inventory, and other assets, which a company has to pay its bills. Condition refers to the environment of your customer's industry economically, legally, politically, and with regard to growth.

DEFINITIONS

The following is a series of definitions used in credit practice. We will be using these terms throughout this book and it might be a good idea to glance through them and to remember where they are for future reference. First, in alphabetical order, are some abbreviations (acronyms) commonly used in credit practice:

CBD Cash before delivery.

CIA Cash in advance.

COD Cash on delivery.

EOM End of the month. If a payment is due in the month following shipment, terms could read "Net 15 EOM." A shipment made in June would be due on the fifteenth of the following month, or July 15.

FOB Free on board. This designation means the point at which responsibility for the freight charges and the title passes. If the terms of the contract read "FOB Factory," "FOB Port of Entry," or "FOB Shipping Point" the customer must pay all shipping costs and receives title to the goods at that point, conversely if the terms read "FOB Destination," the supplier pays all shipping and retains title.

ROG Receipt of goods. If a customer specifies "ROG," it means payment will begin the date the goods are received, not from the date the goods were shipped.

As of the twenty-fifth Some customers, in some industries consider that the shipping and billing month end as of the twenty-fourth. If your customer asks to have invoices dated as of the twenty-fifth, it has the effect of asking for an extra 30 days to pay the bill.

Assets That which a company owns including cash, inventory, receivables, equipment, and the building. This will be discussed in more detail in Chapter 6.

Back orders If orders are not shipped in the total amount requested, the balance not shipped is said to be a back order.

Balance sheet Also called (more properly) statement of financial condition. This document shows what a company has in the way of assets, what it owes as liabilities, and the difference between the two, or net worth. Discussed in Chapter 6.

Bill of lading A document issued by the carrier that is evidence of a contract for carriage and delivery of goods and evidence of title to the goods described. A bill of lading indicates the name and address of the one to whom the shipment is sent (the consignee), a description of the goods shipped, and the terms of the shipping contract.

Chargeback The notice used by your customer telling you what he will deduct from payment for shortages, allowances, freight charges, and returns.

Common carrier A company or individual who transports freight. This usually refers to truckers and airlines, but it can also be railroads, freight forwarders, and express companies.

Credit interchange Interchange of information between companies in your industry. The National Association of Credit Management assembles interchange information for credit checking in a given industry.

Credit ratings The classification of accounts by a rating, either numerical, alphabetical, or both, such as the Dun and Bradstreet credit ratings for businesses.

Discount The percentage your customer is permitted to deduct from the invoice total for early payment.

Financial statement Usually refers to the statement of financial condition and the income statement (balance sheet and profit and loss statement).

Income statement The company's statement of sales, costs, and profit, sometimes called the profit and loss statement (see Chapter 6).

Insolvency Inability to pay off debts when they come due. Companies with a negative net worth are technically considered insolvent. Sometimes used as a synonym for bankrupt and for the situation in which total assets are less than total debts.

Invoices The itemized bills for merchandise that is shipped. They state the total cost and the unit cost. They are either included with the shipment or mailed.

Liabilities What a company owes including payables and notes (see Chapter 6).

Line of credit The amount of money you are willing to let a customer owe you at a given time including invoices, merchandise in transit, new orders, and unfilled approved orders in-house.

Manifest List of the stores being shipped to, especially different stores in a chain being shipped to from one central point. This originally meant a list of goods shipped.

Marginal accounts Businesses with weak credit ratings or a questionable future. Credit managers who ship to marginal accounts watch these customers closely.

Net The full amount that your customer must pay.

Open terms Selling on credit rather than cash terms. The quantity the customer can order is generally limited to a maximum dollar amount line of credit.

Pro forma Latin for as a matter of form. A projection or something made in advance of an official document. If you prepare a financial statement that shows how your sales and expenses will be a year from now, this is a pro forma financial statement.

Proof of delivery A signed receipt indicating the date of delivery to the consignee.

Profit and loss statement Same as an income statement (see Chapter 6).

Requirements account Companies that you deem eligible for any amount of credit they require.

Shipping memo or packing slip This is a detailed listing of the goods shipped to your customer. Style, product names, colors, and sizes appear on the memo, as well as order number, packing marks, and department number.

Statement of financial condition Also called the balance sheet (see Chapter 6).

Working capital Technically defined as the current assets minus the current liabilities, but it basically means the money available for accounts payable (the money owed to the supplier).

THE HUMAN ELEMENT IN COLLECTIONS

There has never been a system designed that eliminates the human element in extending credit and collecting on the goods shipped. A fully computerized system can keep track of orders, perform credit analyses, and send out statements, but it cannot make the judgment concerning who should get credit and how much over what period of time. Credit policy is determined by the people who run the company, and the workability of the policy depends on how people carry these policies out. This and the everyday operation of the system should be kept in mind when making policy.

The word *credit* is from the Latin *credere* which means "to believe or trust." This by itself suggests the human element of credit. Can you believe or trust the judgment of a machine or a rigid system? Credit policy should be flexible enough to let the human spirit trickle through.

The art of gathering credit data and extending or collecting credit is a face-to-face business in the sense that you are really dealing with *other people*, not companies.

2

A Look at Your Credit Policy

The biggest problem for some companies with regard to credit policy is that they have none. Many small businesses are so busy growing that they let their sales staff determine who is qualified for credit. Because of sales representatives' vested interest (a commission), they are a poor choice as your sole source of credit judgment, though a *good* sales person can be a factor in securing outside information for you. Many people in business just set limited criteria for controlling credit: perhaps the owner knows personally (or from past experience) that certain companies create more headaches than profit.

Credit policy may be a written (preferably) or an oral understanding on the part of the credit manager or chief executive. Whatever the form of your credit policies, they should have certain characteristics. Policies should be general enough to apply to a variety of common situations; extend over long periods of time; and provide basic definitions and a basic outlook for a company. A credit policy should balance company

goals of increasing sales, profits, and prestige with credit goals of protecting the corporation's (or business') assets, recovering accounts receivable, and assuring profit. Credit policy should have specific direc-
tives for collections (when to start, when to transfer, and what procedures to follow), especially concerning:

> Payments that anticipate the due date
> Slow-paying accounts
> Bad debts
> Lines of credit
> Cut-off dates
> Unearned discounts
> Incoming orders
> Marginal accounts

All these items and problems will be discussed in greater detail later.
Collecting on slow accounts is covered fully in Chapters 8 and 9.

CREDIT POLICY — CONSERVATIVE OR LIBERAL

Credit policy for a given company, depending on its size, industry, and
management preference, will be either conservative or liberal. If a company is conservative, it is restrictive in granting credit both in the degree
of risk and in the amount it is willing to accept. A conservative company
requires a detailed investigation of every company before it makes a
credit decision. A company with a liberal policy is usually lenient in
giving credit in amount and degree of risk. Liberal companies require
little or no investigation of highly-rated companies and minimal investigation of marginal accounts up to a given limit.

Figure 2.1 is a continuum graph of the industry and economic conditions that could influence your credit decisions or policymaking.

Of course, your credit policy must be flexible, and the conditions of
the economy, your company, and the industry will change from time to
time. When a majority of the conservative conditions exist (there is no
competition, high demand, small volume, low inventory, and a small
profit margin) you would do best to keep your policy conservative. You
should investigate the applicants for credit thoroughly and be very
selective about which companies you allow to buy from you. If conditions (stiff competition, low demand, high volume, excess inventory,
and large profit margins) that prevail indicate a liberal credit policy, it is
best to be less selective and critical.

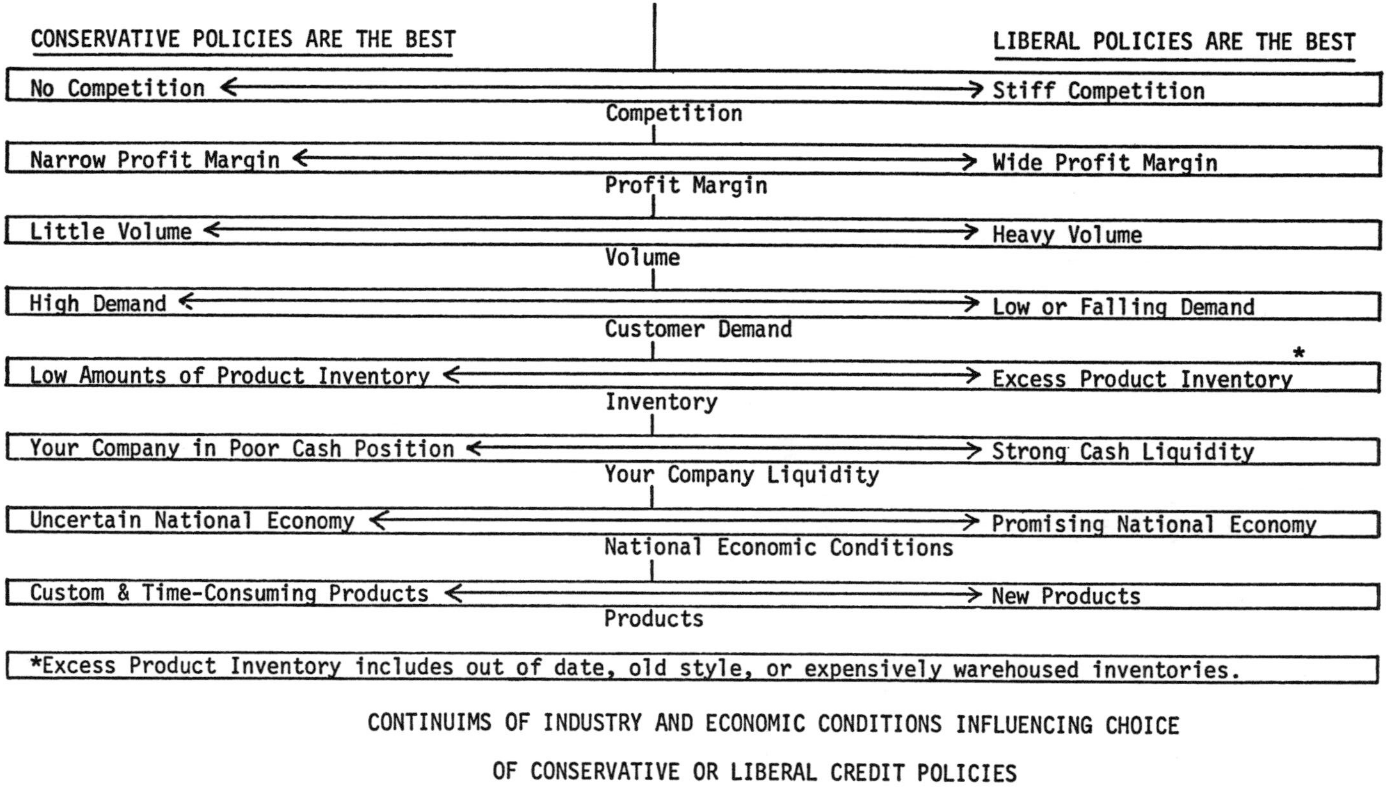

CONSERVATIVE POLICIES ARE THE BEST   LIBERAL POLICIES ARE THE BEST

Competition
No Competition →←→ Stiff Competition

Profit Margin
Narrow Profit Margin →←→ Wide Profit Margin

Volume
Little Volume →←→ Heavy Volume

Customer Demand
High Demand →←→ Low or Falling Demand

Inventory
Low Amounts of Product Inventory →←→ Excess Product Inventory *

Your Company Liquidity
Your Company in Poor Cash Position →←→ Strong Cash Liquidity

National Economic Conditions
Uncertain National Economy →←→ Promising National Economy

Products
Custom & Time-Consuming Products →←→ New Products

*Excess Product Inventory includes out of date, old style, or expensively warehoused inventories.

CONTINUUMS OF INDUSTRY AND ECONOMIC CONDITIONS INFLUENCING CHOICE

OF CONSERVATIVE OR LIBERAL CREDIT POLICIES

FIGURE 2.1
Continuums of Industry and Economic Conditions Influencing Choice of Conservative or Liberal Credit Policies

Besides prevailing economic and industry conditions, there are other factors that influence your credit policies. Conservative policies are more time consuming than liberal policies and this should be taken into consideration. The larger the order, the more conservative should be your policy, because it will be very costly to make a credit judgment error on a large account. If the orders are small, your policy might be more liberal. Some industries are known to be greater risks than others. Retailers represent a greater credit risk than wholesalers, and wholesalers are a greater credit risk than manufacturers. In a given industry (such as retail) different types of businesses have different risks. For example in retailing, the highest failure rate is among retailers of farm implements. In manufacturing, manufacturers of transportation equipment have a much higher failure rate than stone, clay, and glass manufacturers. Figure 2.2 shows relative failure rates of types of retailers and manufacturers in different industries.

Since costs of your operation are directly related to the amount of time your employees have to spend on a given project, and since too much cost can erode your profit margin, it is important to remember that the more conservative your credit policy, the more expensive the costs.

ORGANIZATION OF CREDIT POLICY

One of the first considerations of whether your company's credit policy should be written or not is whether the policy can be understood orally. Credit policy does not have to be written out to be effective, but there are certain advantages to a written policy:

1. Written policy requires the policywriters to think very thoroughly about the procedures and problems of credit policy.
2. It provides a written resource for employees.
3. It makes a precise working tool and eliminates the need to rely on memory alone.
4. It provides a good basis for the regular review of credit operations.
5. It provides a norm of acceptance for the credit manager to apply against any exceptional cases.

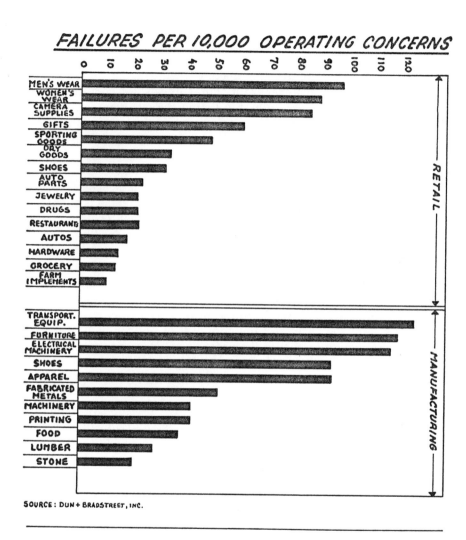

FIGURE 2.2
Failures per 10,000 Operating Concerns

Organization of credit decision making, either written or nonwritten, is very important for all companies so that decisions can be fast, accurate, and routine enough for even new employees. Routinization of credit decision making results in greater employee efficiency and better customer service.

The first step in credit decision making is the organization of information gathering and customer evaluation. This can be accomplished by setting up a chronological index file listing the customers evaluated each month. The files should be arranged so that the customer's name appears twice: once a month as a reminder that requested financial or other information should be obtained; and again as a reminder for the next month that indicates analysis should be undertaken.

Organization of credit approval is also very important, especially for first orders. If your company processes many small orders, it is cheapest to establish an upper limit in dollar amounts for each company and automatically ship all orders up to that limit. Approval can also be based on a Dun and Bradstreet (or other commercial source) appraisal or rating of the company (discussed in detail in Chapter 3). When your company receives an unusually large order exceeding the limit set for your customer or unwarranted by credit agencies' appraisals and ratings, the credit agent should decide what to do according to the following criteria: Does the size of the order and the appraisal of the company warrant further investigation or should the order be rejected outright? Should the customer be extended credit on special terms (such as trade acceptance, to be discussed shortly), accepted as a marginal risk, or given full credit as a result of an investigation?

For repeat orders, the credit department must develop two standard procedures: setting credit limits and determining authorization procedures. A line of credit should be set up for the customer on the first order, a procedure discussed later in this chapter. Credit lines should be based on the amount of credit possible considering the strength of your customer and your own company and the size of the individual order. The authorization procedure for handling repeat orders is usually done by having accounts receivable ledger cards (or records) made for each customer. The purpose of these cards is to show the balance owing by any customer at a given time as well as what and when the most recent order was entered. New orders are checked against these accounts receivable ledger cards to see if they are within the credit limit. If the order is in excess of the credit limit, the limit may be reevaluated or rejected outright.

It is important for a well-organized credit policy to be backed up by information recording and filing systems. A good information (data) recording and filing system should include credit forms; various subject, customer, and sectional files; and a reliable credit library. Credit forms should include credit terms notices, customer summary cards (indicating summary or economic transactions with your company and credit line limit), financial statement forms, and form letters for various usages (see Chapter 7).

Files for your credit department should include, at least, a file of customer ledger cards (or books). This file can be broken down any number of ways, such as alphabetically, by product, division, or number. Every company should also have a file on each customer encompassing all information about the customer including credit reports, correspondence, and analysis worksheets. In companies with just a few customers, all material on one subject for all customers may be kept in one folder. Your company might also consider other special-purpose files, such as a summary file containing basic credit information about each customer to be used for initial screening of incoming orders.

A credit library is a library of various source books on industry information such as Dun and Bradstreet publications, or industry or trade information, including trade magazines.

If for some reason you are just starting a system for gathering credit information and establishing a credit policy, or if you need a refresher course on credit basics, I suggest you consider aging accounts receivable.

DISCOVERING THE STATUS OF YOUR CREDIT
BY AGING ACCOUNTS RECEIVABLE

Aging accounts receivable (sometimes merely called "aging") is not only the most widely used method of checking on collection needs and results, but is also the most effective and essential. Aging accounts receivable is merely the process of listing open accounts to see how long it has been since an order was invoiced: one month or less, two months (overdue accounts), three months, over three months, and so on. This can be done manually by merely stacking all invoices one month old in one pile, two months in another, three months in a third, or by using a written analysis as in Table 2.1.

TABLE 2.1
Sample Aging of Receivables

Account	Invoice	1 Mo.	2 Mos.	Age 3 Mos.	Over 3 Mos.
ABC Manufacturing	1218				$1,213
	1220			$2,318	
	1228			5,700	
	1236		$ 300		
Dixie Distribution	1233		1,450		
	1236	$3,344			
	1247	4,112			
Tomtree Manufacturing	1241	9,000			
	1248	4,000			
TOTALS		$20,456	$1,750	$8,018	$1,213

As you can see from Table 2.1, aging not only tells you who owes what for how long but also gives you the totals for the periods. The aging schedule also tells you the number of customers in each category (period) and the amount (and percentage) of your dangerously past due accounts. Agings should be taken at least once a month. You will want to focus your attention immediately on those accounts that owe a lot of money over a long period of time.

CLASSIFICATION OF ACCOUNTS ACCORDING TO CREDIT RISK

Another technique that will help you in determining your credit policy and in making processing easier is the classification of accounts according to risk. Classification of your customer is a fast and efficient method for processing many credit orders. Classifications of customer according to risk fall into four major categories: automatic (first class, prime, or high-rated) account; semiautomatic (second-class risk, "basically sound, but . . . ") account; the nonautomatic (average to marginal) account; and the marginal (poor to doubtful) account.

Automatic Accounts

Automatic accounts are your customers with the highest financial ratings. These are usually the biggest companies in an industry who historically have proved both a willingness and an ability to pay. These accounts are called *automatic* because they can be automatically approved with little further information. Automatic accounts require no investigation of amount, past dues, or credit-rating checks before processing an order. If this type of account does not pay, it could very well be clerical errors of either your or their employees, not the company itself. However, caution must be taken since any size account should be subject to reevaluation if there is a potential for loss and a trend to slower paying habits.

Semiautomatic Accounts

Semiautomatic accounts are high-rated accounts that should be processed automatically when they order an amount within their credit limit. If they want to order beyond this limit, the credit manager must decide whether accepting the risk or rejecting the account is justified under the terms of your company's credit policy and its financial strength. If orders are over the credit limit it might be a good idea to check with your sales department to see if the orders were solicited or unsolicited and if the customer might have eliminated another supplier and is giving you more orders. You might also check with credit agencies.

Nonautomatic Accounts

Nonautomatic customers are long-term customers who order infrequently, new customers who are established but not known to you, and new customers who are just starting business. Other nonautomatic customers have one of the following characteristics: unstable finances, a poor payment record, or decreasing or negative profits. If you have one of these customers, their orders must be carefully reviewed by some or all of the techniques covered in this book. These nonautomatic accounts can be very profitable to your company if the credit judgment is reliable. Generally, these accounts can be shipped to if they are not in serious financial difficulty.

Marginal Accounts

Marginal accounts are those accounts that run the spectrum from companies that are deteriorating financially or have incompetent management, to companies you are unable to get financial information on, to companies running several months late in their payments. This may mean a top-rated company that makes a habit of slow pay. Marginal companies could have one or more of the following characteristics: unsatisfactory finances; poor to bad payment record; incompetent management; unwillingness to provide credit information; inadequate working capital; legal or tax problems; continuing losses from operations or declining sales; or a drastic change in management. Trading with doubtful accounts is carried out with the expectation of bad-debt losses. In fact, the possibility of such loss is great enough that you should try to persuade these customers to buy on special terms, described later in this chapter. These accounts should be taken on open-book terms only if your company, because of the prevailing industrial or economic reasons mentioned earlier, has a very liberal credit policy. These accounts with special terms might be profitable for your company, but be careful.

Since the most important thing any company can do, regardless of size or industry, is to *create customers*, it is crucial that your company credit policy be geared to new accounts.

ACCEPTING NEW ACCOUNTS

Taking on new accounts is the way a business grows. If a company accepts no new accounts, its growth would certainly stagnate. However, accepting new orders always implies an element of risk. It is the job of the credit analyst to minimize this risk while maximizing his company's growth potential.

One of the best ways to assure a good credit risk on a new order is to conduct a thorough financial and nonfinancial analysis of the new company. This is not always possible, however. Therefore, if the amount of the order is relatively small, the applicant's business is well-known, or if the applicant's company is willing to accept COD or other special terms, little checking need be done. In most cases, however, a more thorough credit check enhances your collection efforts.

Perhaps the most difficult new accounts are from those companies that are just starting up in business. The following list of questions about the new business account should help your judgment.

1. What was the initial investment of the owners in the company?
2. What are the company's total assets, and how much of the assets are secured by loans on equipment?
3. What equipment or other fixed assets are secured?
4. How much initial inventory does the company require from you?
5. What are the company's projected sales over the next year?
6. What kind of legal organization does the company have (corporation, partnership, or sole proprietorship) and who are the principals?
7. What is the business experience of the principals?
8. Is the company's management experienced in this line of business?
9. What does the company's balance sheet look like?

Many of the answers to these questions can be taken from the company's balance sheet (Chapter 6), credit information sources such as Dun and Bradstreet (Chapter 3), nonfinancial techniques of analysis (Chapter 5), or by questioning the principals or purchasing manager of the company.

Of all the factors considered in these questions, perhaps the most crucial is that of the owner's experience. According to an SBA study, *The First Two Years: Small Firm Growth and Survival Problems*, one of the strongest determinants of new business success is the previous business experience of the owners and management especially in the same line. Previous business *ownership* of a similar business is the strongest indicator of successful management and firm survival.

Also, generally speaking, the more money a firm is capitalized with, the better the chance of success. This is especially true with regard to the amount of the owner's cash investment. Firms with large cash investment by an owner (capital, stock, or net worth on the balance sheet) reveal an owner's risk in the business — the greater the personal risk, the greater the desire and willingness to see that the firm is successful.

Besides gathering information on new accounts and analyzing that information, the most important element in accepting new accounts is the task of setting credit limits.

SETTING CREDIT LIMITS

Confusion sometimes exists about the distinction between *credit limits* and *credit lines*. For our purposes, however, there is no distinction between these terms; they are synonymous. Credit limits are the maximum amounts of credit a supplier will grant a customer automatically.

There are several advantages to using credit limits: (1) they expedite collections and cut costs by utilizing personnel time for more difficult accounts; (2) many orders can be approved automatically; (3) managers are released from day-to-day credit decisions so that they can devote their attention to policy matters and difficult cases; (4) cut costs of personnel because of the time and effort (not to mention paperwork) saved; (5) cut costs because they restrict the number of marginal risks your company takes; and (6) prohibit shipments the value of which exceed the limit and force the customer to make a payment first or request a credit line increase.

The disadvantages of using credit limits are the possibility of overextending or underextending credit and the possibility of offending customers. If the methods used to set the credit limit are false, the possibility exists that too much credit will be extended to a risky customer or a good business may be turned away due to a line of credit set too low for a solid customer. Some customers, of course, will be offended by any amount of credit they are allotted or the fact that you are restricting their purchases at all. Most good credit managers inform the customer that the line has been set at a given amount and indicate that if the client requires a higher line of credit the matter will be reviewed. Suggest that the customer supply further financial data to support a review. This helps solve the problem of offending a customer.

Realistically, the customer should be informed of established credit limits as it prevents misunderstanding, may promote sales, and does offer a chance for the customer to discuss the matter with the credit manager. That informing the customer of his credit line avoids misunderstanding is obvious. It is unlikely that your customer will request orders greater than the line of credit extended without first talking to the credit manager. If the credit limit is higher than requested or expected, the customer may be inclined to buy more and more often from your company. Credit limits will immediately inform you of any change in your customer's buying habits if orders exceeding the limit come in regularly. This gives you a good opportunity to talk with the customer about the firm's growth. When you inform your customer of the credit limit, it is also an opportune time to build goodwill toward your own company.

The disadvantage of informing your customer of a credit limit, aside from any personal offense that may be taken with the limit, is that it might discourage prompt payments. If a customer knows what the credit limit is, he may buy up to that limit and delay payment until additional orders are placed. This disadvantage can only be overcome by a favorable personal relationship of the customer with the credit manager, by a strong collection policy, or both.

Credit limits are not set in concrete. They should be used as guides. Orders that exceed the credit limit should not be rejected automatically. The credit department should investigate whether the customer's condition warrants a higher limit or whether the sale might be made on some special terms. Furthermore, credit limits should be revised regularly to take into account the changes that are inevitable with every business. It is best to set credit limits for only a limited period, usually one year or six months.

Factors Influencing the Setting of Credit Limits

There are several factors that influence the amount of credit you extend to your customers; some include the conditions of your company and some concern themselves with the strength of your customer's company. Factors involving your company and the industry include the profit margin of your company, size of your company, amount of competition in the industry, the effectiveness of your collection efforts, and your company's sales policy. If your company's profit margin is large, you can afford a greater risk and higher credit limits. On the other hand, if your profit margin is small, your credit limits should be lower. If yours is a well-financed, large company, you can afford more risk and higher credit limits. If your competitors are extending high credit limits to customers, your company must, to a certain degree, be competitive. If your effectiveness in collecting past-due accounts is high, higher credit limits can be risked. If your company is introducing new products or new territories, credit limits will be higher.

The customer factors that influence the amount of credit are: the financial health of your customer, your customer's inventory needs, and the length of terms the customer requires. Of paramount interest in setting credit limits is, of course, the financial health (strength) of the customer. The stronger the customer's company is financially, the higher the credit limits you can set. Next in importance to the customer's ability to pay is a consideration of how much the customer needs. Credit limits should be commensurate with customer need. Since the longer the terms of credit, the greater the risk, your credit limit for each customer should be proportionate to the length of time allowed before repayment.

Most credit limits are set on the amount of the total outstanding balance a customer is allowed to accumulate. You might also decide to put a limit on the size of the order. Limiting order size would be most useful in cases where a customer is ordering from multiple points. Small orders received in great quantity at many different shipping points should be restricted with regard to number.

Choosing and Setting Credit Limits

Some of the methods you should choose for setting credit limits include analysis of financial statements of the customer (Chapter 6), the overall analysis (Chapters 5 and 6), and credit agency ratings, bank, trade and other information (Chapter 3). Although these criteria will be discussed in detail in later chapters, I will briefly comment on them here.

A credit manager can set a credit limit based on his analysis of a customer's financial statement. On a simplified basis, this would mean a credit limit for 5, 10, or 15 percent, (depending on the business and the prevailing conditions) of the customer's net worth shown on the balance sheet. Some credit managers set a credit line as a percentage of working capital of the customer. In a more complex form, credit limits are assigned on the basis of financial statement analysis using financial ratios and analysis of all elements of a financial statement.

An overall account analysis is the most time-consuming of the various methods, but many times may be required to make a logical credit judgment. An overall analysis involves financial statement, historical, environmental, and character analyses. This method, of course, is usually reserved for the most difficult and complex accounts.

Many credit managers set credit limits on the basis of credit agency ratings. For example, customers with a high rating, such as a Dun and

Bradstreet rating of 5A1, would be supplied with whatever they required as an automatic account. Customers with a lower rating, for example, DD2, would receive a credit limit of $5,000 total outstanding balance. Using agency ratings as the criteria for a credit limit is fast and easy.

Other sources of credit ratings as a guide to setting credit limits include trade, bank, and historical information. Many credit managers set a credit limit identical to the highest limit given by other suppliers to the customer. Some will go less than the highest, some to the lowest, and others to the average credit limit set by their competitors. Knowledge of your customer's bank line of credit may be of some value to the credit manager in setting a credit limit. If the bank sets up an unsecured line of X dollars, you can feel confident in giving the customer a line of credit of X plus. Historical information based on your own accounts receivable ledger cards probably serves as the best guide for credit limits. You may extend credit based on historical data in several ways. One way is to set up an *arbitrary account* that allows a certain limit for a short period of time. During this period, you may note the customer's performance and adjust the line up or down accordingly. Another method is to set up a *no limit* account that grants requirements as long as the customer pays promptly or discounts his invoices. The first time a slow payment is observed, an investigation is undertaken and a credit limit is set.

Some of the questions you might ask yourself about these customers when setting credit limits are:

1. How many other suppliers does the customer have who are competitive with you?
2. How much inventory does the customer normally carry?
3. What are the customer's average bank balances?
4. How much cash does the customer have on hand to meet obligations?
5. What volume of business has been projected for the upcoming year?
6. What kind of payment record does the customer have?

If your customer has several suppliers, as in the apparel industry, much less credit will probably be required from you than would be risky. If, however, you are a major supplier, the credit agency ratings would not work at all because they would represent too small an amount.

If you know the amount of inventory carried by your customer and the vendors used, it is relatively easy to calculate whether the amount being purchased from you is too little or too much. From bank balances, you can estimate your chances of being paid on time, keeping in mind the number of suppliers who must be paid and how much is to be paid to each of them.

Projected business volume for the company in question can tell you whether your share of the business is in line. Past payment records help predict future payments.

TRADE TERMS, SPECIAL TERMS, AND CREDIT INSTRUMENTS

Trade and Special Terms

Trade terms are the agreed upon conditions under which products or services are sold. Trade terms vary from industry to industry and region to region, but there are certain generalities that may be made. Generally, raw materials have shorter terms than finished goods. The food industry usually has shorter terms than other industries, especially on perishable goods. There might be cash terms as long as 10 days, but seldom longer. Seasonal goods, cheaper products, and name brand products are usually sold on shorter terms than other products. There are also other factors influencing length of terms. (See Table 2.2 for a summary of these factors.)

TABLE 2.2
Factors Influencing Length of Terms

Factors Influencing Shorter Terms	Factors Influencing Longer Terms
Raw materials inventory	Finished goods inventory
Name-brand product inventory	New product inventory
Perishable goods inventory	Durable goods inventory
Seasonal product inventory	Nonseasonal products
Less expensive inventory	Expensive inventory
Closeness of business location to plant	Distance of business location from plant
Small quantities of inventory	Large quantities of inventory
Retailer and wholesale buyer	Manufacturing buyer

There are several types (classifications) of trade terms including pre-payment terms, net terms, discount terms, multiple order terms, and consignment terms.

The first, *prepayment terms,* are not rightfully considered credit terms because no credit is involved. The supplier receives cash before or at delivery. Most people are familiar with the terms COD (cash on delivery) and CBD (cash before delivery). These are prepayment terms and are self-explanatory. These "special terms" are not used with regular customers in good financial condition. They can be used with the *marginal accounts* discussed previously in this chapter. These terms are best used with new customers, small orders, and existing customers in poor financial condition or with a poor payment record.

Net terms are those most familiar to everyday business and are the most frequently used. Net terms allow a certain period of time for the customer to make payment and have no discount privilege. When the bill is due, the buyer must pay the full amount. The most common net terms are 30 or 60 days from the date of the invoice. They are expressed as "net 30" or "net 60."

Discount terms allow your customer to deduct an amount of money from the selling price as an incentive for fast payment. Discount terms are usually expressed as a percentage of the total amount on the invoice. A common percentage used is either 1 or 2 percent. The terms are usually expressed as "1/10 net 30," which means that the buyer is allowed a 1 percent discount if he pays in 10 days, otherwise the total amount is due within 30 days. The problem that companies using discount terms run into is that some customers do not pay their bills within the discount period, but still deduct the discount from their payments. If a customer who does this is one of your big customers, what can you do about it without risking their displeasure? It is my opinion that companies should avoid giving discounts unless it is absolutely necessary.

Multiple-order terms are used when a customer orders frequently and one invoice covers several shipments made during a single period. These terms are end-of-the-month (EMO), middle-of-the-month (MOM), or at some specified date in the following month (Prox.). EMO terms mean that orders billed on one invoice are to be paid at the end of the month (usually the twenty-fifth). The period allowed begins on the invoicing date or, more frequently, at the first of the month. MOM invoices are issued twice a month. The credit period runs to the twenty-fifth for the shipments during the first half of the month or to the tenth of the following month for shipments during the second half of the month. Prox. terms are similar to EOM terms except a net period is generally added.

Consignment terms are those that a seller arranges with a buyer for consigning merchandise to the buyer. The seller transfers physical possession of the goods but not legal title. In consignment terms there are certain legal considerations: the merchandise consigned should be kept separate from other goods and clearly labeled, the seller provides insurance on the goods, and proceeds from the sale of the consigned merchandise must be kept separate from the sales of other goods.

Credit Instruments

Credit instruments fall into two categories: promises to pay and orders to pay. Open-book accounts and promissory notes are examples of promises to pay. Checks and trade acceptances are examples of orders to pay.

Credit instruments can be further divided into negotiable and nonnegotiable categories. The principal type of nonnegotiable instrument is the open-book account. The seller agrees to deliver goods, services, or other values to the buyer, upon the buyer's promise to pay them at a future date. Promissory notes, checks, and trade acceptances are usually negotiable instruments. In other words, checks and trade acceptances can be cashed in at a bank, and promissory notes can be assigned to a lender as collateral for financial consideration, but an open-book account can by itself be turned into cash by a third party by assignment. Promissory notes can be cashed, too, on the date named in the note. A negotiable instrument must be in writing, must contain a promise or order to pay a fixed or easily determined sum of money, must be payable on demand at a specific time and unconditional, and must be payable to "bearer" or a named person or entity. A negotiable instrument is a representation of value that can be passed freely from the seller to someone else. Statutory laws in every state but Louisiana prescribe the manner in which negotiable instruments may be transferred and fix the rights and duties of the maker, payee, holder, and endorser of the instrument. These laws are based on, and usually called, the Uniform Commercial Code, even though they differ from each other and from the basic Uniform Commercial Code in important ways.

The elements of a negotiable instrument, then, are: (1) an agreement in writing; (2) a promise to pay X dollars at a specific time; (3) transferable to a third party (like a bank); (4) it discusses who has what rights; and (5) is unconditional (it has to be paid).

Open-book accounts were the earliest and remain the simplest kind of credit. They are memorandum notations made by a creditor as part of his regular bookkeeping procedure. This represents an entry on your ledger card or ledger books that a sale has been made and shipped. This book entry is often the only written evidence of a credit transaction. The main advantage of an open-book account is its flexibility. You can extend the time for payment or make other changes in the terms of the account quickly and without the risk of losing your rights under the law. The major disadvantage of an open-book account is that there is no written evidence of the terms of sale. In the absence of complete agreement on all elements of the transaction, the ledger entry is not conclusive proof of the debt. The seller can in most cases, however, establish a claim upon the buyer by proving delivery and acceptance. Collection on book accounts are, of course, slower than collections on written instruments such as promissory notes.

A *promissory note* is a written promise to pay, on demand and unconditionally, a definite sum of money at a specified time in the future (also called an IOU). It is signed by the maker (the person who promises to pay). The person to whom the note is made payable is the payee. A promissory note may be given by a purchaser in payment for goods or given in exchange for money or credit. Promissory notes are rarely used among manufacturers and wholesalers, but when a buyer is a poor credit risk, a promissory note, especially one guaranteed by someone who is a good credit risk, can be given to the seller. In cases where a buyer is a financially weak corporation, but has an officer or stockholder who is personally wealthy, the promissory note might be a good credit tool. Promissory notes can also be used in extending the time for payment on an open-book account. You might want to grant an extension of time for payment on the condition that the debtor sign a promissory note. A promissory note has the advantage of being good evidence of debt, specifically settling the amount due the seller, and helping insure prompt payment. The holder of the note may endorse it over to a bank for cash, making it more readily transferable than open-book credit. The main disadvantage of requiring a promissory note is that the customer might take offense at being treated as a poor credit risk and might withdraw the account. Promissory notes are one of the special terms mentioned that may be used with marginal accounts.

Checks are the most generally used orders to pay. A check is a written order requesting a bank to pay a certain sum of money. Checks are used for over 95 percent of the dollar volume of payments in the United States today. Everyone knows what a check is, how it is made, and what it looks like, but few business people are aware of the legal ramifications of a check. The bank could refuse to pay the check for several reasons. The check is a promise from the very beginning. The holder (you) can take legal action against the maker (your customer) to collect the amount of the check.

When a customer must establish beyond doubt that the bank will honor their check, they can have the check certified by the bank. A *certified check* is a guarantee by the bank that the depositer has sufficient funds to cover the amount of the check. The bank reserves the amount of the check in the depositor's account. Other checks drawn against the account will be paid only if there are sufficient funds on deposit over and above the face value of a certified check. A *cashier's check* is an order signed by the bank's cashier and is drawn on the bank, not on the customer's account.

Trade acceptances are common only in a few lines of business, notably the fur trade. A trade acceptance is a credit instrument drawn by the seller (you) directing a customer-buyer to pay a certain amount to you, at a fixed future time, to cover the purchase. In most industries, the trade acceptance is used only when the financial position of the buyer precludes, at least temporarily, meeting the normal credit terms of the seller (you). You may extend your normal terms by one or two months if the buyer will accept a trade acceptance. The following steps are necessary to complete a trade acceptance transaction:

1. You prepare and send a trade acceptance form to your customer with the invoice.
2. Your customer (the buyer) makes the obligation effective when he signs it and inserts a payment date and bank name. Your customer then returns it to the seller (you).
3. You (the seller) may hold the trade acceptance until a few days before it is due and deposit it in your bank, just like a check. Your bank will send the acceptance through to your customer's bank as though it were a check. If the holder (drawee) of a trade acceptance needs funds and does not want to wait until the acceptance is due, the holder can discount at the bank or sell it on the open market through trade acceptance dealers.

The advantages of trade acceptances are that they lessen the possibility of returned goods, place pressure on the buyer to pay by the due date, and because they are negotiable instruments can be discounted at the holder's bank.

Bank acceptances are similar to trade acceptances except that bank acceptances are drawn on the customer's (buyer's) *bank* instead of on the customer. Usually they are requested by the buyer, which in effect means the bank is extending credit to the buyer.

3

Your Business and Credit Information

Using credit information from various sources is a basic and necessary part of every good credit decision. No one can make reliable decisions without information and, generally, the more information you have on your customer, the more reliable your credit decision becomes. Information is as vital to credit decisions as shipping invoices are to billing.

Information about your customer can come from several sources. It can come from your customer, from industry (Dun and Bradstreet) ratings, outside people, or from your sales staff. Seven sources of information in all will be discussed in this chapter. If the strengths and advantages of each are understood and intelligently used, no others should be needed.

The important factors in determining the amount of information you need and the number of sources you must contact are: time, location, cost, and amount of risk. If you need a decision quickly, you will be able to contact only a few sources. If the sources of information for a particular account are located far away, you might conclude that it is inconvenient to contact them. The greater your credit exposure, the more you may wish to tap many sources of information. Since gathering credit information is costly in terms of time and energy as well as money, you must make sure that the account is financially valuable in terms of your company's sales *before* you launch a major credit investigation.

It should be mentioned that all credit information is dynamic — it changes from month to month, year to year. January's data may be obsolete by June. If your company gives automatic approval on industry organization ratings (such as Dun and Bradstreet), you should be careful. For instance, an automatic approval of a credit line to ZIP Manufacturing is based on a D & B rating of Cl ½ as per D & B's November rating book. It is reckless to assume that the Cl ½ rating can be considered permanent. Where the rating is the only criterion for acceptance and where no reports are purchased for study and retention, the credit manager should recheck the ratings of all such accounts as each new book is published. This is true of not only D & B ratings, but also of other credit information.

The accuracy of the data you receive on cost should also be considered. Financial statements given you by the customer might be inaccurate or leave out pertinent details, Dun and Bradstreet ratings might be superficial, or your sales staff may be given inaccurate information without knowing it. As a matter of fact, any credit information you receive from any source may not be factual.

There are always people who, for a price, can "fix" any credit report by deleting unfavorable information about a particular company from the storage files. Reports do not have to be deliberately fixed but can still be inadvertently misleading; credit reporting agency employees, in a rush to meet their quotas, may get the wrong information about a company.

Generally, the credit reports you get from the various sources will be accurate, but the credit manager should learn to question all information and only trust that information that agrees with other sources. As a rule of thumb, the smaller your customer is and the younger a company is, the more difficult it will be to get accurate information. A company on a stock exchange probably has the best and most accurate information available concerning its history.

Also, if several sources of credit information agree on their basic assessment of your customer, chances are good that the assessment is a correct one. The higher the correlation of information from different sources, the more accurate the information can be considered. If you get a high rating of your customer from Dun and Bradstreet, a group interchange, banks, and your customer's financial statements, you can be reasonably assured that your customer is a good risk. Perhaps the most important source of information about your customer's creditworthiness is your customer.

YOUR CUSTOMER

Your first step in your credit investigation should be customer-supplied information. Direct contact with the customer affords the advantage of being able to ask for precisely what you want. Person-to-person conversations are likely to get less tangled up than formal communication. It is more difficult for your customer to refuse your requests, and the savings in time and energy are great. Since direct communication with your client is a two-way street, you can take the time to explain requirements until they are fully understood.

Direct contact with your customer gives you the opportunity to set precedents that make credit investigation, evaluation, and collection easier. Some of the things that you should communicate are the extent of information you want from your customer and other sources, the kind of information, and the terms of sale. Express from the beginning that full disclosure of all pertinent details is necessary. Establish the kind of information you want, especially financial statements. If the customer develops the habit of furnishing financial statements to you regularly, your credit operations are that much easier. Explaining your company's terms of sale to the customer at an early time can help you avoid future confusion or disagreements.

The Customer Interview

A well-planned, well-executed interview between you and your customers can be the most effective means at your disposal for obtaining credit information. It can furnish those almost intangible clues that sometimes tell the credit agent more about a company than Dun and Bradstreet can. Of course, interviews are extremely expensive in time and money and should be reserved for those accounts most likely to produce credit problems.

An interview should be well-planned to be successful. The following are important points to consider when planning the interview:

1. Know exactly to whom you should speak by name. Always talk to the top people.
2. Review the information (if any) that you already have at hand.
3. Decide what you must find out from the customer. Ask only for information that is essential to your credit investigation.
4. Decide on the right tactics with which to approach your customer.
5. Jot down the questions you plan to ask. This will save you time in the interview.
6. Have a positive attitude. Positive attitudes generally come from confidence in yourself. This confidence can also keep you from being tense at the interview. In short, be professional.
7. When you ask your questions at the interview, be sure to write down the answers the customer gives you. People love to see you write down what they say as this signifies that what they are saying is important. Writing is a lot more permanent than memory.
8. Stick to the point of the interview. Time is valuable not only to you but to your customer as well.

Letters to the Customer

Letters are an effective and inexpensive way to get information from a customer. They are most often used to procure financial statements. Some techniques for writing such letters are:

1. Make the request seem routine. In other words, you require the same information from all customers.
2. Assure your customer that the information will remain confidential.
3. Point out the advantages to the customer for supplying you information; for example, adequate information will assure the customer of getting enough credit. You might also mention that the information furnished helps assure adequate production of your product for your customer's company.
4. Enclose a financial statement form to make it easy for the customer to supply the information and a stamped, self-addressed envelope for convenience.

Sample Letter 3.1 illustrates the above techniques.

SAMPLE LETTER 3.1
Requesting a Financial Statement

Dear Mr. Platt:

Thank you for your interest in our company and product evidenced by your recent order.

Since one of our prerequisites for considering applicants is an opportunity to review financial statements, we would appreciate your sending us by return mail a current balance sheet and income statement from your firm.

This information will be held in the strictest of confidence by our company and used only for credit purposes.

Sincerely,

INDUSTRY CREDIT INFORMATION

The second most widely used source of credit information is the commercial company that prints credit reports on businesses. These include Dun and Bradstreet, the National Credit Office, the Red Book and the Blue Book used in the produce industry, and other specialized one-line publications.

The most frequently used and the only industry-wide credit service is Dun and Bradstreet.

Dun and Bradstreet

The Dun and Bradstreet reports are usually the starting place for every credit manager in the investigation of marginal and new accounts, or in keeping track of nonautomatic, automatic, and semiautomatic accounts. They are the only credit reporting agency that assigns ratings and prepares reports on any company in any industry, foreign or domestic.

Dun and Bradstreet is also one of the oldest organizations of its kind. In 1841 Horace Greeley founded the *New York Tribune*, the first wagon train arrived in California via the Oregon Trail, and Edgar Allen Poe was first published. It was also the year that Dun and Bradstreet, founded under the name of the Mercantile Agency by Lewis Tappan, commenced operations. Abraham Lincoln and Ulysses S. Grant were two of the early correspondents of the early Dun and Bradstreet corporation. In 1851, a few years after marrying the sister of Benjamin Douglass, owner of The Mercantile Agency, Robert G. Dun started to work for The Mercantile Agency. In 1859, Dun at the ripe old age of thirty-two became the owner and sole proprietor. He ran the company for forty-one years and left a lasting impression on the firm, namely changing the name from The Mercantile Agency to R. G. Dun and Company. Meanwhile, in 1849, about the same time that Dun married his boss's sister, John M. Bradstreet founded a rival credit reporting agency in Cincinnati called John M. Bradstreet and Sons Improved Mercantile Agency. To make a long story short, they joined in 1933 when R. G. Dun Corporation acquired the Bradstreet Company and later changed the name to Dun and Bradstreet, Inc.

Dun and Bradstreet prepares trade summaries by canvassing all subscribers who have ordered reports on the subject company and who are in direct communication with the subject company. Sometimes the survey of a company will include the experience of as many as twenty suppliers. The reporting format shows the highest recent credit extended by each reporting firm, the period of time that the relationship has existed, the amount presently owing, the terms of sale, subjects' manner of payment, and the identification of any past due balances owing. It also shows the manner of payment: discount, prompt, or slow (60 days). When these trade summaries are fresh and representative, the D & B report can suffice for credit support and no further investigation will be required.

Dun and Bradstreet publishes a variety of reports and provides certain services such as *Dun and Bradstreet Reference Book*, The Dun and Bradstreet Report (done on individual companies), and special reports (such as international reports).

The *Dun and Bradstreet Reference Book* lists the general market with nearly three million businesses located in the United States and Canada. The listing is arranged alphabetically, by town or city within their particular state or province. The book is published bimonthly in January, March, May, July, September, and November. Businesses listed in the *Reference Book* are commercial enterprises (manufacturers, wholesalers, retailers, business services) and other types of businesses buying regularly on credit terms. Hospitals, schools, professions (like accounting and law), and certain services are not listed.

A listing in the *Reference Book* gives the following information:

1. The standard industrial classification code (SIC) number. The SIC code number is the standard number used by the federal government to identify companies by industry and function (manufacturing, wholesale, retail, or service). All listings with the same SIC number are in the same line of business.
2. The name of the business used in buying.
3. The date the business was started if it is less than ten years old. This is shown by a one digit number (1, 2, 3, and so on). This number indicates the last number of the year it was started. In 1977, the number 2 would indicate 1972, for example and the number 9 would indicate 1969.
4. A Dun and Bradstreet rating, consisting of letters and a number are also shown. The letters are known as the *capital* rating. They stand for the estimated financial strength of the business. For example, in the rating FF1, the letters FF indicate that the financial strength of the business is between $10,000 and $19,999. The number stands for composite credit appraisals of the business, based upon information contained in the Busi-

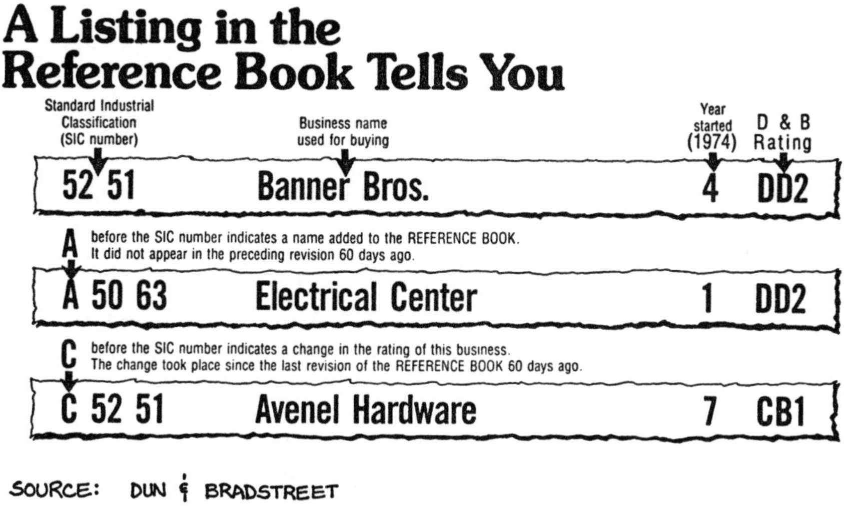

A Listing in the Reference Book Tells You

Standard Industrial Classification (SIC number)	Business name used for buying	Year started (1974)	D & B Rating
52 51	Banner Bros.	4	DD2

A before the SIC number indicates a name added to the REFERENCE BOOK. It did not appear in the preceding revision 60 days ago.

A 50 63	Electrical Center	1	DD2

C before the SIC number indicates a change in the rating of this business. The change took place since the last revision of the REFERENCE BOOK 60 days ago.

C 52 51	Avenel Hardware	7	CB1

SOURCE: DUN & BRADSTREET

FIGURE 3.1
Listings in Dun and Bradstreet *Reference Book*

ness Information Report. In this example, the 1 indicates a "high" composite credit appraisal. In some instances, capital and credit ratings cannot be assigned. Instead, one of the following symbols will be shown: 1, 2, or Inv, the last meaning that a pending investigation was incomplete when the book in which it appears went to press; or the symbol(—)meaning an absence of rating. A more thorough explanation of ratings and symbols is presented in Figure 3.2.

5. In addition to the basic listings described above, the *Reference Book* contains other information such as town population, the county in which the town is located, and the names of officers and the amount of capital of local banks for every town or city in the United States and Canada.

6. Locations of local Dun and Bradstreet offices are also listed in the *Reference Book*.

Dun and Bradstreet Business Information Report (Fig. 3.3) is one of millions of reports that are maintained on businesses and is designed to provide you with the facts most frequently required for your credit decision making. There is a report on file for each name listed in the *Reference Book*, as well as for many others not listed. Reports are revised at least once a year, but frequently several revisions and supplements are needed to tell the story and keep it up-to-date. You can automatically receive copies of these revisions for each name upon which you inquire if you pay a little extra for "Continuous Service."

The elements of the Business Information Report are as follows:

1. The DUNS (Date Universal Numbering System) number is a nine-digit code that identifies name and location of each business. This code may be used by your credit department for record keeping and is well-suited to data processing applications.

2. The summary is a concise analysis, with basic identification of each business appearing across the top of the page, the business' SIC number (describing product line and function), the year the business was started, and the Dun and Bradstreet rating. The summary also digests important report information, usually including payments, sales, net worth, number of employees, history, financing, condition, and trend.

3. The payments section shows how the business pays its bills, as reported by suppliers. This section includes paying record,

Key to Ratings

ESTIMATED FINANCIAL STRENGTH		COMPOSITE CREDIT APPRAISAL			
		HIGH	GOOD	FAIR	LIMITED
5A	$50,000,000 and over	1	2	3	4
4A	$10,000,000 to 49,999,999	1	2	3	4
3A	1,000,000 to 9,999,999	1	2	3	4
2A	750,000 to 999,999	1	2	3	4
1A	500,000 to 749,999	1	2	3	4
BA	300,000 to 499,999	1	2	3	4
BB	200,000 to 299,999	1	2	3	4
CB	125,000 to 199,999	1	2	3	4
CC	75,000 to 124,999	1	2	3	4
DC	50,000 to 74,999	1	2	3	4
DD	35,000 to 49,999	1	2	3	4
EE	20,000 to 34,999	1	2	3	4
FF	10,000 to 19,999	1	2	3	4
GG	5,000 to 9,999	1	2	3	4
HH	Up to 4,999	1	2	3	4

**CLASSIFICATION BASED ON BOTH
ESTIMATED FINANCIAL STRENGTH AND COMPOSITE CREDIT APPRAISAL**

FINANCIAL STRENGTH BRACKET
1 $125,000 and over
2   20,000 to $124,999

: When only the numeral (1 or 2) appears, it is an indication that the estimated financial strength, while not definitely classified, is presumed to be within the range of the ($) figures in the corresponding bracket and while the composite credit appraisal cannot be judged precisely, it is believed to be "High" or "Good."

"INV." shown in place of a rating indicates that the report was under investigation at the time of going to press. It has no other significance.

"FB" (Foreign Branch). Indicates that the headquarters of this company is located in a foreign country (including Canada). The written report contains the location and rating of the headquarters.

ABSENCE OF RATING, expressed by two hyphens (--), is not to be construed as unfavorable but signifies circumstances difficult to classify within condensed rating symbols. It suggests the advisability of obtaining a report for additional information.

**EMPLOYEE RANGE DESIGNATIONS IN REPORTS ON NAMES NOT LISTED
IN THE REFERENCE BOOK**

Certain businesses do not lend themselves to a Dun & Bradstreet rating and are not listed in the Reference Book. Information on these names, however, continues to be stored and updated in the D&B Business Information File. Reports are available on such businesses and instead of a rating they carry an Employee Range Designation (ER) which is indicative of size in terms of number of employees. No other significance should be attached.

**KEY TO EMPLOYEE
RANGE DESIGNATIONS**

ER 1	1000 or more	Employees
ER 2	500- 999	Employees
ER 3	100 - 499	Employees
ER 4	50 - 99	Employees
ER 5	20 - 49	Employees
ER 6	10 - 19	Employees
ER 7	5 - 9	Employees
ER 8	1 - 4	Employees
ER N		Not Available

Dun & Bradstreet, Inc.
99 Church Street, New York, N.Y. 10007

FIGURE 3.2
Explanation of Ratings and Symbols in Dun and Bradstreet

Dun & Bradstreet, Inc.

This report has been prepared for:

BE SURE NAME, BUSINESS AND ADDRESS MATCH YOUR FILE	ANSWERING INQUIRY	SUBSCRIBER: 008-001042

```
DUNS: 04-426-3226                                                    SUMMARY
ARNOLD METAL PRODUCTS CO.              APR 21 197-         RATING   DD1
                                                                   Formerly
53 S MAIN ST                           METAL STAMPINGS             EE1
DAWSON MICH 49666                                         STARTED  1957
     TEL 215 999-0000                  SIC NOS            PAYMENTS DISC-PPT
                                       34 69              SALES    *177,250
                                                          WORTH    * 42,961
                                                          EMPLOYS  10
     SAMUEL B. ARNOLD, PARTNER                            HISTORY  CLEAR
                                                          CONDITION STRONG
                                                          TREND    UP
```

```
PAYMENTS      (Amounts may be rounded to nearest figure in prescribed ranges)
AS OF         PAYING      HIGH       NOW      PAST         SELLING
              RECORD      CREDIT     OWES     DUE          TERMS      LAST SALE
01/7-         Disc        3000       1500     -0-          1 10 30    2-3 Mos
02/7-         Disc-Ppt    2500       1000     -0-          1 10 30    4-5 Mos
03/7-         Disc-Ppt    2000       500      -0-          2 20 30    6-12 Mos
              Disc        800        400      -0-          1 10 30    1 Mo
```

```
FINANCE           On Apr 21 197- S. B. Arnold, Partner, submitted the following statement dated
              Dec 31 197-
              Cash           *     4,870        Accts Pay          *      6,121
              Accts Rec         15,472          Notes Pay (Curr)          2,400
              Mdse             14,619           Accruals                  3,583
                             --------- ---                             -------------
                 Current         34,961            Current               12,104
              Fixt & Equip (*4,183)  22,840     Notes Pay (Def)          5,000
              CSV of Life Ins     2,264         NET WORTH                42,961
                             --------- ---                             --- -------
                 Total Assets    60,065            Total                 60,065
              Annual sales *177,250; gross profit *47,821; net income *8,204.
              Fire insurance mdse *15,000; fixt *20,000.  Annual rent *5,000.
              Signed Apr 21 197- ARNOLD METAL PRODUCTS CO by Samuel B. Arnold, Partner.
                          --0--
                  New equipment purchased last Sep was financed by bank loan.  Monthly payments
              on loan are *200.
                  Arnold reported sales for the three months ended Mar 31 were up 10% compared
              with the same period last year.  Increase was attributed by management to addi-
              tional capacity provided by new equipment.
                  Profit is being made and retained resulting in an increase in net worth   Cur-
              rent debt is light in relation to worth.  Inventory turnover is rapid.

BANKING           Balances average high four figures.  Loans granted to low five figures, secured
02/7-         by equipment, now owing high four figures.  Relations satisfactory.

HISTORY       SAMUEL B. ARNOLD, PARTNER         GEORGE T. ARNOLD, PARTNER
                  Style registered Feb 1, 1965 by partners.
                  S. ARNOLD, born 1918, married, 1939 graduate of Lehigh University, 1939-50 em-
              ployed by Industrial Machine Corporation, Detroit, and 1950-56 production manager
              with Aerial Motors Inc, Detroit.  Started this business in 1957.
                  G. ARNOLD, born 1940, single, son of Samuel.  Graduated in 1963, Dawson Insti-
              tute of Technology.  Served U.S. Air Force 1963-64.  Admitted to partnership Feb 1965.

OPERATION         Manufactures perforated metal stampings for industrial concerns.  Sells on net
              30 day terms.  Has twelve accounts.  Territory greater Detroit area  EMPLOYEES: Ten
              including partners.
              LOCATION: Rents 5,000 square feet in one story cinder block building in normal con-
              dition.  Located in central business section of main street.  Premises neat.

              04-21 (980     /1     )5842/02               1  051
              First National Bank, 80 S. Main St., Dawson, Mich.
```

FIGURE 3.3
Dun and Bradstreet Business Information Report

high credit, amount owing, amount past due (if any), selling terms, and period of time since last sale. A separate line shows supplier comments (for example, Account in Dispute). Associated with each trade experience is a date showing when that particular information was reported to Dun and Bradstreet.

4. The finance section includes essential facts for determining the financial condition and trend of a business. Most reports contain financial information that may represent audited figures prepared by a CPA audit (with or without qualification); unaudited figures from the books of account (not prepared by an outside accountant); or management's own estimate of assets, liabilities, sales, expenses, and profit. Unfortunately, there is no way of knowing if the figures presented are audited by a CPA without qualification or just blue sky dreamed up by the management. Principals of some concerns decline to furnish detailed figures. When this occurs, financial figures may be based on bank and supplier comment, investigation of public records or the D & B business analyst's estimates of certain balance sheet items. Financial information is also frequently supplemented with information regarding leases, insurance coverage, and other pertinent details. Comment in this section is devoted to further necessary explanation of the figures and a description of sales and profit trends.

This financial section is probably the most important and the D & B rating is based to a large extent upon the degree of financial stability and the trend as reflected in this section. If the financial figures given D & B are blue sky, you can see how the rating can be misleading. It is best to check these figures against the information that the customer provides. If there is a big difference between the figures given you by your customer and the D & B figures, look out!

5. The banking section contains information concerning banking relations. It may include an indication of average balances, previous and current loan experience, whether loans are secured or unsecured, length of time the bank had the account, whether or not the bank considers the account satisfactory, and the date when this information was reported. In some instances, names of some or all banks of account are provided, although not necessarily in order of importance. Banks are usually very cooperative with Dun and Bradstreet, so that information tends to be quite accurate.

6. The history section contains the names, year of birth, and past business experience of the principals or owners of concern. This information is usually obtained from the management of the business on which the report is written. Past business experience and outside affiliations of principals are important considerations in evaluating management. In the case of prior business affiliations, D & B files are utilized where feasible to verify and augment the information provided by management. Criminal proceedings that D & B learns about are reported.

7. The operation section describes what a concern does, and under the subcaption "location," describes the premises, the neighborhood, and size of floor space. Also described, whenever applicable, are the lines of merchandise sold or kinds of services rendered, price range, classification of customers, selling terms, percentage of cash and credit sales, number of accounts, seasonal aspects and number of employees. Usually, location information is obtained by the reporter's observation while the balance of the information is provided by management. By describing the machinery of production and the distribution, the operation section helps give the reader of the report a better understanding of the balance sheet and profit and loss figures. Sales departments may use this section to determine whether the subject could be a profitable outlet for their particular lines of merchandise.

The following two sections are optional captions:

8. The special events section highlights those significant occurrences in a business that could vitally affect your present credit relationship or a pending credit decision. Covered here are *recent* changes of chief executive, legal structure, partners, control, business location, or business name. Also included are bankruptcy updates, business discontinuances, criminal proceedings, burglaries or embezzlements, fires, and other disasters. A special events item appears after the heading and summary for quick identification.

9. The public filings section identifies public *civil* filings, such as suits, judgments, Uniform Commercial Code filings, tax liens, and record item updates and releases. Not all public record filings are recorded in this section, only the most significant ones.

Other Dun and Bradstreet reports have been developed in specialized forms to fit the credit and sales requirements of various subscribers. Special reports include key account reports, international reports, analytical reports, and municipal reports. Key account reports are written in direct response to your specific management problems. These reports provide a depth of investigation and a detailed level of information that may not be available in the Business Information Report. International reports are written on overseas business concerns. Analytical reports are written by a staff of analysts familiar with the complicated financial structure of larger firms. Municipal reports are written on most major government units that issue tax exempt bonds.

When to Use the Reference Book

The *Reference Book* provides a quick credit check when an order comes to your desk, a buyer visits your showroom, your salesperson needs information, or before you contact a customer for an interview. The *Reference Book* is not meant as a total credit report, but as an auxiliary source to be used for ready reference where light risk is involved.

When to Order a Report

A detailed Business Information Report should generally be ordered under the following circumstances:

1. When the rating in the *Reference Book* suggests that more data is desirable. (For example, when the customer orders more than the rating would suggest is the maximum.)
2. For new accounts (marginal accounts).
3. For slow accounts (nonautomatic to marginal accounts).
4. When you get unsolicited orders from unknown customers.
5. Where existing buyers want to increase lines of credit.
6. When you notice changes in paying habits (when the customer goes from discounting to slow payments, for example).
7. Where economical for existing accounts (that is, if you get orders of over $1,500 per year).

Specialized Services other than D & B

In a few selected lines of commercial activity, there are reporting agencies that attempt to provide for their particular industry what Dun and

Bradstreet does for the whole business spectrum. They publish rating books and prepare reports for their subscribers. In most cases, they limit their coverage to just one line of activity. An example of this type includes the Red Book and the Blue Book, both of which report only on packers and shippers of perishable vegetables and fruit. Another example is the United Beverage Bureau, which covers bottlers of carbonated beverages. The National Credit Office (a division of Dun and Bradstreet) includes in its coverage several lines, but not all lines. Trinc Transportation Consultants (also a division of Dun and Bradstreet) specializes in providing data on the federally-regulated sector of the transportation industry. Trinc has four directories: *The Dun and Bradstreet Reference Book of Transportation, Trinc's Blue Book, Trinc's Red Book,* and *Trinc's Green Book of Air Freight and Freight Forwarders.*

The National Credit Office (NCO) is the largest specialized credit reporting agency. NCO concentrates on a few lines of businesses, including menswear, dresses, coats, suits, and intimate apparel, converting and household, mill, wholesale and retail (mostly in the fabric business, but some general wholesalers or mass merchandisers), metals, electronics, leather, and chemical. NCO provides reports similar to the D & B Business Information Reports with two exceptions: NCO provides a suggested dollar credit limit for those companies reported and also gives a list of the subject's major suppliers and banks. (See Figs. 3.4(a) and (b) for an example of an NCO report.)

At a modest cost to the subscriber, United Beverage Bureau will provide a "Trade Clearance Report," which is a listing of trade experience and has the added advantages of (1) being current (seldom more than a month or two old); (2) being complete in the number of suppliers reporting; and (3) in identifying those suppliers by the industry in which they are engaged. This identification is a code number for each line of supply — one for bottles, cans, closures, shipping containers, malt, and so forth. Adverse information is also entered on the report by a code number (balances placed for collection, NSF checks, dishonored drafts, and terms).

Specialized industry reporting services are a diverse group varying widely in the quality of their services. The only way for you to reach a conclusion on each agency's reporting of trade experiences is to discuss their coverage with some fellow credit managers who are presently subscribers to a particular agency. If your customers are not within the clearly defined limits of activities on which an agency issues reports, specialized agencies will be of no value. For instance, the United Bever-

nco. specialized credit report

MANAGEMENT & PRODUCTS

FEMINA FOOTWEAR CO., INC.
123 West Kerry Ave.
Buffalo, N. Y. 14020
Phone: 716-477-3602

MFR. SLIPPERS & PLAYSHOES
Dept. 964
Analyst: Jeffrey Jones

JUNE 5, 197-

John W. Sussler, Chairman of Bd.
Peter G. Field, Vice-Pres.
F. J. Richman, Secy.

Edwin W. Delray, Pres.-Treas.
Rosanne S. Dooley, Vice-Pres.

DIRECTORS: John W. Sussler, Edwin W. Delray, George H. Lee, and
Ronald Lockhart.

HISTORY - Established as partnership 1935 as Adorable Shoe Co. Succeeded
1936 by Femina Footwear Co., N.Y. Corp. 1938 change in control
occurred and certain of former interests retired. Charter surrendered
and business re-incorporated under N.Y. laws under present style.
Plant formerly operated at Manchester, Vt., was discontinued 1949.
Moved to caption address 1955.

PERSONNEL - Sussler, born 1910, principal financially, maintains general
supervision over entire operation. Long associated with this
line and officer with subject since 1938. Previously Vice-President
and General Manager of Adorable Shoe Co. Originally employed by
others as an auditor. $50,000 insurance carried on his life with
company as beneficiary. Elected Chairman of the Board 1962.

Delray, born 1921, associated with subject since 1938, in charge of
production. Elected Director 1950. Shortly thereafter elected
Secretary and assumed the additional office of Vice-President 1959.
Elected President and Treasurer 1962.

Richman, born 1930. Employed by subject since 1950. Elected
Assistant Secretary 1955 and Secretary 1962. In charge of purchasing.

Field, born 1928. Associated since 1954. Sales Vice-Pres. since 1963.

Dooley, born 1929. Employed as stylist and designer since 1956.
Elected Vice-President 1959.

Lee, is a local attorney. Lockhart, is also President of Lockhart
Gear Works, Buffalo, N.Y. and has been associated with that company
throughout his business career.

METHOD OF OPERATION - LINE - Manufacture women's and children's turn
process padded sole and cement process hard sole house slippers and
playshoes. Retail price range from $3.95 to $10.95 a pair. Approximately 50% of production is for in-stock and 50% against orders.
DISTRIBUTION - Direct, nationally, about 75% to department stores and
25% to individual retailers. Terms of sale 3/10EOM. Use trade styles,
"Femina", "Kittens", and "Play-Cats".
EQUIPMENT - Lease quarters on first floor of three-story building.
Rents 30,000 sq. ft. Output 2,000 pairs daily. Employs about 125.

BANKS - First Marine Bank, Buffalo, N.Y.
Manufacturers Bank of Buffalo, Buffalo, N.Y.

hl

14695

FIGURE 3.4(a)
NCO Report

nco. specialized credit report

FEMINA FOOTWEAR CO., INC.   MFR. SLIPPERS & PLAYSHOES
123 West Kerry Ave.   Dept. 964
Buffalo, N.Y. 14020   Analyst: Jeffrey Jones
Phone: 716-477-3602

JUNE 5, 197-

CREDIT SUGGESTION - (A) - BECAUSE OF FURTHER PROGRESS AND VERY LIQUID
   CONDITION, REQUIREMENTS ARE NOW SUGGESTED.

NEW INFORMATION - Management recently advised that sales so far this year
   have shown an increase of about 9% over the corresponding period
   of last year with profits also ahead of a year ago.

ANTECEDENT COMMENT - Records clear. Originally formed 1935. Present
   management in control since 1938. Manufacture general line of
   slippers and playshoes. Management experienced and well regarded.

FINANCIAL -

	12/31/6-	12/31/6-	12/31/6-
Cash	$ 5,000	$ 12,000	$ 20,000
Receivables	126,000	114,000	134,000
Merchandise	181,000	239,000	184,000
Current Assets	312,000	365,000	338,000
Current Debts	68,000	107,000	65,000
Working Capital	244,000	258,000	273,000
Fixed Assets	44,000	34,000	32,000
Net Worth	353,000	369,000	388,000
Sales	1,234,000	1,336,000	1,423,000
Profit	28,000	32,000	38,000
Dividends	14,000	16,000	19,000

Auditor: Paul D. Hartman & Co., CPA., Buffalo, N.Y.

TRADE - EXCELLENT

HIGH CREDIT	OWING	PAST DUE	TERMS		PAYMENTS
$ 25,000	10,000	0	2/30		ant
15,000	7,000	0	2/15	prox	dis
11,000	5,000	0	2/30		ant
10,000	6,000	0	2/15	prox	dis
6,000	5,000	0	2/15	prox	dis
5,000	0	0	2/15	prox	dis
2,000	2,000	0	2/15	prox	dis
1,000	0	0	2/30		dis

Union Tanning Co., Boston, Mass.   Smith Leather Co., N.Y.C.
Chelsea Heel Corp., Chelsea, Mass.   Fancy Leather Corp., Boston, Mass.

ANALYSIS - This is a well established business which has shown a consistently progressive trend over the years. Steady increases have
   been shown in both volume and profits in recent years. Financial
   condition has been good for a number of years and was quite liquid on
   the last statement which featured all indebtedness covered more than
   twice by the total of cash and receivables. Financing is assisted
   by unsecured loans from two banks and a small amount was owing to one
   bank at recent investigation date.

cd

FIGURE 3.4(b)
NCO Report

age Bureau does not report on canners of fruit juices because fruit juices do not contain carbonation.

Report Conditions Indicating Further Investigation

There are certain conditions suggested by the credit reports that indicate further research is required on the part of the credit manager. The following list illustrates some of those circumstances that may suggest further research.

1. If the report reflects a condition that you know contradicts current fact. One criticism of industry reports is that they tend to reflect performance more than actuality. Sometimes the information given by the customer is incorrect, or it is possible that the supplier gives only favorable information for fear that the customer will feel obliged to supply the agency with negative information.
2. If the report represents an inadequate number of responses. Where the credit manager knows his client buys from thirty to forty sources, including eight or ten major lines of credit, a summary listing only three minor creditors is too sparce in detail.
3. If the report simply states "generally reported prompt pay," "locally reported prompt." This indicates that the agency has no specific responses to support the generalized conclusion.
4. If information is outdated. Since in most instances, there can be a lag of 60 days or so between the date of a respondent's reply and the actual completion of the report, and the previous detailed clearance may be up to twelve months old, conceivably the data could be over a year old. Businesses can change considerably in one year. In the case of marginal accounts where the affairs are in a constant state of flux, the need for current information is obviously very important.

INDUSTRY CREDIT GROUPS

Credit managers in the same industry have procedural problems and, often, accounts in common. Industry credit groups have proliferated rapidly, particularly during the past thirty years. Most industry groups are organized and supervised by the National Association of Credit Managers, (NACM), although there are others in major industries that are administered by trade association executives. All have strict codes of ethics. Some are national in scope, others regional or local. The one characteristic common to all the groups is the sharing of experience on individual accounts. These groups are valuable sources of information to the credit manager since the information portrays the experience of others in the same general line of activity. For this reason, information reported is likely to be more indicative of performance expectancy than a similar clearance of suppliers in unrelated fields.

The information from the NACM that the average credit agent is most likely to use is the Credit Interchange Bureau or the new National Credit Information Service (NACIS). The National Association also offers other services including *Daily Sheet,* a newsletter that lists recordings of various documents pertaining to assets pledged as securities for loans; a collection division; an Adjustment Bureau that processes the affairs of a debtor in financial difficulty; a fraud prevention service; and a credit education program.

Credit Interchange Bureaus

Local credit interchange bureaus are organized in a system headed by Credit Interchange Bureaus of NACM. The system works as follows:

1. You furnish information on your customers to a local bureau (see Fig. 3.5).
2. When you need information on a customer, you send a request to your local bureau (see Fig. 3.6).
3. The interchange sends you any report it has on file and circulates your request through the system to solicit responses from your customer's other suppliers.
4. These new responses are tabulated and distributed in a new report, which is then placed on file (see Figs. 3.7(a) and 3.7(b) for an example of a Credit Interchange Bureau report).

This allows the interchange to make available to members an accurate, confidential, and factual analysis of the paying record of any customer or potential customer. Bureau reports cover items such as length of patronage, date of last purchase, highest credit recently, amount owing, amount past due, terms of purchase, manner of payment, and

MEMBER INQUIRY
CREDIT INTERCHANGE BUREAU
2300 W. Olympic Blvd., Los Angeles, CA 90006 / (213) 386-8000

Date ____________

Please Secure A Report On:

Firm Name ______________________ Dba ____________

Owner(s) ______________________ Formerly ____________

Address ______________________

City ____________ State ____________ Zip Code ____________

AUTOMATIC REVISION

We Want A Report On This Account Every ________ Months.

OUR EXPERIENCE AS FOLLOWS (REPORT AMOUNTS IN DOLLARS ONLY):

How Long Sold	Date of Last Sale	Highest Recent Credit	Amount Owing (Includes Notes)	Amount Past Due	Unfilled Or First Orders	Terms of Sales	Discounts	Pays When Due	Days Slow	COMMENTS
										Use other side if necessary

IMPORTANT: LIST KNOWN SOURCES OF SUPPLY BELOW. THE BUREAU WILL MAKE EVERY EFFORT TO OBTAIN THEIR INFORMATION AND INCLUDE IT IN THE REPORT.

NAME	ADDRESS	CITY

Customer Banks With ______________________

Member

PLEASE INCLUDE YOUR EXPERIENCE

FIGURE 3.5
Customer Information Form

MEMBER NO

BUSINESS CLASSIFICATION

PLEASE GIVE EXPERIENCE WITH ABOVE:

DO NOT FOLD OR BEND

ACCOUNT INACTIVE OVER 1 YR. ☐ NOT SELLING ☐

HOW LONG SOLD

PAYING RECORD ☐ DISCOUNTS

DATE OF LAST SALE

SLOW ____ DAYS ☐ PAYS WHEN DUE

HIGHEST RECENT CREDIT $ .00

TREND OF PAYMENTS:

NOW OWING (INCL. NOTES) $ .00

☐ IMPROVING ☐ NO CHANGE ☐ SLOWER

PAST DUE (INCL. NOTES) $ .00

OMIT CENTS

COMMENTS:

TERMS OF SALE: DISC. & NET ________ ☐ C.B.D. ☐ C.O.D. ☐ OUR REQUEST ☐ CUSTOMER REQ.

☐ SEND US COPY OF THIS REPORT

RETURN
SAME DAY RECEIVED

CREDIT INTERCHANGE BUREAU
2300 W. OLYMPIC BLVD
LOS ANGELES
CALIF 90006

FIGURE 3.6
Information Request Form

Form 7 (b)

CREDIT MANAGERS ASSOCIATION of SOUTHERN CALIFORNIA
Credit Interchange Bureaus

2300 WEST OLYMPIC BLVD.
LOS ANGELES, CALIFORNIA 90006
(213) 386-8000

Affiliated with
the NATIONAL ASSOCIATION
of CREDIT MANAGEMENT

REG. U. S. PAT. OFF.

82

DIS-DISCOUNTS
PWD-PAY WHEN DUE

Report on

JOHN DOE APPLIANCE STORE

PAGE 82

THE ACCURACY OF THIS REPORT IS NOT GUARANTEED. ITS CONTENTS ARE GATHERED IN GOOD FAITH FROM MEMBERS AND SENT TO YOU BY THIS BUREAU WITHOUT LIABILITY FOR NEGLIGENCE IN PROCURING, COLLECTING, COMMUNICATING OR FAILING TO COMMUNICATE THE INFORMATION SO GATHERED.

BUSINESS CLASSIFICATION	HOW LONG SOLD	DATE OF LAST SALE	HIGHEST RECENT CREDIT	NOW OWING	PAST DUE	TERMS OF SALE	PAYING RECORD			COMMENT
				INCLUDING NOTES			D I S	P W Q	DAYS SLOW	

THIS REPORT IS FOR EXTENSION OF COMMERCIAL CREDIT ONLY

INFORMATION HEREIN IS STRICTLY CONFIDENTIAL FOR THE EXCLUSIVE USE OF YOUR CREDIT DEPARTMENT.
UNDER NO CIRCUMSTANCES SHOULD LEDGER INFORMATION BE SHOWN OR REVEALED TO THE REPORTED SUBJECT.

ENT. BANK 18%

2 1 76 SUED BY A D C CORP 2656 PROM NOTE

5 18 76 COLLECTION DEPT ITEM v25

NUMEROUS FINANCING STATEMENTS FILED 4 72 THROUGH 7 75

7167   6488

BI 45

FIGURE 3.7(a)
Credit Interchange Bureau Report

CREDIT MANAGERS ASSOCIATION of SOUTHERN CALIFORNIA

Credit Interchange Bureaus

2300 WEST OLYMPIC BLVD.
LOS ANGELES, CALIFORNIA 90006
(213) 386-8000

Affiliated with
the NATIONAL ASSOCIATION
of CREDIT MANAGEMENT

81

DIS-DISCOUNTS
PWD-PAY WHEN DUE

Form 7 ®1

REG. U. S. PAT. OFF.

Report on

JOHN DOE APPLIANCE STORE

2300 WEST OLYMPIC BLVD

LOS ANGELES CALIF   L A COUNTY   APR 1 1976

THE ACCURACY OF THIS REPORT IS NOT GUARANTEED. ITS CONTENTS ARE GATHERED IN GOOD FAITH FROM MEMBERS AND SENT TO YOU BY THIS BUREAU WITHOUT LIABILITY FOR NEGLIGENCE IN PROCURING, COLLECTING, COMMUNICATING OR FAILING TO COMMUNICATE THE INFORMATION SO GATHERED.

BUSINESS CLASSIFICATION	HOW LONG SOLD	DATE OF LAST SALE	HIGHEST RECENT CREDIT	NOW OWING	PAST DUE	TERMS OF SALE	PAYING RECORD D's	PAYING RECORD W's	DAYS SLOW	COMMENT
				INCLUDING NOTES						

THIS REPORT IS FOR EXTENSION OF COMMERCIAL CREDIT ONLY

INFORMATION HEREIN IS STRICTLY CONFIDENTIAL FOR THE EXCLUSIVE USE OF YOUR CREDIT DEPARTMENT.
UNDER NO CIRCUMSTANCES SHOULD LEDGER INFORMATION BE SHOWN OR REVEALED TO THE REPORTED SUBJECT.

LOS ANGELES #323 510									
#1060	ELEC		UNFILLED ORDER 1500						
#2236	ELEC .	270	276	280	183	183	210PX	30 60	
1059	ELEC	271	176	5052	3200	3200	10PX	60	NTH CK
#1077	ELEC	569	276	600	208		110PX	X	
1519	ELEC	470	376				COD	OUR REQ	
#2069	RADIO	YRS	176	4485	835	835	21030	60 90	FLOOR
#2235	ELEC	370	1175	923	923	923	10	120	
		ACCT TURNED OVER FOR COLLECTION							
#2274	RADIO	YRS	1175	197	191	191	COD	150	
2389	RADIO	YRS	276	3306	1627	1156	11030	30 120	
147	BANK	CUSTOMER 1 TO 3 YRS SM 4 FIG							
		SEC LN MED 4 FIG NUMEROUS LATE CHARGES							
		ITEM OF RECORD 11 1 75 WT & FICA TAX LIEN 3529							
		12 20 75 RELEASE OF WT & FICA TAX LIEN 3529							
		1 76 S B A LOAN 40000 GUARANTY PARTICIPATION—MINORITY							

FIGURE 3.7(b)
Credit Interchange Bureau Report

such comments as the credit grantors may have to make. Figure 3.8
illustrates how to read the report.

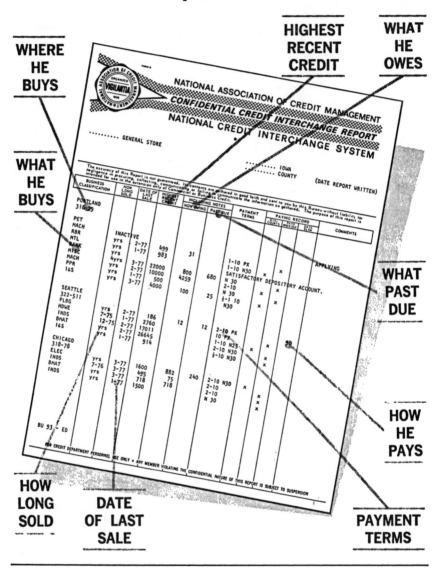

FIGURE 3.8
Reading a Credit Report

HOW TO ANALYZE A CREDIT INTERCHANGE REPORT

Business Classification

This column reveals the markets in which the subject is buying, the business classification of each contributor of information, and the period the experiences cover. Under each market is a code date showing exactly when members in that market were canvassed for information. Example: "402 – 40," under Des Moines. The 402 denotes that Des Moines contributors received requests from the Bureau and supplied the information on or after April 2. Buying in too many markets or in markets that are not customary sources of supply may indicate creditor lack of confidence. Buying one line from too many suppliers may indicate a badly broken stock of nominal sales value.

How Long Sold

This is a measure of the confidence creditors have in the subject. When a subject not just starting in business is found making first purchases from a large number of creditors within comparatively recent time, it is usually a signal of (1) refusal of credit accommodations on the part of his former suppliers, or (2) deliberate preparation for an overbuying fraud scheme.

Date of Last Sale

Lacking the date, the information should not be accepted as reliable. This is vital in times when there are certain to be variations in the fortunes of business institutions.

Check variations in "paying records" against "last sale" dates; they indicate the trend of the account. Check activity for indications of wise or speculative buying. Compare "how long sold" with "date of last sale." Unusual activity with a large number of new suppliers does not ordinarily indicate stability.

Highest Recent Credit

If not understood, this can easily be misleading. To illustrate: suppose a customer's normal requirements from a given source amount to $100 every ten days. If the customer buys on 2 percent 10, net 30 and discounts the bills, that customer will never owe the supplier more than $100. That would be the "high credit." If the customer does not discount but pays when due, the average indebtedness and accordingly the "high credit" shown might be $300. If payments are 30 days slow, the "high credit" may vary from $400 to $600.

Thus the "high credit" may be more a matter of necessity rather than exact measure of confidence. A large "high credit" may thus become an unfavorable rather than a favorable factor. Always check "highest credit" with "terms" and "manner of payment."

Highest Credit against Amount Owing

This indicates whether the subject of the report is owing the maximum accommodation recorded by its creditors or whether the subject is within the limits previously established. This appraisal should consider seasonal activities, and general trends in business.

Amount Owing

This is often of value in checking financial statements. Although Credit Interchange does not claim that reports cover the total indebtedness of the subject, frequently the "amount owing" (as shown on the report) is greater than that shown in the financial statement. Comparison of "amount owing" on reports over a period of time indicates the trend of the subject's affairs. Comparison with "high credit," measured against business trends, indicates whether the subject maintains a reserve or has exhausted credit accommodations. It discloses whether the subject is generally indebted to all sources of supply or whether a reasonable number of his accounts with creditors are in balance.

Amount Past Due

This is the first indicator of financial difficulty. Checking "date of last sale" and "paying record" usually indicates any refusals of further credit. A report showing little indebtedness, when checked as to "paying record," often indicates a definite lack of confidence in the subject. The information being secured from impartial sources, a comparison of "amount past due" with "amount owing" provides an accurate rating for determining what percentage of the total known indebtedness can be assumed as being past due. If a single item is past due it may indicate an honest dispute — not inability to pay.

A large amount "past due" should not be immediately accepted as indication of an unfavorable trend. A check against "amount owing" and "highest credit," together with "comments," will sometimes disclose that the subject is rapidly overcoming a period of adverse experience. If the "amount past due" is approximately equal to "amount owing," that can generally be accepted as a danger signal, indicating a time when those not presently suppliers might profitably refrain from becoming involved.

As a subject goes through the usual period of difficulty prior to failure, it is always noted that Credit Interchange subscribers are collecting and closing their accounts. The total "amount owing" on the reports grows correspondingly less. Thus a report on an involved subject may show a considerable number of creditors reporting, but the total "amount owing" may be very small. Under such conditions, Credit Interchange often cannot secure the major indebtedness, which usually rests with nonmembers. This situation should be construed as definite proof of the service. The "paying record" in such cases invariably discloses why members discontinued selling, and should be sufficient evidence for others to follow the same procedure.

Terms of Sale

This is frequently called the yardstick of the report. Variations in terms and discounts often explain variations in "paying record." In some instances it will be discovered that a good record in the home market is an indication that the subject is being held closely to terms for definite reasons. COD and CIA terms, which often indicate restrictions in credit accommodations, should not always be accepted as such. They are standard terms for certain industries and products. Often these terms are established at the subject's request and are, accordingly, a favorable instead of unfavorable factor in appraising the subject's business methods.

Manner of Payment

This is not the substance of the report, but merely a summarization and explanation of facts disclosed by other information. It is the guide to discovering important facts and details regarding the subject shown elsewhere in the report. A slow-paying record may indicate a highly unfavorable account, or it may indicate an account in temporary difficulty but in which creditors have high confidence. The distinction can always be established by referring to other facts in "amount past due" and "comments."

Averages are misleading in appraising "paying record." When a part of a creditor's report shows an account slow, and another part reports it as paying when due; or where there is a variation in the degree of slowness, a study of all the facts will often show the reasons, and disclose how erroneous a summary can be which shows so many discounting, so many paying when due, and so many slow.

Comments

This column provides space for pertinent facts not clear from routine figures as taken from the ledger page. Trend of payments, as appraised by the Credit Executives, will also appear in this column. Whether an account shows no change, is improving, or getting slower, is valuable information in determining the stability of the customer. Listed here will be "unfilled" or "first orders," maintained to protect against overbuying, fraud, or inexperience on the part of the subject. Excepting instances where a subject is just beginning in business, or where logical expansion is anticipated or under way, a report showing a large number of unfilled orders is always a signal for careful investigation. Care should be exercised in appraising comments such as "collected by attorney," or "refused," particularly when they are in conflict with the general record of payment. (Often a check on the date of the transaction in question will disclose the experience to have taken place at some much earlier date.)

Date

The date at the top of the report discloses when the report was written. The dates of the experiences shown in the report should always be determined by referring to the "market dates" (shown under market headings) and the "dates of last sale." This is particularly important in lines of industry where short discount terms prevail.

The totals of "amount owing" and "amount past due" columns should not be assumed as the totals representing the status of the customer. They are incorporated into the report for the convenience of members in arriving at percentages appraising volume of business.

THE NATIONAL CREDIT INFORMATION
SERVICE (NACIS)

The National Association of Credit Managers and TRW, Inc., recently developed and implemented a nationwide computerized business credit reporting system designed to assist credit managers in reducing the costs of carrying overdue accounts receivable. There were about two million firms in the information file when the system became operational in 1976. NACIS trade payment information is obtained only from contributing companies whose accounts receivable are automated. For the next few years this will restrict the data collected but as more companies become automated, the data base will increase.

Credit data showing the paying habits of specific firms are extracted from the automated accounts receivable to contributors to the service and sent on magnetic tape to the data center where it becomes part of the NACIS file. Information is put directly into the NACIS file as received in electronic form. Updated NACIS trade payment information is collected from contributing companies every 90 days.

A Credit Interchange Report is factual, it never offers recommendations or opinions. Personal comment not based on actual experience and outside party opinions are not included. Each report is confined to a clear, uncolored, impersonal statement of facts as recited by creditors, properly presented for quick intelligent analysis. Each column and detail of the report is valuable in the proper appraisal of credit responsibility.

For a clearer insight into the debtor's situation, various items on the report may be compared with others. The following suggestions for such analysis will be helpful.

There can be no short cuts or restrictions. Any service procedure that permits a creditor to secure information without giving his information promptly and completely as requested is founded on error and inequity. Continued support of this principle of "getting" without "giving" means the complete breakdown of that exchange of ledger experience information so vital to business under modern conditions.

If you should need additional information about Credit Interchange Service, contact:

> Credit Interchange Bureaus
> National Association of Credit
>   Management
> 1198 Arcade Building
> St. Louis, Missouri 63101

The NACIS report (Fig. 3.9) contains information on open credit accounts, date of last sale, payment terms, recent high credit, amount currently owing, and past-due dollar amounts in 30-, 60-, and 90-day categories. The bulk of information on a NACIS report consists of trade payment data taken directly from the accounts receivable records of their suppliers. Each contributor is shown on the report by its business category (chemicals, machinery, or other). Each trade line reported shows the customer's account balance and an aging of that balance into current and past due accounts.

All trade lines reported by NACIS are summarized on each report, so you can see at a glance how many contributors reported on the company in question (the total account balances reported) and an aging of that total into current and past due amounts. In addition to showing the total of the current account balances, they also show how these compare to the total account balances in any of the previous six months.

Costs of NACIS reports for contributors are about $3.55 for each NACIS report ordered over your own terminal or $3.95 for each report ordered through a NACM Association (costs are for 1977 only).

Responsibility of Members of Credit Interchange Bureaus and NACIS

Sometime ago there was a fad with jigsaw puzzles. The preparation of a Credit Interchange Report is quite like working one of those puzzles, with this difference: the worker of the puzzle has all of the pieces spread out, ready for placing as they fit into the picture. In Credit Interchange, the experience of each individual creditor is one piece of the credit picture the report will portray; therefore, when a member instructs the Bureau to prepare a report, there are two elements essential to the quick

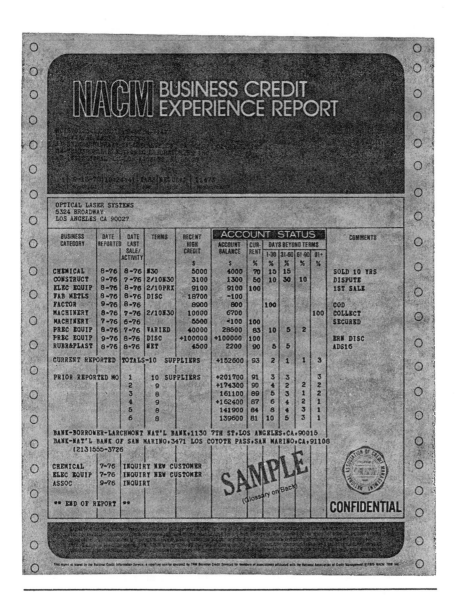

FIGURE 3.9
Business Credit Experience Report

assembling of that complete credit picture: first, the Bureau must know where to go for the pieces of the picture; second, the Bureau must have all the pieces before it can complete the picture. Therefore, to make the service effective, the member should (1) notify the Bureau of the accounts he is selling and/or follow the established procedure of the local Credit Interchange Bureau; (2) give the Bureau the names of all known creditors when making inquiry; (3) respond promptly and in complete detail to all requests for information received from the Bureau.

If that procedure is adhered to consistently and conscientiously, the member is contributing fully to a speedy, complete, and satisfactory service. If the member fails in that responsibility, satisfactory service is impossible.

BANK INFORMATION

Your customer's relationship with a bank is one of the most important. A customer's standing at a bank is important to you, the credit manager. Because banks are intimately involved with the activities of a company, they can furnish trade, ownership, and operating information that you may have been unable to locate elsewhere. The larger urban banks may not know an individual customer on a personal basis, but their files contain a wealth of information. The smaller banks in rural areas may have less complete files, but their views are supplemented by their acquaintance with the client on both a business and a social level. The following is a discussion of the type of information you may want to request from the bank.

1. How long has the bank had the account? This information puts the bank's evaluation of your customer in perspective. If the business is an existing one but the account is new, find out why the customer changed banks.
2. What is the average account balance? The average balance a customer keeps in a bank account helps you judge liquidity. When you compare this balance with the balance of other companies in the field, you can see a situation that would require future investigation. Knowing the opening balance of a customer who is a new business can help you determine if there is adequate financing to launch the enterprise. Finding the current balance is always necessary to verify a company's cash position. Banks tend to generalize when they give you

information about account balances (or loans). Rather than tell you the exact figures they will use the following generalizations with the corresponding meanings: low four figures ($1,000 to 2,000); moderate four figures ($2,000 to 4,000); medium four figures ($4,000 to 7,000); high four figures ($7,000 to 9,999); low five figures ($10,000 to 12,000).

3. Is the account a borrowing or nonborrowing account? If the account is nonborrowing, it is important to determine why. Since most companies borrow from their main bank, you could be getting information from your customer's secondary bank. The other reason that the account may be a nonborrowing one is that the company is a poor credit risk. The customer may be depending on outside financing rather than cheaper bank financing. Outside financing and no bank financing could indicate a serious situation for the customer. If the account is a borrowing one, you might want to find out the following information:

a. How much is the loan amount outstanding and how long does the customer have to pay it back? This information is necessary to determine if the customer's bank obligations will conflict with trade obligations with you.

b. How often does the customer borrow? If payments are promptly met with no damage to the trade record, a regular borrowing account can be a reliable customer for your company. Frequent large borrowings, however, could mean the company is undercapitalized.

c. Is the loan secured or unsecured? An unsecured loan is granted with no collateral put up by the company. Unsecured loans are usually a good indication that the bank has faith in the company. A secured loan may be secured by liquid assets (cash or securities), accounts receivable, inventory, warehouse and trust receipts, notes payable, equipment, or real estate.

d. Are there any overdrafts or have drafts been presented to the bank for collection?

Care must be taken in requesting information from a bank because their first responsibility is to their depositors. The following are some guidelines that should be considered when corresponding with a bank either in writing or over the phone:

1. If possible deal through your own bank. The most effective results can generally be obtained on a bank-to-bank basis. It is a great help if you can ask your company's bank to conduct the investigation for you. Bankers feel that they can be more honest with a fellow banker than with an unknown outside trade supplier.
2. Be sure to state the purpose of the inquiry. Is it due to increased slowness? For a new account? For heavier purchases?
3. Develop personal contacts with your bank and other bankers.
4. Be specific and limit your request. If inventory turnover for your customer appears extremely sluggish from your review of the figures, does the bank share this view?
5. Check to make absolutely sure that the name, address, and account number you furnish the bank is correct.
6. When you communicate by letter use only company stationery.

To find the name of your customer's bank you need only ask, look at the checks, or require that every new account that is sold furnish this information.

Bank furnished information is usually very reliable and banks are generally forthright and prompt in their replies.

INFORMATION FROM YOUR COMPANY SALES REPRESENTATIVE

Since the sales representative knows each account personally, his information is of great value to the credit manager. The sales representative from your own company can gather essential information when the order is taken, and on a continuing basis, he can develop helpful facts and impressions. Sales representatives are the credit manager's primary means of obtaining credit information directly from customers. Moreover, sales representatives are in an ideal position to measure the customer's plant and equipment, management, local and industry conditions, and location.

Sales representatives should be able to acquire from the customer certain credit information that you might need such as financial statements, references, and recent changes in management or operations. They can fill out financial statements or leave forms for the customer to fill out. It is probably a good idea if you develop a credit application form for your customer. The form could include customer's name, address, telephone number, bank, type of legal form of ownership (corporation, proprietorship, or partnership), owners' names, specimen purchase order request, commercial references (names and addresses), date business established, other pertinent business history, and a sample profit and loss and balance sheet.

Because sales representatives visit the plants of many different companies in the same field, they can get a good view of any one company's equipment and production. They can compare equipment and production to other companies in the same field. In the retail field, representatives can evaluate the merchandising abilities of managers as well as the quantity and quality of the products sold. Seeing the premises also gives a sales representative an idea of how productive and up-to-date the company is.

Sales representatives have a good idea of an industry in general because they frequently sell to many companies in the same industry. They usually sell in one particular geographic area, which gives them a handle on local conditions such as strikes and product tastes. Such an overview of the geographic area as well as the competition in that area is a good barometer of the adequacy of a particular customer's location.

Sales representatives who are successful know how to "read" people, they understand what they want and where they "are coming from." Even poor sales representatives know people better than the average person. Their opinions of a customer's management attitude may be quite accurate.

Although sales representatives are potentially a great source of information, they are sometimes reluctant to provide it. Their main objections to securing information are: the time required, fear of offending the customer, and losing a sale because of adverse credit information. The best way to overcome these objections is to know your representatives personally, emphasize and explain credit policies to all new representatives as well as veterans, and inform them of your credit decision on every case. Notifying your sales representative in the event of an unfavorable decision will be to your advantage. If a sales representative finds out about an unfavorable credit decision from a customer first, he will be very embarrassed and upset.

Above all, when you are using sales representatives for acquiring information, remember that they always want the sale and the money or prestige it brings, so they will tend to act as the customer's advocate whenever possible.

INFORMATION FROM REFERENCES

The term *references* includes the names of suppliers submitted by the applicant and other sources provided by your sales representative or your own personal experience.

The media used in the inquiry of references has a great bearing on the results attained. Most inquiries about payment experience are made by mail. These are made by either a standardized routine form or a letter inviting a reply by letter. Since the latter method will be answered by a credit manager, it is probably the better of the two. If you use mail inquiry, it should be restricted to routine investigations of basically sound automatic or semiautomatic account customers or to cases that do not warrant the cost of a telephone call.

Unfortunately, a form inquiry or even a personal letter will probably produce the barest of results. If you feel the need for other than skeletal information, you should use the telephone, regardless of the location of the reference. It is far less costly for a skilled credit manager to spend ten minutes discussing a marginal situation with another supplier than to send out a hundred form inquiries.

You should also be aware that the list of references you are calling is supplied by *your customer*, who obviously is not going to supply any negative references.

OTHER SOURCES OF INFORMATION

Two other sources of credit information about your customer are other suppliers in the same industry (in addition to the ones your customer gives you as references) and the companies who buy from your customer.

Information from other suppliers can be obtained from credit interchanges, such as the NACM (National Association of Credit Managers) credit interchange, mentioned earlier. You may also get information by direct interchange. This means communicating in some form (letter or telephone) directly with one supplier to obtain that supplier's ledger experience with your customer. This is a very expensive method, however, and should be reserved for large, risky accounts, accounts for which information is not available from other sources, and accounts that have outdated information. Apply the same rules for this inquiry as with bank inquiries: ask specific, short questions; check for the exact name, address and account number; and so on.

Group meetings with other suppliers are excellent and inexpensive direct interchanges between suppliers. More suppliers can supply more information about more customers at the same time. Group meetings are usually enjoyable, offer the opportunity to meet other credit people and to learn some of the latest credit and collection techniques. Sponsors of group meetings include NACM, credit associations, Dun and Bradstreet, the National Credit Office, other industry credit publishers, local trade associations, and sometimes the large universities.

Another source of information, one which is not often tapped by the credit manager, is your customer's customers. Knowing who a company's customers are can tell you a lot about the company and its future ability to pay your bills. If the company's clients change rapidly, if they consist of only small, unreliable accounts, or if one of the large clients is in legal or financial straits, then your customer will have trouble paying you. If your client's customers, on the other hand, are large, reliable, financially solid, and have bought from the company for a long time, chances of your being paid are quite good.

4

Credit Managers and Reports to Management

Unfortunately, in this country top management has been slow to recognize the importance of the credit manager's functions. Usually the position of credit manager falls into a subdivision of the financial or sales departments. This is unfortunate, and could be devastating, because a good credit manager can mean profit for a company in both the recovery of loss or prospective loss and increased sales. Still, in how many companies is the credit manager awarded an executive vice presidency, or whose chief executive officer is a former credit manager? Lately, credit managers have been coming into their own as important participants in overall company policy and management and are now more often contenders for higher executive posts.

Today credit managers not only have to be tough, tactful, and well-trained, but they must have skills and knowledge in several different fields. A credit manager must know about accounting, financial statement analysis, collection techniques, commercial law (including bankruptcies, tax, and negotiable instruments), management, psychology, purchasing, finance, and communication. Formal training of a credit manager usually includes a college degree and, more and more, an MBA. In addition, credit managers probably have years of on-the-job training in addition to their academic degree(s).

THE CREDIT MANAGER AND THE COMPANY

Because of the functions of the credit department and its effect on the operations of other departments in a company, the credit manager must interact with members of several departments.

The department in the company that the credit manager must interact with most is the sales department. Credit is important not only in making the sale but in collecting later. A good relationship between the credit manager and the sales manager as well as the top sales representatives is not only a good idea, but can save the credit manager time and energy in the long run.

The finance department and the legal department depend on the credit manager for good cash forecasting and a fluency in credit law. Sometimes the credit manager can tell the finance department a thing or two about patterns of payment and show the legal department some interesting points about bankruptcy law and laws dealing with negotiable instruments and taxes.

Because a credit manager and the credit department are in frequent contact with customers, the public relations people are generally interested in their impact on sales and company goodwill. The credit department can provide valuable help to the purchasing people because of the credit department's ability to appraise a supplier for stability and responsibility.

In a small company, the credit manager should have an ongoing relationship with (or in some cases is one-and-the-same as) the company president, sales manager, and/or accountant.

A credit manager's responsibilities include maintaining good relations with customers; formulating credit policy; assisting in formulation of general company policy; staffing and training of the credit department; cash forecasting; protecting company interests; and administrating the credit department.

The most important duty of the credit manager is collecting receivables. This seems obvious, but with all the things that you as the credit manager have to do, it is easy to lose track of your main reason for being there.

The factors that affect the way you collect receivables vary from the way you (and your boss) set up credit and collection policies, to your use of collection devices, to establishment of collection schedules. Once an account becomes delinquent, the credit department must make the necessary telephone calls or visits and write the necessary letters to bring in the money.

The other main function of the credit department is extending credit. The credit department evaluates the credit worthiness of the company's customers and decides whether merchandise or services can be sold on credit terms. The department (or you) must then establish a credit limit for each customer. Assuming that company credit policy is already in existence, the major part of extending credit is collecting credit information.

MEASURING AND EVALUATING COLLECTION RESULTS

A credit manager should occasionally (at least once, preferably twice, a year) review credit policy, clients, and the cost effectiveness of the credit department. This should be done for two reasons: to find out how effective your department is in terms of profit to the company and to let the boss know how you are doing.

The first step in determining the effectiveness of the credit department is to review present policy and activities to see if changes are in order. A change in any one of the variables that you used to set credit policy can mean that your policy will swing in one direction or another, liberal or conservative. You should concern yourself with whether current policy is being carried out properly. This can be done by checking on client files and ledgers. Changes in the industry or the type of customers you have or any new products that your company is pushing will also have an effect on whether credit policy is adequate. Many times changes will take place to correspond with changes in the collective financial condition of your company's customers.

As we illustrated earlier, the relative amount of trade receivables in business is growing rapidly. Collecting on these receivables is not only important to cash flow of a company — it is crucial. Additionally, sales representatives know that profitable sales to marginal risks, which require extreme skill in handling, are a major source of increased company revenue. For these reasons, the head person in any organization has become extremely interested in how effectively the credit department is operating. The measures of this credit efficiency are collection results, bad debt losses, administrative efficiency, and credit rejections.

Collection Results Measurements

There are basically three measures of collection results: aging of receivables, day's sales outstanding (DSO), and receivable turnover.

Aging of receivables, which we discussed in Chapter 2, is one of the oldest, simplest, and most effective methods of determining collection efficiency. An aging is a schedule that shows all the accounts that owe you money, how much, and for how long. The firms that owe you the most money for the longest time are the ones that should get most of your attention. An effective collection effort will be reflected in the great majority of the accounts paying within the required current period (say 30 days). An accounts receivable aging that shows 95 percent of the accounts or more as current indicates a very effective collection policy. Some companies age their accounts receivable monthly or weekly (and unfortunately, some companies do it only quarterly). For the greatest efficiency and feedback to you, the credit manager, accounts receivable should be aged daily.

Day's sales outstanding (DSO) is a measure of credit department efficiency calculated by dividing the closing accounts receivables balance by the average daily credit billings.

The closing accounts receivable balance is the amount of accounts receivable outstanding at the end of a period (say on a quarterly balance sheet). The average daily credit billings is the total billings for a period divided by the number of days in that period. For example, Your Company, Inc., has an accounts receivable balance at the end of the first quarter of $100,000. The total billings for the three month (90-day) period is $300,000. (If all sales of Your Company are on credit, the total credit billings would equal the total sales). Dividing $300,000 by 90 days you get average daily credit billings of $3,333. DSO would be calculated: $100,000 ÷ $3,333 = 30 days.

In the case of Your Company, Inc., 30 days is the period required by the terms of sale, so the collection efficiency is right on. If the DSO is considerably longer than the period provided by the terms of sale, it is a sign that collection efforts should be improved. DSO is also useful in comparing your credit department's performance with that of other companies in your field. (Information is available from the Credit Research Foundation's publication National Summary of Domestic Trade Receivables.) Comparing your present DSO with previous periods DSO in your same company will give you an idea of what your trend in collection is — up or down.

Receivable turnover and collection period can be determined in several different ways. Receivable turnover is an indication of how long it takes in days for you to collect an "average" receivable, how much receivables are in relation to sales, or how many times your accounts "turn over" in a given period.

The best known receivable turnover ratio shows the average number of days it takes you to collect an average account. This is called the average collection period ratio and is essentially the same as the DSO. It is a two-step ratio and looks like this:

Step 1: $\dfrac{\text{net sales for the period}}{\text{number of days in the period}}$ = average sales per day

Step 2: $\dfrac{\substack{\text{accounts receivable} \\ \text{at the end of period}}}{\substack{\text{average sales per} \\ \text{day (from Step 1)}}}$ = average collection period in days

For example, Your Company, Inc., has sales at the end of the second quarter (six month or 180-day period) of $180,000. The accounts receivable outstanding at the end of the same second quarter is $45,000. The average collection period in days would be calculated as follows:

Step 1: $\dfrac{\$180{,}000 \text{ net sales}}{180 \text{ days}}$ = $1,000 average sales per day

Step 2: $\dfrac{\substack{\$45{,}000 \text{ accounts} \\ \text{receivable}}}{\substack{\$1{,}000 \text{ average} \\ \text{sales per day}}}$ = 45 days average collection period

If the terms of sale for Your Company is 30 days, then Your Company's collection efforts would be too slow at 45 days. Provision would have to be made for stronger collection procedures. If the average collection period is longer than it is supposed to be (say 90 days in the case of Your Company), you *know* you are in trouble.

How long should the collection period be? Ordinarily, the collection period should be no more than one third greater than the net selling terms required by your company on an open-book account. The formula for this is:

$\substack{\text{Safe average} \\ \text{collection period}}$ = net selling terms + $\dfrac{\text{net selling terms}}{3}$

If you are selling on net 30 day terms, the collection period should not exceed 40 days. With net 60 day terms, the collection period should not exceed 80 days.

Another technique for calculating receivable turnover is the *net sales to accounts receivable ratio*. This can be calculated by dividing the closing accounts receivable (after deducting reserve for bad debts) into the net sales for the period.

In other words, this ratio tells you how many times you collect all your receivables during a period. If you use the example of Your Company, Inc., above ($180,000 sales and $45,000 in receivables) you will clear out your receivables, or turn them over, four times during the period. Unfortunately, this ratio by itself does not tell you all that you must know unless you compare it to industry information or to your own company history to get a trend. The higher the number of times that the receivables turn over in a given period, the more efficient your collection operations are.

A *collection index* may be calculated by dividing receivables outstanding at the beginning of a period into collections during that period.

This collection index shows you how efficiently you have collected all those accounts that were outstanding at the beginning of the period and how much you have done in addition to that. If the collection index is 1, that is, it took you the whole period to collect receivables that were outstanding at the beginning of the period (unless the period in question is only one month) you know that your collection effort is weak. Generally speaking, the lower the collection index number, the stronger your collection effort. The problem with this ratio, like the net sales to accounts receivable ratio, is that it is relative. It makes real sense only when compared to others in the same industry or your own historical trend.

Changing credit policy could be one factor to be considered when looking at losses. If the credit policy has become more liberal lately, you can probably expect more *bad-debt loss* than before. If policies have become more conservative, there should be a decline in bad-debt loss. If your credit policy has become more conservative and your losses are increasing, this might be an indicator that something is wrong. Of course, general economic and industry conditions may also affect a company's bad-debt losses, and this should be taken into consideration. Perhaps of more help than just the absolute number and dollar amount of loss is bad-debt loss per risk category (automatic, semiautomatic, nonautomatic [average], and marginal). You expect some losses in your marginal accounts, but if your automatic accounts are showing losses, perhaps it is time to re-examine your whole program.

Bad-debt losses are generally measured as a percentage of total sales, or (more properly) as a percentage of total credit sales. Bad-debt losses as a percentage of sales, sometimes called a bad-debt ratio, is calculated by dividing total bad debt by credit sales.

According to a Credit Research Foundation study, the average bad-debt loss for wholesalers was 0.13 percent, the average for manufacturers was about half as much at 0.06 percent; wholesalers varied in their loss between 0.11 percent and 0.4 percent; manufacturers' bad-debt loss varied from 0.026 percent to 0.62 percent. This study was for large companies with good credit departments and big clients, but it can give you an idea of what percentage is allowable. How much of a percentage loss to bad debt is acceptable in your company is relative, but offhand I would say losses above 3 percent of credit sales is dangerous in most companies. Banks, for instance, consider a loss of more than 1.5 percent of their loans as intolerable. The only time that a company can withstand bad-debt losses in excess of 3 percent is if the product they are selling has a very large gross margin.

Administrative Efficiency and Credit Rejections

Administrative efficiency can be measured by the volume of work, volume of active credit accounts, and cost comparisons.

The number of orders processed, letters written, and calls made measure the volume of work within the department. If you take these numbers and compare them with an equivalent previous period, you can get a good idea of relative work volumes. If you have done a larger volume of work with the same number or less employees, it indicates that your efficiency is getting progressively better. You might go one step further and take the total volume of work and divide it by the number of employees, which will give you the volume of work per employee. This is easily compared to the same volume per employee in previous years.

The volume of active credit accounts can be used to calculate average profit per account, sales per account, accounts receivable per account, and credit department costs per account. These figures by themselves do not mean much, but when you compare them to those of previous periods they give you a feel for any current improvements or defects.

Cost comparisons in the credit department mean making a comparison of the current period's cost of operating the credit department with the cost of the prior periods and against budgeted costs. The problem with this is inflation. Personnel, rent, supplies — everything that cost so much last year is going to cost so much more this year. Comparing the costs of operation with budgeted costs is not a bad idea, but there are still a lot of things that can increase costs that are beyond your control.

Credit rejections may be calculated on the basis of orders, total dollar amounts, or both. Calculating the number of credit rejections as a percentage of total applications or the dollar amount of rejections as a percentage of total dollar amount of credit applications might be helpful. Basically, this ratio will only show you that you have a large or small percentage of credit applications rejected. The only time this would be useful is if the company purports to have a conservative policy yet has very few rejections. That would tell you that something is haywire. If the policy purports to be liberal yet has a lot of rejections, this would also indicate something is awry.

CREDIT MANAGER REPORTS TO MANAGEMENT

If the credit manager and the owner of the business are not the same person, management will from time to time want reports from the credit manager on the effectiveness of the credit operation.

Measuring the effectiveness of the credit department is not only important to the boss, but it is important to you. If the credit department has done poorly, it is important that the boss knows why. It could be that the credit policy is insufficient, the sales department is uncooperative, the new product introduction is too costly in credit losses, or several other factors that can be improved through planning and cooperation.

If you, the credit manager, do not make reports, there are no milestones that tell you where you are, where you have been, and where you are going. In short, no one can tell if the policy and the department are good or bad, effective or ineffective.

There are two basic problems in making a report: it has to be readable by someone who does not have day-to-day contact with the credit department, and it has to include all the facts.

Some companies may already have a reporting format well thought out by management, and designed to meet their needs. Other companies have no format at all or an existing format that is inadequate. Partially because of the different needs of different companies, no book on credit and collections has any sample format that the credit manager can use for reporting. This is unfortunate because one of the most crucial factors in a smooth-running credit department is good communication with management.

Therefore, based on my experience as a financial analyst, manager, management consultant, and long-time researcher on credit and collection problems, I propose the following format. The format emphasizes clarity and facts and minimizes confusion.

CREDIT DEPARTMENT REPORT FORMAT

The format for reports (see a sample report from Hero Manufacturing, Inc., at the end of this chapter) includes the following sections: performance data, collection efficiency ratios, summary, comparisons of performance data, comparisons of collection efficiency ratios, and special problems and considerations.

The first two sections, performance data and collection efficiency ratios, are the numbers that result from the department records, financial statements, and analysis. The other sections starting with summary and ending with special problems and considerations are sections explaining why the numbers fell as they did, how they relate to previous years and the industry averages, and any special problems that you might want to bring up with management.

The sections are organized in the order most managers want the information so that a busy executive need read only the first few sections and get the necessary data. The detail is sufficient enough so that financial control-minded management can get all the explanation it needs.

Performance Data

The performance data section includes all the raw numbers from financial statements and credit department records. It includes the amounts for sales, accounts receivable, average daily collections, bad-debt losses, work volume, number of accounts, department costs, and credit rejections. It also gives special details about some of the categories. For instance, volume of work is divided into number of orders processed, letters sent, calls made, and so on. Bad-debt losses are broken down into number and dollar amount, and so forth. The numbers are given not only for the present period, but also for previous periods.

Collection Efficiency Ratios

The collection efficiency ratios section includes all the performance ratios for the current period, previous period, and industry average. This section includes average collection period, day's sales outstanding, receivable turnover, bad-debt losses both as a percentage of sales and of total orders processed, and the collection index.

Summary

The summary section is a brief discussion of what the data and the ratios indicate about present operations and their relationship to historical and industry information. The information that is particularly good or especially bad should be emphasized here. This section is a written explanation to management of what your operation has accomplished over the featured period. Comments should be brief and easily understood. This is probably the most important section.

Comparisons of Performance Data

This section should be a detailed description of what the data means, how it relates to previous periods, and how the information was compiled. In this section as well as the next one, you might want to list the data and explain it one figure at a time, emphasizing increases or decreases from the previous period.

Comparisons of Collection Efficiency Ratios

This section, like the previous one, should give a detailed explanation of what the ratios mean. Unlike the previous section, however, this section must not only talk about current and previous periods of your own company, but also how it compares to the industry averages. A detailed explanation, item-for-item, of every ratio that is more or less than the industry or previous period figures should be undertaken.

Special Problems and Considerations

This section is the credit manager's sounding board for any special problems that have occurred in the department during the period. The discussion should include relations with other departments such as sales, any results of policy or operation changes, or any difficulties that arise from extending credit for a particular product. I suggest that you also list the ten slowest or problem accounts that you dealt with (or are still dealing with) during the period. The problems discussed here should be problems that will have an effect on management, sales, or profits and any personal problems that you might be having currently. You can also take a look into the future for the next period to predict what kind of results you expect and what changes you think should be made.

Sample Format

On the following pages is a sample of how the format works for a company, in this case, Hero Manufacturing, Inc. The sample should give you a good idea of how the report functions and what things it usually covers.

The following sample may be too complicated for your particular operation or may be too simple. You need not use all the data, ratios, and explanations featured in this sample. You may want to add some information. This format is flexible and meant to cover most circumstances, but not all. Eliminate those parts you do not like or add to it things that you think are more relevant to your own company.

CREDIT AND COLLECTIONS
DEPARTMENT REPORT
FOR THE YEAR ENDED 12/30/1978

HERO MANUFACTURING, INC.
Ronald Roper, Credit Manager

Summary

This year the credit department processed more orders, collected more, and billed more than the previous year. We also had more personal visits to customers and more telephone calls than the previous year. Our average dollar sales per account was higher than before although our gross profit per account dropped (due primarily to the company's overall lower gross margin than the previous year). Even though we had a slightly larger dollar credit loss than last year, losses were for a fewer number of accounts. The credit department had higher costs than the previous year, but this is partially due to inflation and an increase in staff. With the present growth rate of the company (30 percent per year) the fixed cost of credit operations should remain low as a percentage of sales. Credit department costs were over the budget this year, but this may be partially due to the unforeseen growth in sales the company has been experiencing. Cost per account is also higher than in the previous year. The number and dollar amount of credit rejections has increased over the past in an effort by the credit department to cut down on the number and dollar amount of bad-debt losses.

All of the credit department's collection efficiency ratios are better than the previous year and a good deal better than the industry averages. Our average collection period dropped from 44 days last year to 37 days this year, well below the industry average. Our receivable turnover is more rapid than last year and much better than the industry average. Bad debt as both a percentage of sales and a percentage of total orders processed is less than the previous year and better than the industry average.

The disappointing area of last year's performance was the cost of operations increase and the slight increase in dollar amount of bad-debt losses. Currently I am planning a reevaluation of the department's costs to see if they can be cut to some degree in the area of supplies, telephone calls, and travel. Even though bad-debt losses increased in dollar amount, the number of accounts that had to be considered bad debt has dropped from the previous year. The department also experienced an increase in credit rejections, but we in the department consider this a necessary procedure in order to keep bad-debt losses in line.

Comparisons of Performance Data

Average daily billings are calculated by dividing the total sales, since all sales are on credit, by 360 days. Average daily billings increased 30 percent over the previous year. The dollar amount of bad-debt losses increased only 7 percent over the previous year and the number of bad-debt loss accounts decreased by 27 percent. We processed 20 percent more orders than last year, made twice as many phone calls, and made slightly more personal visits. We wrote about half as many letters.

We had 12 percent (or 15) more accounts at year end than we had at the beginning of the year (year-end 1977). Each account bought 9 percent

TABLE 1
Performance Data

Item	Present Period 12/30/1978	Previous Period 12/30/1977
Sales	$5,620,000	$4,323,000
Accounts receivable	$580,000	$528,367
Total collections during period	$5,300,000	$4,020,000
Average daily billing	$15,611	$12,008
Bad-debt losses	$80,000	$75,000
No. Bad-debt losses	11 accounts	15 accounts
Volume of work:		
Orders processed	2,070	1,730
Letters sent	1,022	2,316
Telephone calls	8,640	4,310
Personal visits	380	310
Number of accounts at year-end	138	123
Average sales per account	$38,406	$35,146
Average gross profit per account	$9,774	$10,192
Cost of credit department:		
Actual	$51,500	$42,750
Budgeted	$45,000	$40,000
Cost per account	$373	$346
Credit rejections:		
No. of credit rejections	75	38
$ of credit rejections	$462,000	$216,000

more product than in the previous year, although profit per account dropped 4 percent.

The costs to run the credit department include salaries and payroll tax for three employees ($49,500) and supplies and postage ($2,000). The costs of operations increased 20 percent over the previous year and the cost per account increased by 8 percent. Actual costs of operation were $6,500 over budget. The over budget costs can be accounted for by unexpected volume of sales and inflation not taken into consideration.

Credit rejections were high when compared to the previous year. We had 75 rejected applications, a 97 percent increase over last year. The total amount for the orders that we turned down was $462,000, a 114 percent increase over last year. The credit department decided last year, and management agreed, that our credit policy had to be more conservative in order to keep down the number of bad-debt losses, which we have done for the most part.

Comparisons of Collection Efficiency Ratios

All collection efficiency ratios showed better performance this year than the previous year, and also better performance than the industry averages. The industry averages were taken from Credit Research Foundation's *National Summary of Domestic Trade Receivables.*

Average collection period and day's sales outstanding are calculated by the following ratio:

$$\frac{\text{accounts receivable}}{\text{average sales per day}}$$

Receivable turnover is calculated by the following ratio:

$$\frac{\text{net sales}}{\text{accounts receivable}}$$

The average collection period dropped from 44 days last year to 37 days this year. The turnover of receivables increased from 8 times a year

TABLE 2
Collection Efficiency Ratios

Ratio	12/30/1978	12/30/1977	Industry
Average collection period	37.15 days	44 days	48 days
Days sales outstanding	37.15 days	44 days	48 days
Receivable turnover*	9.69 times	8.18 times	7.5 times
Bad debt as a % of sales	1.4%	1.7%	2.0%
Bad debt as a % of total orders processed	0.5%	0.9%	N/A

Receivable turnover is calculated by the net sales to accounts receivable ratio.

to 9 and one half times. Bad-debt losses dropped as a percentage of sales and total orders processed.

Our success in collections is due to the new tough policy the credit department instituted at the beginning of the current period.

Special Problems and Considerations

Ten slowest accounts at year-end: Rotten Distribution, 95 days; Goose-creek Mfg., 91 days; Darsten-Disken, 86 days; Tie Top Tennies, 84 days; Sarranch Supply, 79 days; Tushi Distributors, 79 days; Miniola Mile-stones, 76 days; Sloopi Supply, 71 days; Slap Supply, 63 days; and Realrock Distribution, 59 days.

Results of credit policy changes: Credit policy was more conservative and an increased effort was made in collections at the beginning of this year. As a result of this change in policy, a smaller number of accounts have become bad-debt losses and our collection period has decreased to only 37 days from 44 days last year. The policy change has also caused an increase in the number and dollar amount of credit rejections, but we believe this to be a necessary part of the restrictive credit policy.

Increases in department costs: This year we experienced a 20 percent increase in credit department costs over last year, but only an 8 percent increase in costs per account. We think these increased costs are reasonable in view of the increased sales and work due to a more restrictive credit policy. The difference between budgeted and actual costs can be attributed to the unforeseen increase in company sales.

Relations with other departments: The sales department had difficulty adjusting to our new conservative credit policy at the first of the year, and it caused some friction between our departments. The sales representatives, however, have since adjusted and are themselves becoming more selective about the customers they sell to. I would suggest that if any changes in the credit policy be made in the future that we have a long interchange between the credit and sales departments before the policy goes into effect. Relations with other departments remained good throughout the year.

5

To Whom Should You Extend Credit — Nonfinancial Analysis

The job of a credit agent is to know whether a customer or a prospective customer will pay the bills. When you are right about the customer, your company makes money, you save a lot of time and energy, and you look good to management. When you are wrong, you and your company lose. Your company loses money to bad debts and ties up working capital, and you lose prestige. The better your judgment, the better off everyone is.

There are two ways to judge an account: on a nonfinancial analysis basis and on an in-depth financial basis. Nonfinancial analysis is less expensive in time and money, but it is not as accurate as financial analysis in predicting success of the credit. In most cases, fortunately, nonfinancial analysis is all that is required to make a good judgment. This chapter will discuss nonfinancial judgments and Chapter 6 will discuss the various financial analysis techniques used to make credit judgments.

Nonfinancial judgments are based on account credit information (discussed in Chapter 3), payment performance and antecedents, owners' and managers' experience and background, business age and growth, impressions of company employees, financing and adequacy of capital, business trends, and other factors including attitude of the customer.

AGENCY REPORT INFORMATION

A typical agency report indicates when a business started, when the present owners took over, and when and if it was incorporated. The report also gives you a brief biography of the principals.

By reading the reports you will find that Hero Manufacturing, for example, started ten years ago, came under its present management control two years ago, and was incorporated in California last year. John Hero, the president, is forty-eight and married. Before he became president of Hero, he worked in the aerospace industry making space-age hamburger containers. Before that he had two more enterprises that were sold to large conglomerates. Hero has a MBA from University of Southern California. The report also tells about the comptroller, vice president, and other executives.

If there was any derogatory information about anyone in the firm such as convictions for fraud, it would be reflected in this report. Any bankruptcy in the past would also be listed in the report. Reports also tell you the location, appearance of buildings, and legal composition of the company.

In short, industry and agency reports briefly cover management and the age of the company. The reports identify, but do not reveal, the growth trend, the extent of expansion, the potential for success, and the ability of the employees.

If the company you are investigating is very large with good credit, you probably do not need any more than what the agency reports will tell you. But consider this: the Dun and Bradstreet Reference Book lists over three million businesses in the United States, and well over half of them are worth less than $50,000. Only 5 percent of the businesses they list are worth over $500,000. So the majority of companies you will be dealing with are small businesses. Accordingly, there is a lot more involved with evaluating a small business than a brief history. The main characteristic of a small business is there is one individual, usually not a professional manager, who is running the show.

PAYMENT PERFORMANCE AND ANTECEDENTS

All credit persons know how important it is to know the history of potential customers. There is no better indicator of the future than an analysis of the past. If the owners have been hardworking, prompt, and ambitious in the past, there is little reason to believe that this will change in the future. We are told by psychologists that a child has his moral pattern set for life by the time he is nine years old. Surely the way people handle themselves morally when they start their very first business is an indicator of their future business behavior. Since businesses do not run themselves, the most important indicator of business behavior is the behavior of the owners.

Payment Performance

Probably the best indicator of a business's payment ability in the future is a review of its historical payment ability and past payment record. If you have information about the business's payment performance with other companies, it is a good idea to review this information. You may also discover any special financial arrangements a company may have, and, most important, where a company buys. Historical payment performance is available in agency reports.

It is important to gather a representative sampling from other suppliers when you are evaluating the payment performance of a business. A company's payment record may vary widely with different suppliers. Even though a company may be in trouble, it may maintain a few prompt accounts for reference purposes. It is also possible that a customer could be prompt with others but slow with you.

A careful look at suppliers will also indicate a pattern of taking discounts, paying on a geographical basis, and sometimes a pattern of no patterns. The amount of high credit that is extended to a customer is something to consider as well as the amount currently owing. It is okay for a customer to have a high percentage owing during seasonally busy times when the credit limit is high and a low percentage during the seasonal lulls. Any deviation from this pattern, however, should provoke your investigation.

Past due accounts should always concern you. Be aware, though, that the slowness might be temporary. You know the reasons for slowness and the inability to repay: financial or legal problems, management turmoil, the owner drawing too much money, overbuying, disasters, etc.

Sometimes, however, the slowness is just temporary due to misunderstandings between shipper and buyer on terms, amounts shipped, etc., and slowness due to inadequate accounts payable to personnel. If the customer is slow, it is a good idea to find out why.

In summary, usually a supplier will report that an account either takes discounts, anticipates (pays in advance of the discount period), is slow or is prompt. The report that concerns you the most is that the account is slow. If you get this in a report, try to find out for how long, and, if possible, why.

Antecedents

Before undertaking an evaluation of a business's antecedents, verify if the business has activities conducted under other names, any gaps in the owner's history, and owner's previous employment.

When you boil down non-financial credit analysis to the most important factor, that factor is *character* — the character of the owners. As we discussed in the first chapter, good character is a pretty undefinable quality, but most people can tell you what bad character is. These facets of character, while not appearing on an agency report, can be determined by talking to other suppliers and company employees. These factors of character do not usually appear on agency reports, but you can find them out fast enough by talking to other suppliers and the company employees.

Any history of business failure should be of particular concern to you as a credit manager. Business failures include bankruptcies, general compromises and extensions, and informal discontinuances. We will discuss bankruptcy and general compromises and extensions (creditor actions) in Chapter 9. An informal discontinuance is when an owner gives (or sells for $1) the business to someone else to take over, thereby removing himself from the situation entirely. It is important to determine the type of failure, the cause of failure, and the settlement with creditors. Whether the bankruptcy was voluntary or involuntary may expose a great deal about the owners. A voluntary bankruptcy is a bankruptcy requested by the owners of the business. An involuntary bankruptcy is a bankruptcy initiated by creditors selling goods to the business. Knowing how much the creditors received and how willing management was to meet most of their obligations is important. If the cause of the bankruptcy was bad management (94 percent of all manufacturing bankruptcies are), how has management improved since then?

If there has ever been a fire, investigate the facts involving this fire. Even the most innocent fires cause delays in collections and can often result in credit losses because fire insurance policies, even though they do cover the damage, do not always result in 100 percent coverage of loss. There is usually a time delay before compensation is made, fixed expenses continue, and business activities are disrupted. The loss of business momentum alone will cut a company's sales and profits. Many times business records are lost and the company has to request duplicate invoices. Unfortunately, sometimes fires and losses are suffered because a desperate person turns to arson to solve a company's problems. For these reasons it is important that you find out if a business has had a fire before, or worse yet, several fires. You should determine the date of the fire, insurance recovery, cause of the fire, assets damaged, whether it was a partial or total loss, and if the business continued operations or temporarily suspended operations after the fire.

A history of civil and criminal proceedings against the business, its officers, or its employees should receive further investigation. A civil proceeding is a law suit in which one party claims that he has been damaged by the company, its employees, its officers, or its products or services. The fact that a suit has been filed in the courts does not mean that the defendants are liable for anything. A pattern of suits brought against or brought by a customer, however, can be a good indication that payment problems might be encountered. To guard yourself against any unwanted legal problems, you must ask: Has payment of a judgment caused an impairment in the financial condition of the company?

Criminal proceedings against officers or employees can have an effect on the business for several reasons including excessive financial drain and time away from the business. If the customer is judged innocent or pardoned, but has a pattern of criminal charges, the credit risk can still be considered high. A person continually defending himself does not have the time and energy to run a business properly.

OWNERSHIP AND GENERAL MANAGEMENT
EXPERIENCE

Ownership

Who owns the business you are analyzing? The answer to that question may seem simple. Yet, according to Dun and Bradstreet's figures about 20 percent of the businesses operating at the beginning of this year will have either changed ownership or vanished by the end of this year. Remember also that Totsmith's Horn Manufacturing might not be owned by Mr. Totsmith, and may not even manufacture horns anymore. Ownership is a legal issue and generally whoever holds title to the capital of a business is the owner of the business. In some cases the owner might be an estate or the bank. Be aware of an agent or manager acting for the owner, if the company is not a corporation, or worse yet there may be a hidden ownership. An agent is a person appointed to transact the business of someone else and who derives authority from that someone else. It is possible that the owner confers such wide power to a manager that the manager has almost total control over the assets. If this is the case, you will want to deal with the agent rather than the owner. Hidden ownership occurs when someone, who might have provided all the capital for the business and owns the major interest and shapes all the policies, gives someone else technical ownership. To find out who the real owner is ask these questions: Who makes the important decisions? Who is authorized to sign on the bank account? Who authorizes large purchases? None of these will lead to the legal owner in many cases.

The legal liability of the owner is directly related to the type of legal organization the business has: sole proprietorship, partnership, or corporation. If a *sole* proprietorship (an unincorporated business owned by one man), runs up debt and cannot pay from the assets of the business, the owner's personal assets are subject to suit and claim. Legal responsibility puts a sole proprietorship between a rock and a hard place. A *partnership* (an unincorporated association of two or more persons) makes each partner severally and jointly liable for all the debts of the business; partners, like proprietorships, put their personal assets at risk when partnerships are sued. A *corporation* is an artificial body created by law and endowed by law with the power of acting as a single individual. It acts in all respects like an individual when carrying on the business authorized in its articles of incorporation. Unlike a partnership or a sole proprietorship, shareholders and managers of a corporation are *not normally liable* (except in case of fraud) for the debts of the business.

Other types of business ownerships are joint ventures, trusts, and estates. A *joint venture* is a partnership created to carry out a projection limited in time and scope. The legal responsibility of a joint venture is similar to that of a partnership. A voluntary trust exists when the title to a business' assets is given to trustees to be managed in accordance with instructions given in the trust investment. Many politicians put their business interests into trusts while they are holding public office. A trust is generally considered to have the legal liabilities of a corporation.

When a person dies his *estate* (in the person of the executor or adminis-trator) is the owner of his property, including any businesses he owned at his death. The estate will manage the business until it is sold or disposed of in accordance with the will. Claims against a business owned by an estate are no riskier than while the owner was alive, unless the total assets of the owner are less than the total claims brought against the estate. Satisfying a claim with a trust, joint venture, or an estate should require no different procedure or effort than with claims against a sole proprietor, partnership, or corporation.

The three major forms of business organizations (sole proprietorship, partnership, and corporation) each have special credit features. In a sole proprietorship, credit risk is enhanced or weakened by the personal assets of the proprietor, by having to rely on the management skills of just one person, and by the life span of the business depending on the well-being of the owner. In partnerships, credit risk is enhanced or weakened by the personal assets of all the partners, by the possibility of dissension between the partners, and by the managerial skills of the partners. A corporation has no assets except those owned by the corpo-ration itself, corporations have perpetual life, and changes in manage-ment can be made quickly by the board of directors or stockholders.

If you find it necessary to track down the actual ownership status of a company, there are several sources to use. In the office of each state's Secretary of State you will find corporation records; through these you can find out if the company is a corporation. In state Secretary of State offices, county clerk offices, or town clerk offices you can find records of fictitious business names; if the company operates under a name other than that of the owner(s), you will find ownership information in these records. A check with a public library reference department may lead you to other reports that contain ownership information about the com-pany.

Management Experience

According to a Dun and Bradstreet survey, the major pitfall of small businesses is lack of experience on the part of management. That man-agement has had prior experience in the same field is, by itself, in-significant; it is not only the time spent that matters, but also the knowl-edge acquired. The amount of experience required for success varies with the type of operation.

Balanced experience is the key. The owner needs knowledge of products, finance, buying, and selling. Finance and buying are the two most important factors of money management. A business that cannot manage money will soon be in trouble. Yet it is the exceptional rather than the average owner who understands this. A Dun and Bradstreet pamphlet, *The Pitfalls in Managing a Small Business,* quotes a plumbing wholesaler on buying: "The golden bit of advice a businessman can give a beginner is 'get experience.' Due to the ever increasing competition in this line even the new man must be thoroughly familiar with all the aspects. Buying ability is the keynote, plus a thorough knowledge of what his customers want." A manufacturer of screw products explained: "The first trouble I encountered was in the correct buying of machinery."

So the main thing that the credit manager should look for in the management of his customer's business is not only experience, but balanced experience. The agency reports will give you some idea of experience, but a talk with management will give you the best details on balanced experience. When you talk with your customers, test their total knowledge of business, not just their knowledge in one area.

BUSINESS HISTORY AND GROWTH

History

The age of a business (its history) and its growth potential are both bits of knowledge that are of considerable importance to the credit manager in rating an account and reaching a decision. As far as the credit manager is concerned, the age of a business is determined by the number of years under its *present* ownership. With major industrial giants, a change of management is of little concern because they have strong built-in stability through the continued tenure of other senior management personnel. In small- to medium-sized companies, however, a change of ownership or a change in the top administrative control means the start of a new company.

It makes little difference whether the original founding date of the company was fifty or one hundred years ago, a new management is certain to change the pattern of business through new personalities, new decisions, and a new philosophy. In most cases the successive management will start out with advantages over new companies — prestige, goodwill, a functioning organization, and a higher capital base. But these can be quickly dissipated by unwise management judgment.

Dun and Bradstreet or other credit reporting agencies give the dates of the formation of a company to coincide with the time of takeover of new ownership. In the case of family owned firms, the original date of founding is carried forward despite the fact that the company may now be run by second, third, or fourth generations.

The age of a business is significant to you, the credit manager, as an indicator of the probability of survival. Statistically, most failures occur in the first two to five years of a business. Usually, a company that has functioned with at least moderate success for eight or ten years represents a lesser degree of risk than a new company. Dun and Bradstreet figures show that more than half of the businesses that fail do so within the first five years; and of these, most fail within the first three years. To be exact, 32 percent of all businesses that are started fail within the first three years and 56 percent within the first five years. Only 22 percent of the businesses over five years old will fail before their tenth birthday. Figure 5.1 shows the percentage failure related to age over the periods from 1945 to 1972.

It is interesting to note in Figure 5.1 that in the 1940s when failure rates for businesses less than five years old were up as high as 78 percent, failure rates for businesses more than five years old were lower than at any time in the past half century. Lately, failure rates for businesses between six and ten years old and more than ten years old are running neck and neck.

Because of the failure rates for new businesses, these pose a problem for evaluation by credit managers. To evaluate new businesses properly you should try to find out the amount of starting capital and the source of starting capital. Starting capital should be of an amount sufficient to finance the kind and extent of operation that the management plans. Starting capital can come from one of the following sources: savings, borrowings, inheritance, sale of prior business, or disposal of real property. Remember that the attitude of a person risking his own money can differ from that of a person using someone else's money. If the money is borrowed it is a good idea to find out from where it is borrowed and what percentage it is of total capital.

If your customer is a company in its first year of operation, the company's most crucial problem will be adequate funding to get through the year. Of course, the new business usually has production or distribution problems and personnel problems, but these will be solved with time if capitalization is adequate.

After the first year, companies face the problems of having exhausted their original funds (which have hopefully been replaced with funds from operations or outside money). After the first year "settling down"

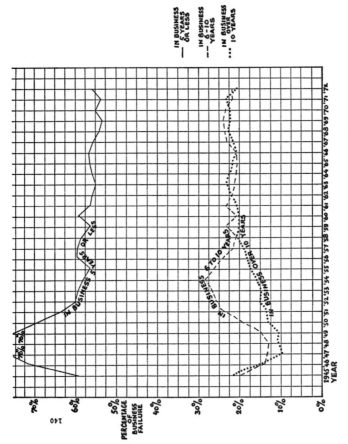

DATA: U.S. DEPARTMENT OF COMMERCE

FIGURE 5.1
Percentage of Business Failures Related to Age

time, the second year company is probably on the verge of rapid growth, which might put strains on working capital.

The characteristics of firms three to five years old, according to Donald E. Miller and Donald B. Relkin[1] are:

1. The capital structure will usually be much less than that of the average firm that has been in existence longer.
2. Past industry conditions that were abnormally favorable and allowed a new company to "ride the crest of a wave" may subside. (Consider the recent market history of the hand-held calculator.)
3. There may be management differences over future objectives that could cause disruption.

Businesses more than five years old have been statistically better risks. You cannot, however, assume that an old business of this sort is a good risk. Recently, the trend has been toward a greater number of failures in companies older than ten years as shown in Figure 5.1.

Besides being concerned with how long the company itself has been in business, you should also consider the length of time it has been in that particular line of business. This is illustrated by the following story.

> I was president of a novelty manufacturing concern. We had made a lot of money for many years, but suddenly demand for our products dropped sharply. We had $200,000 in cash. I took a quick look ahead and decided we would manufacture ranges. I bought out the other stockholders with part of my cash and plunged right in. Shortly thereafter, rising costs and decreasing prices, due to competition, took the rest of my cash, and another $200,000 besides. Then creditors took the manufacturing plant. Moral? There is no substitute for experience.[2]

If the business you are investigating has just been acquired in a merger, you might want to ask yourself some questions: What was the purpose of the merger (plant, talent, market, trend)? Will the result of the acquisition strengthen the company? How strong is the new parent company? Will the merger result in any legal problems?

Growth

Indications of your customer's growth generally come from two sources: your company's sales representative and your own analysis using industry agency reports and the customer's financial statements.

---

[1]Donald E. Miller and Donald B. Relkin, *Improving Credit Practice*. (New York: American Management Association, 1971).

[2]Published as a pamphlet by Dun and Bradstreet.

Alert sales people usually know when a company has grown because they have seen an increase in their orders, either from your company or a competitor. If they do not know offhand, all they need do is consult past sales records.

You can draw conclusions from agency reports by comparing the high credit amount for previous years reported with the high credit currently reported. If the highest credit for most of the companies to your customer was $50,000 on the average last year and is $60,000 this year, this shows a growth trend.

If you have present financial statements on your customer as well as financial statements from a previous period, you can compare the increase in sales or profit from period to period.

Trends in growth are important because the credit manager's role is to predict tomorrow's results, since a credit decision is, by the nature of the beast, oriented toward the future. Pinpointing where your customer stands financially today is important, but it is the trend that will best predict the future. Is your customer, Hero Manufacturing, moving up or down or are they at a plateau? For example, let us assume that you have two customers: Hero Manufacturing and Rotten Distribution who both had sales of $2 million last year. The fact that they had the same sales does not mean they will do equally well in the future as a glance at their historical sales performance (Table 5.1) will tell you.

Even though the sales are the same today, you can easily see that Rotten Distribution is heading downhill, while the other, Hero Manufacturing, has a continuing upward trend in sales. A company could have about the same sales each year, with possibly a 2 or 3 percent increase. This is a mature company and you cannot reasonably expect much more increased volume from it, but it is probably stable enough to pay debts and creditors.

TABLE 5.1
Comparing Historical Sales Performance

	Hero Manufacturing	Rotten Distribution
Last full year 1978	$2,000,000	$2,000,000
1977	1,700,000	2,400,000
1976	1,100,000	2,800,000
1975	700,000	3,200,000
1974	500,000	3,200,000

CUSTOMER FINANCES

Problems

There are four financial problems that can cause difficulties in businesses and sometimes can cause them to go under. These problems are: lack of sufficient money (working capital), inventory mismanagement, a strong concentration of company funds in fixed assets, and poor credit granting practices.

Lack of Money

Insufficient capital to keep a firm operating smoothly can be caused by a number of factors. The firm can be capitalized initially at too low an amount, there may be negative cash flow from operations (caused by net operating losses or poor collections), the firm may not be able to borrow or obtain equity money, and/or the firm may have a poor capital structure (too much equity versus debt, or more likely, too much debt versus equity).

Inventory Mismanagement

Inventory mismanagement is another problem for many businesses. Control of finances means knowing how much money the company has and how to handle it. That the capital is managed properly is more important than the absolute amount of capital itself. Too much inventory or the wrong kind can be a stumbling block for any business, but can be especially problematic with small businesses.

Many times a businessperson will order inventory that does not sell well, but will nevertheless be able to handle it. If the same businessperson orders a great deal of the wrong inventory, or just more inventory than can be sold quickly, it is inevitable that the bills will be paid slowly, because of the high payables and inadequate receivables.

Too Much Capital in Fixed Assets

Dollars put into fixtures, equipment, and real estate either come out of working capital or from borrowed funds, which puts a drain on working capital. If the fixed assets (equipment, fixtures, or real estate), are used for expansion purposes, you should be aware that expansion creates a need for more working capital, not less. Even if funds to purchase assets are borrowed, down payments from working capital are required. The seeming paradox of needing to invest money to expand and needing that money and more to fuel the expansion, causes many problems in a business. Take the example of Hero Manufacturing. They are doing so well that they know they need to expand, to buy another plant. They take half of their $100,000 cash as a down payment on another plant. To put the plant in operation they have to hire more employees who will not be totally efficient at first because of the learning curve time required for them to adjust to the new machines and operations. Add to that the fact that they now need more inventory and have an increase in receivables, and suddenly the money they had left over from the down payment, and then some, is gone.

Poor Credit Granting Practice

You as a credit manager know the importance to your own company's cash flow, of granting credit to the right customers, and having a good collection record. Unfortunately, a lot of people are in the credit business without knowing how to read a Dun and Bradstreet report. This is a very common problem with small businesses, especially those with less than $1 million in sales. The ironic thing is that even though you may be a great credit manager, you may take a loss on an account because the customer does not have a good credit manager.

Effects of Type of Operation on Financial Statements

When the credit manager goes over a customer's financial statements, it is important to remember that the type of operation the customer has (wholesale, retail, manufacturing, or service) will effect some items on the profit and loss statement and balance sheet. If your customer varies from the following norms, this will indicate that something is amiss.

Wholesalers will have no manufacturing costs, large amounts of inventory, narrow profit margins, and only a moderate investment in fixed assets.

Retailers have more expenses as a percentage of sales than wholesalers, higher rents and advertising expenses, inventory as a major expense, and generally higher gross profit margins than wholesalers.

Manufacturers' costs are labor and materials, financing for fixed assets is often necessary, gross margins are higher than wholesalers, and adequate working capital is necessary to meet their operating expenses.

Service industries have very little inventory (mostly supplies), high labor costs, short collections (because of the immediate cash flow needs for paying labor), and generally short credit terms.

CUSTOMER'S DISTRIBUTIVE STRENGTH

How strong is your customer's distribution? If you can answer that question, you have an important key to your customer's future success. If your customer is not successful in the future, you will not be paid in the future.

Your Customer's Customers

One of the elements of your customer's distributive strength is who its customers are and how dependent your customer is on any one of them. It is a good sign if your customer is the sole supplier of a national restaurant chain, but if your customer has to depend on them for over 50 percent of total sales, it is not such a good sign. Has your customer developed other commercial, institutional, or industrial accounts to the point where these businesses could withstand the loss of that major customer? The possibility of losing an account that represents 50 percent of your total business would frighten any company.

The situation of having only one major customer is very common in the case of small businesses that do the majority (some up to 95 percent) of their business with the federal government. Most items sold to the government are bought on a one-year contract at a very low price, and the bidding for government contracts is extremely competitive. The government-produced items usually require a high degree of quality control and require very exacting standards. Collections with the government are usually very good and advances are allowed, so a customer whose majority of work is done for the government can be profitable, but the year-to-year nature of these contracts and the price and standards they exact makes your customer's future uncertain.

You should be interested in your customer's terms of sale if for no other reason than to compare them with the terms that you require. Unless your client has a strong position of liquidity or unlimited borrowing capacity, it may be difficult to pay on 10 day terms to suppliers while granting 60-day terms to customers. Further, you should compare these selling terms to others in the industry. Are they competitive, too restrictive, too liberal? In addition to comparing the terms of sales with the industry, it is important to note whether your customer is collecting in a period not longer than his own terms.

The seasonal nature of a customer's business is also important to you as a credit manager for two reasons. If you obtain your customer's statement it is important to know if the figures were prepared at the high or low point of annual activity. When projecting the maximum exposure for your customer, knowing the seasonal cyclical fluctuation lets you know if the ceilings you establish are excessive or inadequate.

OTHER IMPORTANT FACTORS IN EVALUATION

Other factors that tell you about the credit strength and repayment ability of your customer include the number and type of accounts that your customer has on the books, the competition, the facilities and equipment owned, and the general industry conditions.

Number and Type of Accounts

The number of accounts your customer has is a good indication of the popularity of their products. If the customer's company sells an important percentage of total sales to a subsidiary, parent, or affiliate, it is important to note the selling terms and percentage of total sales represented concerning such sales. If they sell to a large number of accounts, make sure that they have the necessary staff, facilities, and procedures to handle the load.

Knowing the type and class of trade sold helps you evaluate the quality of the company's receivables. You may also observe from knowing this the problems that your customer — if a manufacturer — may encounter according to whether their output is distributed by jobbers or retailers, or is sent directly to consumers. Jobbers tend to require longer payable periods of their suppliers than retailers, but usually have shorter payable periods than manufacturing customers. If a company supplies a retail consumer directly, its receivables will be negligible and the company will have better cash flow.

Competition

Without a consideration of the competition, no prediction of a customer's success can be accurate. Your customer's product must be evaluated with reference to the competition. Also your customer's paying habits, selling terms, pricing, profit margin, and trend must be analyzed in light of what others in the field are doing. Other comparisons to consider are research talents, budgeting equipment sophistication, available financing, and marketing and advertising expertise.

Facilities and Equipment

To be able to service their debts, a company must have adequate facilities and equipment. Consider whether equipment and facilities are leased or owned outright. The physical appearance of the premises, including fire or accident risks, meeting OSHA (for Occupational Safety and Health Administration) standards, management efficiency, inventory control, and employee attitudes, can be an aid in understanding the operation.

Industry Conditions

Usually if the industry as a whole is successful your customer is more apt to be successful. Outside influences on an industry such as increased government control and increased automation will affect your customer. All industries will have peculiarities that reflect on its financial statements, selling terms, seasonal fluctuations, and paying habits. Components of an industry's condition include regional influences, stage-of-business maturity, sensitivity to economic conditions, required technical skills, overall strength, and required raw materials.

6

To Whom Should You Extend Credit — Financial Analysis

GENERAL FINANCIAL INFORMATION

To do a financial analysis on your client, one source of information is required above all others — the client's financial statements. Without financial statements, nothing can be done in this area.

Financial analysis is probably the most accurate way to predict repayment, but it takes more time than just ordering a D & B report and talking a few minutes to a sales representative. Ratio and other financial analyses used to be very time consuming, but now, with the advent of the calculator, programmable calculator, and the minicomputers, the time involved has been minimized. Calculators make the job of doing ratios, trend analyses, and financial comparisons relatively easy. Programmable calculators (like the Texas Instruments SR-52 and Hewlett-Packard HP-65 in 1977) make ratios and most analyses a snap because all the "number crunching" can be done at the push of a button. In the future, as these electronic devices come more into the budget of the average person, almost all credit applications will be analyzed quickly and inexpensively (see Appendix A).

The things that you should be most interested in as a credit manager are your customer's working capital, receivables, inventories, debt structure, and how the company looks in comparison to others in the industry.

> *Working capital:* A company should have sufficient working capital to support its volume of business. Working capital should handle the volume without extending the company to a degree that it cannot remain current on its payables and is unable to clean up bank debt occasionally.
>
> *Receivables:* Any unusual build-up or continuing trend of increasing collection time should be noted. Supplemental periodic agings may be revealing. Accounts may be converting into notes. There should not be too much of a dependence and concentration of receivables with one company (like the government).
>
> *Inventories:* Any unusual build-up of inventories should be investigated. An adverse trend in the rate of inventory turnover may be cause for concern. Profits should stem from normal operations and not from speculative undertakings.
>
> *Debt:* Term debt should not be considered to be a satisfactory substitute for equity capital. There should be a reasonable balance between debt and equity.
>
> *Comparisons to other companies in the same industry:* Is the company maintaining its position in the industry in terms of both volume and profit margin? If not, the reasons for this should be investigated. Is the company moving with industry trends? Research and development investments in its field and services of consultants can give you a clue to the answer.

Interpretation of Financial Statements

As I previously mentioned, financial statements from your customer are absolutely necessary to a financial analysis. Unfortunately, not all the statements that your customer supplies will be accurate. Although they are supposed to represent a true financial picture of the firm, financial statements are subject to accidental or deliberate misrepresentation.

Everyday Credit Checking suggests: "To be truly valid, a financial statement should be certified, preferably by the accountant who has audited the figures. If your customer prepares the statement himself, without the benefit of an accountant, he at least ought to have it certified by a notary public, so that you can be fairly certain he isn't offering fraudulent figures. And he ought to sign the statement . . . . Another thing you ought to verify is whether the accountant has made a physical audit of your customer's assets, or whether he's simply accepting his client's book figures."[1] (Whether a physical inventory of assets is taken or not will be stated on the front page of the statement if it is done by a CPA).

Realistically, though, most clients will not have audited statements. In some cases you are lucky to receive a statement at all. Surveys of credit managers, as a matter of fact, consistently reveal that many will accept unaudited and uncertified statements. From marginal accounts you may even want to demand an audit as a condition of the sale.

Even if you are able to obtain adequate statements, remember that everything in life is relative, and the financial statement is no exception. An isolated figure means nothing. To say that the cost of a pair of socks is exorbitant today compared to twenty years ago cannot be proven simply by comparing the present price to the earlier price. It is more important to consider whether our expendable income is high enough to afford the difference and still be able to buy other things.

Whether you have audited or unaudited figures, certified statements, or the customer's guesses to analyze, there are certain techniques to check the accuracy of the figures. One of the best checks of the balance sheet figures is the sales amount. Can your customer actually produce the amount of sales indicated with the assets indicated? This varies from industry to industry, so it should be considered in view of the industry. Sometimes new businesses will say that their assets are worth $50,000 when the purchase price of the business was only $35,000. One way to dispel this problem is to remark to your customer that $50,000 seems a high price for the company. Many times he will reply: "I got a good deal, I only paid $35,000 for it."

Sometimes assets are reported at one amount and the insurance carried on them is shown at a different amount. This could be a clue that the assets are inflated or that the insurance coverage is inadequate. Compare the present net worth to see if it is higher or lower than the net worth from a previous period.

Find out if the obligations as reported by the trade on the Dun and Bradstreet or other industry reports are reasonably close to those indicated on the customer's balance sheet. You can also check with outside people, such as the previous owners, to confirm the purchase price. Debt and secured borrowings, as previously discussed, are public record.

[1]Sol Barzman, *Everyday Credit Checking*. (New York: Thomas T. Crowell & Co., 1973).

Physical Appearance of Financial Statements

Illustrated below is a sample balance sheet form. Note that on a balance sheet all assets are listed on one side and all liabilities and owner's equity is listed on the other. The accounting equation is that assets must equal liabilities plus net worth. Or put another way, assets minus liabilities equal net worth.

$$\text{Assets} = \text{Liabilities} + \text{Owners' Equity}$$
$$\text{Assets} - \text{Liabilities} = \text{Owners' Equity}$$
$$\text{Assets} - \text{Owners' Equity} = \text{Liabilities}$$

TABLE 6.1
Profit & Loss Statement
Monroe Manufacturing Company[1]

Balance Sheet
December 31, 19__

Assets

Current assets:			
Cash		$40,000	
Accounts receivable	$90,000		
Less allowance for doubtful accounts	10,000	80,000	
Inventories:			
Finished product................	75,000		
Work in process	75,000		
Raw materials	20,000		
Supplies	10,000	180,000	
Prepaid expenses		10,000	
Total current assets			$310,000
Fixed assets:			
Furniture and fixtures	$10,000		
Less allowance for depreciation	5,000	$5,000	
Machinery and equipment	$30,000		
Less allowance for depreciation ..	16,000	14,000	
Buildings.......................	$45,000		
Less allowance for depreciation ..	9,000	36,000	
Land		15,000	
Total fixed assets...............			70,000
Investments			20,000
Total assets			$400,000

[1]Not a real company.

TABLE 6.1 (cont.)

Liabilities and Equity

Current liabilities:

Accounts payable		$40,000	
Notes payable.....................		80,000	
Accrued liabilities:			
Wages and salaries payable	$4,000		
Interest payable	1,000	5,000	
Allowance for taxes			
Income tax	$16,000		
State taxes......................	4,000	20,000	
Total current liabilities			$145,000
Equity:			
Capital stock.....................		$200,000	
Surplus		55,000	
Total equity			255,000
Total liabilities and equity			$400,000

Switching one asset for another (accounts receivable for cash, cash for inventory) of the same value does not alter the total value of net worth. When more is added to the assets than to the liabilities, net worth increases. When more is added to the liabilities than to the assets, net worth decreases. Financing an asset 100 percent with a debt, or with a cash down payment and debt, does not affect net worth. The first process merely swaps an asset for a debt, and the second swaps an asset for a debt plus another asset (cash).

A crucial question for a credit manager is which assets were paid for with debt money and which with equity money? Two companies, both with $100,000 in assets, may be in very different circumstances as far as claim to assets. If Company A bought the $100,000 in assets with $30,000 in cash (owner's equity) and $70,000 in borrowed money, and Company B did just the opposite ($70,000 in owners' equity, $30,000 in debt), which do you think is the strongest company?

Profit and loss statements (a sample from *A Handbook of Small Business Finance* is illustrated in Table 6.1) show income (sales) plus the expenses and cost of sales (which decrease the income), and what is left over after expenses (net profit).

The income statement and all its parts, as well as a balance sheet and its parts, will be illustrated in this chapter from the standpoint of what it all means to the credit manager. Before you read all the details, you might want to look at the balance sheets and income statements for Hero Manufacturing, Inc., and Rotten Distribution, Inc. in Tables 6.2, 6.3, and 6.4.

TABLE 6.2
Statement of Financial Condition
12/30/78

| | Hero Manufacturing | | Rotten Distribution | |
	Present Year 12/30/1978	Previous Year 12/30/1977	Present Year 12/30/1978	Previous Year 12/30/1977
ASSETS				
Current Assets:				
Cash	200,000	353,400	(5,000)	50,000
Securities	900,000	623,483	-0-	-0-
Accounts Receivable	580,000	528,367	690,410	712,300
Allowance for Uncollectables	(30,000)	(27,300)	(60,000)	(61,000)
Inventory	330,300	386,000	583,310	551,300
Prepaid Expense	69,500	69,500	-0-	
Total Current Assets	2,049,800	1,933,450	1,208,720	1,252,600
Fixed Assets:				
Furniture and Fixtures	75,000	75,000	12,000	12,000
Equipment	520,500	303,503	195,000	195,000
Vehicles	90,000	85,000	55,000	45,000
Buildings & Leasehold Improvements	350,000	350,000	200,000	200,000
Less: Accumulated Depreciation	(302,000)	(191,453)	(52,000)	(43,000)
Land	100,000	100,000	30,000	30,000
Total Fixed Assets	833,500	722,050	420,000	439,000
Other Assets:				
Investment in Subsidiary	-0-	-0-	271,280	238,000
Organizational Expense	40,000	40,000	50,000	50,000
Less: Amortization	(35,000)	(32,000)	(20,000)	(17,000)
Trademarks	-0-	-0-	40,000	40,000

Notes Receivable from Officers	5,000		200,000	178,000
Total Other Assets		8,000	541,280	489,000
TOTAL ASSETS	2,888,300	2,663,500	2,170,000	2,180,600
LIABILITIES				
Current Liabilities:				
Accounts Payable	209,490	129,950	512,000	507,800
Payroll Taxes Payable	57,010	48,000	35,000	39,000
Provision for Income Tax	60,300	42,250	12,600	52,800
Notes Payable	162,900	156,500	510,000	469,582
Accrued Wages	10,062	10,000	10,062	9,518
Other Accruals	-0-	153,400	11,458	10,000
Total Current Liabilities	499,762	543,700	1,091,120	1,088,700
Mortgages Payable	320,338	331,000	160,000	173,000
Notes Payable	339,000	285,000	218,880	208,300
TOTAL LONG-TERM LIABILITIES	659,338	616,000	378,880	281,300
TOTAL LIABILITIES	1,159,100	1,159,100	1,470,000	1,870,000
Net Worth:				
Common Stock	300,000	30,000	810,600	801,400
Preferred Stock	50,000	50,000	N/A	N/A
Paid-In Surplus	150,000	150,000	N/A	N/A
Retained Earnings	1,229,200	1,004,400	29,400	79,200
Less: Owner's Draw	N/A	N/A	75,000	50,000
Principal Debt Repay	N/A	N/A	65,000	20,000
TOTAL NET WORTH	1,729,200	1,504,400	700,000	810,600
TOTAL LIABILITIES AND NET WORTH	2,888,300	2,663,500	2,170,000	2,180,600

TABLE 6.3
Income Statement

| | Hero Manufacturing | | Rotten Distribution | |
	Present Year 12/30/1978	Previous Year 12/30/1977	Present Year 12/30/1978	Previous Year 12/30/1977
Sales and Revenue				
Net Sales of Product	5,620,000	4,323,000	4,200,000	4,620,000
Interest Income	51,750	40,100	-0-	-0-
Total Income	5,671,750	4,363,100	4,200,000	4,620,000
Less: Cost of Sales				
Merchandise	1,067,800	767,333	2,940,000	3,194,083
Wages	2,135,600	1,534,665	185,000	201,062
Factory Overhead	640,680	460,399	65,000	70,594
Selling Costs	427,120	306,933	212,000	230,261
Total Cost of Sales	4,271,200	3,069,330	3,402,00	3,696,000
Gross Profit	1,400,550	1,293,770	798,000	924,000

Operating Expense:				
Wages General	400,000	380,000	400,000	420,000
	80,000	70,000	N/A	N/A
Payroll Tax	43,200	40,500	43,200	48,700
Insurance	90,000	82,000	45,300	47,000
Accounting and Legal	42,000	36,000	25,000	27,000
Administrative Costs	85,000	81,000	10,446	22,200
Supplies & Postage	3,500	3,200	5,000	6,100
Rent for Premises	65,000	55,000	26,000	26,000
Utilities and Phone	7,200	6,900	12,010	11,600
Travel and Entertainment	41,700	40,900	63,000	74,200
Leases	28,000	24,000	12,200	10,900
Tax and License	3,800	3,200	2,600	2,700
Dues and Subscriptions	4,500	4,600	3,100	3,700
Depreciation & Amortization	3,000	2,900	1,700	1,700
Interest	65,779	71,460	176,444	90,200
Commissions	39,140	30,110	-0-	-0-
TOTAL OPERATING EXPENSE	991,823	921,770	756,000	792,000
NET PROFIT	408,727	372,000	42,000	132,000
Less Reserve for Taxes	183,927	167,400	12,600	52,800
ADJUSTED NET PROFIT	224,800	204,600	29,400	79,200

TABLE 6.4
Cost of Sales Schedule

	Hero Manufacturing		Rotten Distribution	
	12/30/1978	12/30/1977	12/30/1978	12/30/1977
Merchandise:				
Furnished Goods Inv. — Beginning	176,000	145,320	551,300	550,200
Work in Process Inv. — Beginning	95,000	78,311	N/A	N/A
Raw Material Inv. — Beginning	115,000	94,503	N/A	N/A
Material Purchases	991,000	817,829	2,875,890	3,153,583
Freight-In	21,100	17,300	32,100	41,600
Less:	90,000	115,000	N/A	N/A
Less: Finished Goods Ending	150,000	176,000	583,310	551,300
Less: Work-in Process	90,300	95,000	N/A	N/A
Total Cost of Materials	1,067,800	767,333	2,940,000	3,194,083
Direct Labor Costs				
Factory Salaries	1,312,260	939,216	107,000	119,000
Shipping Salaries	498,000	356,042	55,000	59,000

Payroll Tax & Benefits	161,113	118,169	16,200	17,800
Bonus and Vacation	164,227	121,238	6,800	5,262
Total Direct Labor Costs	2,135,600	1,534,665	185,000	201,062
Factory Overhead:				
Rent and Equipment Leases	320,000	280,000	25,800	25,800
Utilities	93,133	39,399	1,200	1,300
Supplies	60,000	56,000	4,000	6,000
Repairs and Maintenance	57,000	43,000	5,000	11,494
Equipment Depreciation	110,547	42,000	29,000	26,000
Total Factory Overhead	640,680	460,399	65,000	70,594
Selling Expense	265,000	201,200	120,000	129,000
Payroll Tax Payable	26,500	20,120	12,000	12,900
Travel and Transportation	35,620	10,613	26,000	29,000
Bad-Debt Losses	80,000	75,000	40,000	47,800
Advertising	20,000	-0-	14,000	11,561
Total Selling Expense	427,120	306,933	212,000	230,261
Total Cost of Sales	2,271,200	3,069,330	3,402,000	3,696,000

Assets

Assets are a company's resources — what the company owns. Assets are in the form of cash, inventory, accounts receivable, equipment, fixtures, and real estate. Assets fall into the general groupings of: current, fixed, and other assets. Current assets are those items that are already cash or are readily convertible into cash. Fixed assets are those items that cannot easily be converted to cash in a short period of time at their true value (equipment or buildings, for example). Other assets are items that are considered neither fixed nor current, such as goodwill, long term investments, and research and development.

Assets appear on the left hand half of a balance sheet in order of descending liquidity (convertibility to cash).

Current assets are the assets that the credit manager is most concerned with. For the most part, when your customers pay their bills, they pay with their current assets. Current assets are items of economic value that can be converted to cash within one year or within the normal operating cycle of the business. Current assets consist of: cash on hand and in the bank; marketable securities, that is, securities and bonds that are immediately convertible to cash; accounts receivable; and inventory (merchandise).

There are other types of current assets such as trade acceptances, promissory notes, and revenue stamps. If your customer has notes receivable (promissory notes) or trade acceptance it may mean that there is a problem with a few customers and accounts receivable had to be converted to notes receivable. Yet this may also be an accepted procedure of your customer's industry.

Cash is the most important of all assets to the credit manager. Cash includes money in safes and banks, checks, money orders, and other cash convertible instruments accepted at a bank for cash. Cash does not include postdated checks and IOUs.

If the total cash position is very light — for example, $5,000 in cash out of $185,000 in total assets — your customer is operating in an unbalanced condition. This would mean that most of the current assets are in accounts receivable and inventory. A light cash position taken out of context does not necessarily mean disaster. Since a company constantly generates new cash to meet its obligations, a temporary light cash position is acceptable, but it generally means the company will run late in its payments.

A heavy cash position, where cash is the majority of the current assets, is usually a sign of a healthy company. However, occasionally a heavy cash position can mean something else. If a large cash balance is carried as "cash on hand" it may include IOUs and postdated checks, which in fact is not cash. Heavy cash can also be the result of overly conservative buying policies.

A couple of other things that you should be alerted to when examining cash is amounts in foreign currency and the possibility of the customer's bank using cash to offset a loan. If your customer has loans outstanding from this bank, the bank may have the right to offset the loans against deposits. If there is a bank loan on the statement, you should be aware of this possibility.

Marketable securities include, in order of their liquidity: U.S. government securities, state and municipal securities, and corporate securities. Securities and bonds of this short-term nature can be considered to be the same as cash. U.S. government securities include bonds and Treasury notes. These are the most marketable of the marketable securities. State and municipal securities, usually in the form of bonds, are next in liquidity to U.S. securities. There have, however, in the past been a few defaults on these types of securities. Corporate securities can bring additional profits to a company, or considerable loss. These investments are usually carried on a company's balance sheet at cost, but their market value could be either more or less. If the company's investment in any one business is larger than the norm, this may represent an eventual attempt to control the activities of that business. If this is the case, your customer might be reluctant to sell its investment in order to pay off trade debt.

Accounts receivable include customer (trade) accounts receivable, accounts receivable from subsidiaries or affiliated companies, trade acceptances, and accounts receivable from lessors of leased departments.

Trade accounts receivable are amounts of money due from customers as a result of the sale of goods or services. Under accounts receivable this should be the largest entry. Your customer should have a reserve for bad debts listed on the balance sheet under accounts receivable. If there is no such reserve, you should automatically reduce accounts receivable by some reasonable amount before doing any calculations. Sometimes your customer's accounts receivable will be pledged. This means that whoever they are pledged to has first claim, not you. If they are pledged, they have to be registered with the public authorities. If your customer provides you with an aging of accounts receivable, you will be able to tell what percentage of the receivables are way overdue.

Accounts receivable from affiliates or subsidiaries should be carefully examined, especially if they seem large in relation to the rest of the receivables. This item could represent advances, loans, or goods delivered on consignment, and really should not be considered current. (Trade acceptances represent a very liquid asset *if* it is the custom of the industry to require them.) If, on the other hand, the industry practice is to sell goods on open-account, then trade acceptances generally represent the effort of a company to ensure payment from a doubtful risk.

Receivables from lessors of leased departments apply only to retailers who operate individual departments in someone else's store. If your customer is running such a department, your customer is the lessee (tenant) and the owner of the store is the lessor (landlord). Under normal arrangements, the lessor processes all income from sales, cash or charge, and credits this income to the lessee. Occasionally, a lessor will experience financial difficulty and will be unable to pay everything owed the lessee. This will hamper your customer in meeting his obligations.

Inventory (merchandise) is difficult to evaluate because it presents many problems. You must consider the reliability of the physical inventory count, condition of the inventory, its value, and whether the amount shown is reasonable for the industry.

Inventory includes different items for different types of companies (manufacturer, wholesaler, retailer). Inventory for retailers and wholesalers consists of finished goods or goods that can be sold without further processing (except shipping). Manufacturers, on the other hand, have three kinds of goods: raw materials, work-in-process, and finished goods. Raw materials can be sold easily, so from the credit standpoint, raw materials inventory is considered the most valuable of the three. Work-in-progress is considered to be the least valuable inventory because it requires labor to turn it into finished goods. After the goods are finished, a sales effort is still required to turn the inventory into cash. If finished goods are popular products in good condition that can be easily sold, they are worth their valuation. If the goods have questionable salability (such as new or custom products) then their value on the financial statements may be too high. Salability is the key factor in evaluation of any inventory. And remember, forced sales bring less money than sales in the normal course of business.

How the inventory figure was arrived at — by physical count or estimate — has bearing on the accuracy of the dollar amounts. Actual physical counts, especially those taken by CPAs in an audit, give the most accurate figures.

Unlike cash, inventory can have differing valuations, depending on the formula used. Inventory should be valued at *lower of cost or market*. Your customer can inflate the value by appraising it at the current market value, which might be higher than the original cost, or vice versa. There are many other ways of evaluating the cost of inventory on hand as well. These methods include: first-in-first-out (FIFO), last-in-first-out (LIFO), and retail method. FIFO, LIFO, and the retail method are formulas that accountants use in computing possible obsolescence of merchandise.

In the FIFO method (see Table 6.5) the accountant assumes that inventory items bought first are those that are sold first. Therefore, the entire inventory is valued at the cost of the most recent purchases. When prices rise, the value of the inventory increases and profit is higher because cost of sales (beginning inventory plus purchases less ending inventory) is lower. The reverse is true in times of declining prices.

With the LIFO method (see Table 6.5), the accountant assumes that the last articles bought are the first ones used (or sold). Because there is a base (beginning inventory) whose valuation is not affected by recent purchases, inventory valuation tends to be low in periods of rising prices. LIFO is opposite of FIFO in this respect. Since for the last few decades we have had nothing but rising prices, this method of inventory valuation tends to be the most conservative, thus preferred by credit managers.

To recapitulate these two methods: under FIFO, inventory is overvalued in times of increasing prices and under LIFO, inventory tends to be undervalued.

Retailers sometimes use an entirely different method to arrive at inventory valuation. This is an estimation of value by percentage. The retailer enters the cost and the selling price of each article of merchandise. At the end of an accounting period, the difference between the sums of the cost and the sales price of all items is calculated. This difference is the gross margin or markup. This figure is then calculated as a percentage of sales price (markup divided by average sales price). The remaining inventory is added up at the most recent sales price. The total inventory dollar amount at retail (sales price) is then multiplied by 1 minus the gross margin (or markup percentage). This method is very common among small retailers who do not have perpetual inventory systems. The important factor is that this method tends to be inaccurate and results in overvaluation of inventory in times of rising prices.

Inventory pledged to a loan and the age of the inventory are two other things the credit manager should be concerned with. Pledged inventories do not pay the bills your customer owes you in case of liquidation and inventory that is out of style or outdated does not sell well.

Fixed assets are tangible equipment, property, and fixtures that are used in the production of the company's goods. They are always shown

TABLE 6.5
Comparison of Inventory Methods

	LIFO	FIFO	Retail Method
Balance sheet valuation as an indication of current value	Poor	Good	Fiar
Income statement effect:			
During periods of rising prices	Lowest earnings	Highest earnings	Lower than FIFO, higher than LIFO
During periods of falling prices	Highest earnings	Lowest earnings	Higher than FIFO, lower than LIFO
Inventory value:			
During periods of rising prices	Lowest value	Highest value	Between LIFO and FIFO
During periods of falling prices	Highest value	Lowest value	

on the balance sheet below the current assets. They usually are not available for the payment of current trade obligations except in bankruptcies and other cases of financial embarrassment. In certain industries, the fixed assets constitute a major share of the total assets. Printers, for example, have up to 89 percent of their total assets in fixed assets. Most fixed assets have liens against them because very few businesses pay 100 percent cash for fixed assets.

Fixed assets include plant equipment, furniture and fixtures, automotive equipment, real estate, buildings, leasehold improvements, and other equipment. These items are usually carried on the books at the cost when purchased (original cost). All fixed assets except land are depreciated. Be aware that the original cost of the equipment, especially when depreciation is considered, may be entirely different from the market price. Land usually has a value in excess of the amount at which it is carried on the books. Specialized buildings and equipment, on the other hand, may be of no use to anyone except the present owner. All this makes evaluating fixed assets very difficult. Add to that the fact that sometimes assets are reappraised upward, either by a qualified appraiser who would give a truer picture of the market value, or by the owner to make the statements look better.

The main value to the credit manager in understanding a company's fixed assets is knowing the sources of paying back the indebtedness the customer has as a last resort. The credit manager can also see that if the company has a large amount of assets tied up in fixed assets, little is left for working capital to pay off trade obligations.

Other assets, also known as *intangible assets,* include investments, goodwill, copyrights and trademarks, development costs, prepaid expenses, and officers' loans and advances. Credit managers sometimes refer to prepaid expenses, officers' loans and advances as "slow" assets. All these assets are lumped together under other assets because they cannot be rightly considered either current (since none are easily convertible to cash) or fixed (since they have little to do with the production of the company's goods). Intangible assets also include, besides the items mentioned above, patents, formulas, organization expenses, treasury stock, and catalogs. As described in the *Dun and Bradstreet Handbook of Credit and Collections,* "Intangible assets are characterized by their great value to ongoing concerns and their limited value to firms in bankruptcy."

Investments (under other assets) are those placements of a company's cash into long-term investments, whose yield will not occur within the next year. These include investments in subsidiaries or affiliates; stocks and bonds that will take more than a year to mature; cash surrender-value of life insurance policies; pension or profit-sharing funds; and fixed assets that are not used by the business for production of its goods. These investments will generally become available to creditors only in the case of financial difficulty.

Slow assets include prepaid insurance, taxes, rent, interest, and advances to officers, employees, and subsidiaries. Prepaid expenses are of no use to creditors because they cannot be converted to cash to pay trade bills. These assets are already committed. They have been paid in one accounting period but are applicable to a future period. Advances to subsidiaries are usually made on a more or less permanent basis. Advances to officers or employees are of doubtful value because most companies will not press important personnel for payments. If any of these assets are unusually large, careful investigation is absolutely necessary.

Liabilities

Liabilities are what a company owes — its debts. Liabilities will be in the form of obligations for merchandise purchased (trade debts), taxes, or loans. Liabilities are either current or long term. Current liabilities are those debts that must be paid within one year such as trade obligations, taxes, accrued expenses, and the current (within the next year) indebtedness of a loan. Long-term liabilities are the amount of loans due after the current year, such as mortgages.

If a customer has more liabilities than assets, technically the customer is bankrupt. This is called a *negative net worth* and is a condition that is more common than you would suspect. The higher your customer's liabilities in relation to assets, the smaller the likelihood that granting additional credit will be of any help. There is a close relationship between the creditworthiness of your customer and his current liabilities (due within one year). Current liabilities also include accounts payable, accrued expenses, and advance payments.

To a credit manager, the most important liability is *accounts payable* because that is the amount owed for purchase of merchandise on open-account trade terms. Are the accounts payable in line with cash and with the inventory? If they are too close in value, there may be trouble. If your customer has $20,000 in cash, $150,000 in merchandise inventory and $150,000 accounts payable, there are serious problems. This will be especially true if the customer has equal amounts of accounts payable and inventory and is saddled with slow-moving inventory. If accounts payable exceed the amount of cash and inventory combined (with no accounts receivable), the company is not only in trouble, but on the verge of bankruptcy. A light accounts payable position in relation to current assets is generally a good sign.

Notes payable, another important liability for the credit manager to consider, includes notes payable to banks; trade acceptances, and notes payable to companies or individuals other than banks.

Use of short-term financing by banks is not only a common but in many ways a favorable method of generating working capital for a company. A large amount of notes payable to banks could be an indication that the loans are secured by some asset, usually accounts receivable. Disproportionately small bank borrowings could indicate that bank financing was not available, which is a negative credit factor. Notes payable to banks include secured and unsecured loans and lines of credit. Unsecured loans are a sign of a bank's confidence in the company because banks usually only make unsecured loans to their best customers. Secured or guaranteed (by the owners) bank financing means that the business is an average risk. If your customer has a bank line of credit, this indicates that the bank regards the company as a good credit risk.

Companies can borrow from individuals or concerns other than banks either for convenience or because bank financing is not available. It is a smart idea to find out which is the case. Be aware that often notes given by individuals are backed by private, sometimes oral, agreements that the debt will be retired first if financial disaster strikes. Nonbank notes may either be secured or unsecured like bank loans. Unless it is the practice of the industry to require trade acceptances, trade acceptances are an indication that other suppliers consider this company a doubtful risk.

Accrued expenses are expenses that have not been paid, but will have to be paid within the next year (usually within the next quarter). The most common accrued expense is taxes payable (payroll, sales, and income taxes). Taxes payable can be a key element in evaluating the short-term future of your customer, and we will discuss it more thoroughly later in the ratio analysis portion of this chapter. Other common accrued expenses are wages payable (money owed to employees at the end of a period), insurance, rent, and interest expenses. In other words, an accrued expense is money that should have been paid out but has not been. For this reason, it is not good if the accrued expenses are a major portion of current liabilities. Many accrued expenses, especially accrued taxes (or taxes payable), mean that the customer is having trouble meeting required payments.

Advance payments are payments made by your customers in advance of work completed or performed. This is common among companies manufacturing products for the government (the space shuttle and defense weapons systems are examples) that have long completion times. Even when the amount of these advance payments (money received before the product was finished) is large, this should not concern the credit manager.

Long-term liabilities are obligations of a company that will be due later than one year from the date of the financial statement. Long-term liabilities do not affect your customer's ability to repay current obligations such as trade debt, but it does affect net worth. The stronger the net worth, the better shape your customer is in financially.

Long-term liabilities include only three things: long-term notes payable, mortgages, and bonds. All three are long-term written loans.

Long-term notes payable, sometimes called installment notes, are long-term obligations that represent the promise of the company to pay money at some date later than a year from the current date. Long-term notes payable are usually from a bank or other private or company source.

Bonds, on the other hand, are generally underwritten for general sale to the public. Bonds, too, are long-term commitments, but the source is the key factor. If your customer is strong enough to issue a public bond sale, the Securities and Exchange Commission probably knows more about your customer than you ever need to know. If you have trouble evaluating this kind of company, consult the SEC reports for information. Bonds and long-term notes payable both can either be on a secured or unsecured basis.

Mortgages are always secured by an asset. Mortgages are either real-estate secured or secured by equipment (called a *chattel mortgage*). Real estate mortgages are generally viewed with favor by credit managers. (In any case, the company will have more money for working capital if they do have a mortgage on their building than if their building is free and clear). Remember, your bills are paid with working capital, not the sale of an asset.

In summary, the important thing to remember is that current liabilities have to be paid within the next twelve months and accrued liabilities have to be paid within (usually) the next quarter. Long-term liabilities do not really affect short-term payment to you as a supplier.

And most important, remember that you as a supplier (an accounts payable to your customer) are paid from current assets.

Net Worth of Owner's Equity

Net worth (sometimes called equity or capital) is the owner(s)'s share of a business. Net worth is equal to the initial amount the owner puts into the business plus the profits they have made while in existence minus what the owner took out or any net losses. Net worth is usually described by the following formula: net worth = total assets − total liabilities.

The fact that net worth is on the liabilities side of the balance sheet confuses some people. If net worth is equity then it must belong to the owner. Wouldn't that make it an asset? The usual explanation is that it is listed on the liabilities side of the balance sheet because the company "owes" the owner that much. If all the assets are sold or liquidated and all the liabilities are paid off, the owner is given what is left because the company owes that. If the explanation does not make sense, you may feel like C. Northcote Parkinson in the preface to *Parkinson's Law and Other Studies in Administration*. He wrote: "Heaven forbid that students should cease to read books on the science of public or business administration — provided only that these works are classified as fiction. Placed between the novels of Rider Haggard and H. G. Wells, intermingled with volumes about ape men and space ships, these textbooks could harm no one."[1]

Composition of Net Worth

For partnerships and proprietorships net worth is generally just one figure — the difference between total assets and total liabilities. Corporations break net worth down into capital stock, paid-in surplus, earned surplus, and appraisal surplus.

Capital stock is the total of the owner's transferable interest (stock) in the corporation. This stock is either common stock or preferred stock. Capital stock has voting power, preferred stock does not, but preferred stock has a provision that dividends be paid first to them. Treasury stock is stock (either preferred or common) that has been bought back by the corporation.

[1]C. Northcote Parkinson, *Parkinson's Law and Other Studies in Administration*. (Boston: Houghton Mifflin Company, 1957), p. vii.

Paid-in (capital) surplus is the value of assets (including cash) given to the firm for which no stock has been issued. Earned surplus is the amount of earnings (net profit) kept in the corporation and not issued as dividends. When a corporation reevaluates its assets, the amount of this reevaluation should appear as appraisal surplus.

Aside from knowing what makes a balance sheet balance, the net worth section of your customer's statement has little significance to you as a credit manager in terms of repayment of trade obligations. It is, however, important in relation to the rest of the statement, and as a barometer of your customer's present condition and trend. This will be discussed later in the chapter.

Other Balance Sheet Items

Reserves and contingent liabilities are balance sheet items that do not fall into the categories of assets, liabilities, or net worth. Reserves can appear anywhere on the balance sheet, but they are never listed as an asset. Contingent liabilities usually do not appear on the balance sheet at all except as a footnote. Sometimes contingent liabilities will appear as "other liabilities" on balance sheets of very large companies.

Reserves are funds that have been set aside for special purposes. Reserve for Depreciation and Reserve for Bad Debt are two common types of reserves. Reserves can be conveniently divided into three types: valuation reserves, liability reserves, and surplus reserves.

Valuation reserves are used to reduce the values of related assets to amounts indicative of their present-day values. Valuation reserves include reserves for depreciation, bad debt, discounts, amortization, and depletion. A valuation reserve will appear after an asset on the balance sheet with the legend "less?" or with the dollar amount of the reserve in parentheses ($12,000).

Liability reserves are put in a balance sheet to provide for known liabilities within the next three to twelve months. Liability reserves include reserves for income tax and contract renegotiation charges. Surplus reserves are set up to restrict the use of surplus funds to specific programs. They are considered part of the company's net worth. Surplus reserves include reserves for decline in asset values, expansion, insurance, and contingencies.

Contingent liabilities are a company's possible future obligations resulting from some action that is ongoing today for which there is no known outcome. If the company is now involved in a lawsuit it may have a contingent liability in case the suit is decided against them. Other contingent liabilities are for returns and cancellations, guarantees or endorsements, contracts and commitments, and discounted accounts or notes receivable.

Contingent liabilities may not be shown on the balance sheet but they are usually indicated by footnotes, offsets to contingent assets, and special reserves.

Income Statement (Profit and Loss)

The income statement (profit and loss or operating statement) is a listing of the total income, costs, and profit for a given period. The income statement shows the movement of a company from one period to another whereas the balance sheet shows the company at one point in time. The moving train analogy is often used to illustrate the differences between the income statement and the balance sheet. When a train is moving across the countryside, the income statement is like a moving picture of the train that shows the entire journey from its beginning to present. The balance sheet is like a still picture of where the train is now. Income statements usually bear the legend "year-to-date December 31, 19XX" whereas balance sheets will just have the date "December 31, 19XX."

In practice, many balance sheets are submitted without the income statement and credit agencies assign lines of credit based solely on the balance sheets and annual sales figure. To many credit agents the balance sheet alone is the financial statement. Of course, income statements give the whole picture of a company, and whenever possible they should be required. An income statement has six basic parts: (1) sales; (2) cost of sales; (3) gross profit; (4) operating expense; (5) operating income (net profit before tax); and (6) net income after tax and other items. (See Table 6.3 for an illustration of an income statement.)

Income Statement Items

Sales (or gross sales) represent the total income of a company. This sales figure includes both cash sales and credit sales. Sometimes you will see the item "net sales" after "gross sales," or just "net sales" alone. Net sales is the remaining amount after returns, allowances, and discounts have been deducted from gross sales. For purposes of ratio analysis and any other credit analysis, the net sales figure should be used.

The sales figure is a helpful reference for the credit manager in many ways. It may show the probable purchases by your customer in your own line. This is done by examining sales together with a breakdown of the products the customer buys and uses. Taking sales in conjunction with the balance sheet can help you test certain assets. If asset inventory is $50,000 but sales for an entire year are only $70,000, you know something is wrong. It could be that your customer is in an industry that requires large, slow-moving inventories, but it is more likely that the inventory is excessive and/or stale.

Cost of sales (or cost of goods sold) is the amount in dollars that was required to buy or produce the goods that were sold during the period. The formula used to calculate this figure is: cost of goods sold = inventory at the beginning of the period + dollar amount of goods purchased or produced − ending inventory.

In a retail or wholesale operation, the goods are usually purchased. In a manufacturing operation, the goods are made (produced at the factory). For a manufacturing operation, the cost of goods sold formula would be: cost of goods sold = beginning inventory + raw materials + labor + factory overhead (including shipping, rent, and sometimes selling expense) − ending inventory. (See Table 6.4 for an illustration of how this works).

Gross profit is the amount left over after deducting the cost of goods sold. This is sometimes called the "gross margin," especially when discussing the figure in terms of a percentage of sales. Many retailers and wholesalers use the expression: "The shop is cutting X percent" which means that the store has X percent gross profit margin. The gross profit is also called the "mark-up" (the amount over and above costs that the product sells for). This is a significant figure because this is the money from which the company must pay all its nonproduct-related expenses (such as office and administrative expenses, interest, taxes, and utilities). The formula for determining gross profit: gross profit = sales − cost of sales.

Operating expenses are all the costs not directly related to sales. Regardless of whether sales are $10,000 or $1 million, these expenses (costs) have to be paid. Operating expenses include rent, utilities, insurance, office and administrative salaries, supplies, taxes, legal and accounting fees, leases, and (generally) advertising, travel, entertainment, dues and subscriptions, repairs and maintenance, depreciation and amortization, and bad debt. Some of these expenses may appear as costs of sales (such as bad debt, depreciation on production machinery, and advertising) because they are considered to be a cost of production and marketing.

Operating income (net income on sales or net profit before taxes) is the amount earned after all expenses of the business' operation have been deducted from gross profit. This measures the operating success of the business before other (nonoperating) income and expense or taxes is considered. For smaller businesses, there is no "other" income and expense.

Net profit after tax (net profit after tax and other items) is the amount of money that is left over after all obligations are paid. It can be taken out by the owners in the form of owners' draw or dividends or reinvested in the company. Note that on interim statements (not year-end statements, but for a period shorter than one year) the taxes are just an estimate and may in fact be higher or lower than shown.

RECONCILIATION OF NET WORTH

Recently CPA associations and some government agencies have recommended or required that a business, in addition to the income and balance sheets, have a reconciliation of net worth statement. In theory this reconciliation is considered part of the balance sheet, but in fact it serves as a bridge between the two statements. It shows what happened to the net worth over the last period, but it also shows income obtained or disbursed by the company that does not appear on the income statement. For instance, if the company sold some machinery, this adds to the net worth but is not considered to be income from operations.

Table 6.6 is an illustration of the format of the reconciliation of net worth statement.

Table 6.7 details which items are additions to net worth and which are deductions from net worth.

Net worth increases when earnings are retained, assets are revaluated upward, new capital is added, or liabilities are paid off at less than the amount owed (written down). Retained earnings (not withdrawn from the business) is the source of increase most favored by credit managers because it means operations are healthy. Revaluing assets to their market value, as we discussed before, may either be totally legitimate or could be done to present a false picture. This type of increase in net worth should be a cause for concern. An addition of more capital is usually considered a favorable sign, write-down of liabilities is usually not.

TABLE 6.6
Sample Reconciliation of Net Worth Statement

Net worth at the beginning of the period   —————

Add:
  Net income after taxes   —————
  Sale of stock   —————
  Sale of equipment   —————
  Receipts from tax refunds   —————
  Excess from reevaluation of assets   —————

Subtract:
  Net loss for period   —————
  Loss on sale of asset   —————
  Purchase of treasury stock   —————
  Dividends   —————
  Withdrawals   —————

Net worth at the end of the period   —————

Net worth decreases when losses are incurred, assets are written down, capital is withdrawn, or liabilities are "written up" or purchased at a premium.

RATIO ANALYSIS

Probably the most accurate way of finding out information about the strength or weakness of your customers' financial condition is by doing a series of ratio analyses on their statement information. Trend analysis is a further predictive technique but not as important or as accurate as ratios.

Ratios are numbers or percentages that show the relationship between two items. Ratios can be used for internal analysis of the relationships of different items on the financial statements. (See Table 6.2.) Ratios can also be used for comparative analysis, that is, how your customer's ratios compare to the industry's, to your customer's own historical ratios, or to an "ideal" ratio.

TABLE 6.7
Changes in Net Worth

Item	Additions to networth	Deductions from networth
Capital stock:		
Sale of	X	
Exchange of asset for	X	
Repurchase of		X
Cash:		
Given in the form of dividends		X
Taken in exchange for stock	X	
Credits to surplus	X	
Debt:		
Retirement at less than value owed	X	
Retirement at more than owed (premium)		X
Incurred to repurchase company stock		X
Equipment:		
Sale of, for more than book value	X	
Sale of, for less than book value		X
Income Tax:		
Additional assessments		X
Refunds	X	
Losses (from operation or otherwise)		X
Owner's draw		X
Profits	X	
Real Estate:		
Sold for more than book value	X	
Sold for less than book value		X
Retained earnings	X	
Revaluation of assets:		
Upwards (increase)	X	
Downwards (write-down)		X
Treasury stock:		
Purchased		X
Sold	X	
Withdrawals (for whatever reason)		X
Write-down or write-offs:		
Of assets		X
Of liabilities	X	

Each ratio has a certain meaning to you as a credit manager because it tells you something about your customer's financial strength that the customer either will not or can not tell you. Ratios (1) have "predictive" qualities that can tell you what financial strengths and weaknesses your customer will have in the future; (2) tell how your customer's operation looks when compared to other customers in the same industry; (3) can "test" or check up on certain items in your customer's balance sheet or income statement to see if they may be false or misleading. Moreover, by just taking the financial statements of your customer and using the right ratios you can tell about the company's distribution strength, financial strength, quality of management, efficiency of collections, profitability, current (short-term) liquidity, and capital structure. In short, ratios are very useful to the credit manager who knows how to use them.

Ratio analysis by credit managers consists of two parts: doing the calculations and comparing and interpreting the results. The calculations can be easily programmed into a calculator or computer. This will save you some time. The most important thing is that you spend your time interpreting these ratios. Therefore, I have included as Appendix A a flow chart of the programming steps required, as well as the actual key strokes involved, in programming these ratios into a calculator.

But before we get into the ratios themselves, it is a good idea to discuss the importance of industry comparisons. Figures 6.1a and 6.1b are industry ratios from the Dun and Bradstreet *Key Business Ratios*. These pages illustrate what Dun and Bradstreet's industry surveys found to be the high, average, and low results of ratios calculated from financial statements of companies in selected industries. Since ratios may be different in different industries, it is best to compare the results you got on your customer with others in the same industry. For instances, in the meat packing industry an average collection period is only 15 days whereas in the manufacture of transmission and distribution equipment the average collection period is 68 days. If a company has a collection period of 30 days it would be doing very poorly if it were a meat packing company, but fantastically well if it were manufacturing transmission equipment. There are many industry publications that have industry ratios. To find the best book, you should talk to other credit managers in your industry or visit a good library.

When you do the ratios all you need is eleven numbers: seven from the balance sheet, two from the profit and loss (income) statement, and one that is calculated by subtracting two balance sheet figures from each other. The figures you need are:

Line of Business (and number of concerns reporting)	Current assets to current debt	Net profits on sales	Net profits on tangible net worth	Net profits on net working capital	Net sales to tangible net worth	Net sales to net working capital	Collection period	Net sales to inventory	Fixed assets to tangible net worth	Current debt to tangible net worth	Total debt to tangible net worth	Inventory to net working capital	Current debt to inventory	Funded debts to net working capital
	Times	Per cent	Per cent	Per cent	Times	Times	Days	Times	Per cent	Per cent	Per cent	Per cent	Per cent	Per cent
3821-22 Instruments, Measuring & Controlling (53)	4.32	5.71	15.30	18.03	3.14	3.81	51	5.8	28.4	21.3	47.5	56.1	45.6	23.7
	2.83	4.00	9.28	11.80	2.29	3.05	64	4.1	40.4	44.3	90.3	74.1	69.6	38.1
	2.28	1.41	3.29	4.80	1.71	2.17	83	3.1	57.9	71.8	130.4	89.4	97.9	64.5
3321-22-23 Iron & Steel Foundries (56)	3.45	4.86	15.92	33.38	3.59	8.13	40	21.6	47.9	22.6	33.1	31.5	77.3	16.8
	2.37	3.19	8.38	15.40	2.71	5.30	44	10.3	63.4	30.7	58.8	83.1	115.4	39.2
	2.02	2.07	5.55	12.08	2.09	3.72	60	5.9	79.0	53.8	80.5	89.1	177.6	75.1
2253 Knit Outerwear Mills (56)	2.94	3.91	19.97	27.82	6.46	8.73	30	9.9	13.2	35.8	58.4	58.3	80.0	12.8
	2.01	2.87	11.71	16.33	4.04	6.40	49	6.9	28.4	60.6	89.0	96.8	114.9	33.8
	1.55	1.35	5.77	9.18	2.84	4.18	68	4.7	54.8	126.9	163.1	147.2	154.9	61.7
2082 Malt Liquors (30)	2.92	5.08	9.84	32.80	4.16	12.75	11	18.3	53.7	17.8	40.0	34.1	129.5	39.8
	2.31	1.65	4.97	12.64	2.49	8.95	16	15.1	70.7	24.9	58.2	55.8	137.4	94.4
	1.74	(0.55)	(1.61)	(6.23)	2.07	5.69	25	11.6	103.8	44.0	91.4	77.9	210.0	138.8
2515 Mattresses & Bedsprings (46)	3.36	3.03	12.24	15.35	6.05	8.18	41	11.3	14.4	24.6	65.6	55.8	65.8	13.0
	2.58	1.36	5.12	9.18	3.76	5.70	50	7.7	29.1	46.2	95.2	76.7	101.1	30.9
	1.69	0.55	3.39	4.17	2.36	4.00	61	6.4	50.0	92.3	131.8	103.9	140.8	76.5
2011 Meat Packing Plants (92)	3.70	1.33	14.79	25.89	19.05	34.13	12	55.1	42.9	23.9	58.2	34.1	87.3	16.5
	2.00	0.67	8.57	17.96	10.45	19.79	15	30.1	63.2	52.7	95.9	60.0	143.3	47.6
	1.47	0.20	2.59	5.73	7.00	12.57	20	21.2	90.0	100.6	184.5	111.4	227.7	88.4
3461 Metal Stampings (104)	4.35	4.90	12.16	21.75	4.39	8.16	34	11.1	30.9	17.4	44.0	44.4	64.5	26.4
	2.55	2.84	7.93	13.33	3.11	5.06	43	7.3	54.1	34.6	71.6	71.6	105.7	59.2
	1.67	0.72	2.59	6.72	1.94	3.48	58	5.2	82.2	72.0	153.5	102.4	162.4	85.6
3541-42-44-45-48 Metalworking Machinery & Equipment (124)	4.36	5.93	12.76	20.02	3.23	5.54	46	13.4	34.8	18.9	38.8	36.2	56.4	15.0
	2.83	3.06	6.94	11.21	2.13	3.46	61	5.9	48.3	29.6	71.4	66.2	91.1	43.1
	1.96	0.62	0.93	1.75	1.49	2.29	76	3.2	69.6	62.0	114.8	92.5	161.0	76.8
2431 Millwork (55)	4.14	4.25	21.08	29.04	6.25	8.56	34	10.9	23.7	26.0	58.9	52.6	72.0	17.1
	2.27	2.61	10.08	16.83	4.10	5.74	48	8.1	39.0	51.3	106.0	73.9	94.5	44.7
	1.75	1.37	5.40	6.08	2.92	4.09	59	5.5	61.8	87.8	204.9	118.2	144.6	77.7
3599 Miscellanous Machinery, except Electrical (90)	4.45	5.75	14.65	28.54	4.03	7.14	33	23.8	32.7	19.0	29.7	22.5	61.8	7.9
	2.71	3.20	6.87	12.70	2.76	4.67	46	9.4	51.1	32.8	59.1	54.2	103.1	27.5
	1.84	1.23	3.89	7.49	1.83	3.44	61	5.0	70.8	65.4	113.3	87.3	194.7	70.1
3714 Motor Vehicle Parts & Accessories (89)	3.70	5.72	16.23	26.74	3.60	5.91	35	9.0	27.2	25.6	55.2	55.2	54.8	27.8
	2.77	4.26	11.53	19.20	2.68	3.93	44	5.8	44.3	37.1	78.4	73.3	80.3	47.4
	2.19	2.96	8.22	11.21	2.16	2.87	54	4.1	62.5	55.4	117.9	96.0	116.7	73.1
3361-62-69 Nonferrous Foundries (47)	4.03	5.65	14.63	29.96	4.05	8.71	42	18.9	33.3	18.6	34.2	27.6	74.2	12.9
	2.75	2.74	8.63	17.46	3.01	5.28	47	13.4	54.5	29.1	84.9	44.5	130.4	30.0
	1.59 ·	1.08	1.41	5.79	2.15	4.00	53	6.7	77.8	73.6	175.3	83.7	260.4	122.5
2541-42 Office & Store Fixtures (60)	3.54	5.66	16.00	26.81	4.80	9.50	36	12.2	20.2	30.8	79.2	45.1	74.6	25.4
	2.22	2.45	8.58	12.85	3.52	4.86	58	7.7	42.6	55.8	114.3	75.8	116.4	46.9
	1.59	0.48	2.21	2.34	2.23	3.32	70	4.5	70.6	91.2	155.5	123.7	174.4	109.0
2361-63-69 Outerwear, Children's & Infants' (58)	2.70	2.46	15.29	18.50	8.83	12.11	30	12.9	6.8	46.9	55.7	51.1	81.1	7.4
	1.89	1.40	8.31	10.16	5.88	7.84	42	7.5	11.2	92.1	116.9	89.9	126.8	18.7
	1.46	0.49	2.54	2.72	3.69	4.50	60	5.9	24.2	175.5	315.8	146.5	208.7	37.5
2851 Paints, Varnishes, Lacquers & Enamels (112)	3.81	3.96	12.91	20.55	4.60	6.80	35	8.7	25.4	23.3	44.4	58.1	53.3	15.6
	2.92	2.61	8.87	13.50	3.40	4.85	46	6.4	40.8	40.1	72.6	73.3	81.3	33.1
	2.13	1.50	5.39	6.87	2.51	3.43	59	5.0	55.4	64.2	106.8	89.3	109.7	56.1
2621 Paper Mills, except Building Paper (55)	3.52	4.91	10.01	28.19	2.56	6.22	34	11.4	67.8	19.0	50.5	46.7	68.0	39.9
	2.82	3.28	6.27	14.02	1.97	4.30	43	7.8	87.4	22.1	75.4	60.6	98.0	117.4
	2.17	1.56	3.27	6.85	1.67	3.78	54	6.2	117.5	40.5	121.4	82.7	172.3	156.7
2651-52-53-54-55 Paperboard Containers & Boxes (61)	4.17	3.87	19.66	30.20	4.37	10.80	33	11.7	46.7	17.1	59.1	54.3	64.4	40.3
	2.22	2.63	7.38	14.20	3.06	6.45	36	8.0	70.5	38.3	75.2	80.0	92.8	67.5
	1.64	1.35	4.28	7.95	2.06	4.76	44	6.2	101.2	64.1	129.1	140.9	162.7	124.5
3712-13 Passenger Car, Truck & Bus Bodies (46)	3.54	3.14	14.02	19.64	6.78	7.67	29	9.0	18.5	25.6	47.6	59.4	64.1	17.3
	2.07	1.82	8.48	10.11	4.21	5.35	41	6.1	30.5	69.2	116.0	88.6	90.8	31.9
	1.49	1.16	4.21	6.14	2.46	3.92	56	4.3	66.3	128.5	218.6	141.1	151.9	48.1

( ) Indicates Loss

FIGURE 6.1(a)
Industry Ratios

Line of Business (and number of concerns reporting)	Current assets to current debt	Net profits on net sales	Net profits on tangible net worth	Net profits on net working capital	Net sales to tangible net worth	Net sales to net working capital	Collection period	Net sales to inventory	Fixed assets to tangible net worth	Current debt to tangible net worth	Total debt to tangible net worth	Inventory to net working capital	Current debt to inventory	Funded debts to net working capital
	Times	Per cent	Per cent	Per cent	Times	Times	Days	Times	Per cent	Per cent	Per cent	Per cent	Per cent	Per cent
5097 Furniture & Home Furnishings (81)	2.98	3.40	14.42	20.14	6.85	7.82	40	9.5	6.8	42.3	74.1	58.0	66.6	16.0
	2.10	1.56	8.42	10.09	4.83	5.50	49	6.8	13.5	75.4	140.2	88.1	108.7	31.7
	1.67	0.94	4.17	5.94	3.24	4.33	70	4.6	30.7	138.3	198.4	117.8	138.3	43.9
5041 Groceries, General Line (196)	3.15	1.21	13.86	16.81	20.27	25.58	8	18.0	11.7	39.7	83.1	86.8	49.7	20.9
	2.00	0.57	7.77	9.79	12.43	15.08	12	12.5	32.3	80.2	138.1	123.8	76.8	37.4
	1.51	0.23	3.49	4.30	7.69	9.45	17	8.7	67.7	139.7	224.8	172.8	108.6	83.2
5072 Hardware (174)	4.08	2.62	10.81	13.08	5.71	7.20	32	6.6	6.3	26.3	55.5	75.2	38.4	6.5
	2.62	1.76	7.02	8.34	3.80	4.61	43	4.9	13.6	50.9	96.7	97.1	67.0	19.0
	1.81	0.80	3.64	4.07	2.73	3.31	52	3.7	25.1	98.2	152.9	130.0	100.6	36.2
5084 Industrial Machinery & Equipment (97)	3.27	3.78	17.24	23.65	7.90	8.80	34	11.2	8.4	35.5	79.6	62.5	65.4	13.5
	2.12	2.03	8.50	11.03	4.73	5.50	48	6.6	18.8	69.5	134.0	92.1	103.0	41.7
	1.59	0.75	4.17	4.76	3.24	4.04	59	4.0	46.6	139.7	216.8	125.1	150.3	67.9
5098 Lumber & Construction Materials (146)	3.60	3.05	16.67	23.17	8.64	11.36	36	11.3	8.8	32.5	75.3	52.5	60.3	14.0
	2.20	1.85	11.00	13.02	5.73	6.18	47	8.0	21.9	68.5	125.6	83.7	104.4	33.0
	1.64	0.94	6.18	7.00	3.38	4.01	64	5.8	39.5	124.6	247.4	118.4	173.2	64.7
5047 Meats & Meat Products (48)	2.93	1.33	21.62	22.58	25.38	29.41	15	76.4	9.6	37.2	65.9	33.5	133.5	12.8
	2.03	0.74	12.13	13.75	16.94	20.44	22	42.0	29.9	79.2	114.5	50.3	197.1	36.7
	1.45	0.23	3.54	4.72	9.36	14.67	30	24.2	50.0	175.3	256.6	104.1	378.0	71.3
5091 Metals & Minerals (76)	4.03	3.54	14.13	21.01	6.34	7.46	39	7.9	11.2	28.9	54.1	57.8	54.1	11.5
	2.36	2.07	8.44	10.51	4.04	4.96	47	5.3	22.2	66.2	110.5	93.3	85.9	27.3
	1.51	1.21	5.11	6.57	2.38	3.45	60	3.7	43.5	134.7	172.7	141.1	130.5	59.4
5028 Paints & Varnishes (38)	6.13	3.56	12.92	19.35	4.74	6.29	33	8.0	6.1	17.7	33.8	45.0	42.4	7.0
	3.50	2.55	5.52	8.09	3.29	4.26	41	6.4	16.1	25.6	68.1	69.4	60.4	16.1
	2.00	1.13	3.10	4.76	2.52	3.27	48	5.4	27.7	70.9	93.7	93.0	99.9	40.3
5096 Paper & Its Products (121)	3.88	2.33	11.31	14.92	8.06	10.73	31	11.8	7.8	30.4	67.6	57.1	57.5	12.2
	2.34	1.21	7.00	8.79	5.39	6.66	40	8.1	14.5	59.8	107.4	83.2	95.9	23.1
	1.70	0.60	3.43	4.26	3.63	4.61	51	6.1	35.7	104.2	177.6	102.2	146.6	53.8
5092 Petroleum & Petroleum Products (66)	3.45	3.21	14.52	37.55	7.70	15.38	25	35.4	26.6	20.7	42.3	23.1	112.7	18.9
	2.07	1.31	9.09	16.02	4.80	9.40	34	24.2	48.5	38.8	90.3	47.9	174.0	62.3
	1.50	0.69	3.53	8.79	3.08	5.59	52	13.7	86.7	86.5	189.1	84.3	287.5	130.0
5033 Piece Goods (128)	3.17	2.39	11.04	13.84	8.13	8.91	29	9.1	2.1	43.9	61.1	62.5	59.4	8.7
	2.10	1.36	6.35	7.22	4.74	5.96	47	6.1	5.0	84.1	122.2	91.2	100.0	17.4
	1.64	0.67	3.68	3.89	3.25	3.51	68	4.6	15.2	132.8	176.8	124.3	146.5	41.2
5074 Plumbing & Heating Equipment & Supplies (179)	3.66	3.13	13.04	16.30	6.58	7.62	36	8.4	6.8	31.4	59.8	65.4	53.0	9.8
	2.63	1.77	7.76	9.72	4.50	5.24	45	6.0	13.2	53.3	97.9	82.5	79.9	20.4
	1.94	0.99	4.28	5.39	3.32	3.70	58	4.8	28.4	99.2	158.6	106.1	120.0	44.1
5044 Poultry & Poultry Products (45)	3.39	2.21	15.79	31.97	14.44	25.90	14	66.7	12.1	27.1	61.0	24.7	111.9	19.4
	2.09	0.83	8.11	10.77	10.52	16.16	21	31.1	26.5	59.3	104.2	49.4	157.8	95.4
	1.39	0.26	2.55	3.50	6.47	8.17	31	15.0	80.8	108.7	263.0	100.0	248.2	187.0
5093 Scrap & Waste Materials (61)	4.10	3.37	12.11	24.18	7.32	10.61	20	30.0	19.3	21.3	36.3	28.5	50.1	15.9
	2.41	1.59	6.95	12.57	3.74	7.91	30	11.5	36.0	37.2	103.1	63.0	127.3	47.5
	1.54	0.80	4.72	8.09	2.67	4.39	48	7.1	59.4	88.3	182.8	103.6	229.5	107.7
5014 Tires & Tubes (44)	2.58	3.09	14.15	17.50	6.11	8.26	32	9.7	13.8	50.1	101.2	60.7	84.6	8.9
	1.93	1.80	7.69	10.00	4.51	5.87	42	6.0	24.9	87.3	122.3	94.8	116.7	30.4
	1.58	0.93	3.67	6.21	3.43	4.33	63	4.4	45.1	125.7	251.6	137.0	150.0	66.7
5094 Tobacco & Its Products (97)	2.71	1.04	13.94	23.78	21.35	27.49	13	25.6	9.4	46.2	81.0	60.7	81.2	8.8
	1.97	0.73	9.65	13.12	12.40	17.28	16	18.5	17.3	82.5	118.2	93.0	114.1	20.9
	1.43	0.40	5.40	7.02	7.48	10.42	24	12.3	31.9	152.0	170.1	141.5	164.0	40.9

FIGURE 6.1(b)
Industry Ratios

From the balance sheet:

1. Total current assets
2. Accounts receivable
3. Inventory
4. Total fixed assets
5. Total current liabilities
6. Total all liabilities
7. Net worth

From the income statement:

8. Net sales
9. Net profit after taxes

Calculated:

10 & 11.   Working capital (current assets minus current liabilities).

Standard Business Ratios

Credit agents differ as to what the best ratios are, although traditionally the current ratio, sales-to-inventory ratio, and debt-to-worth ratio have been the most widely used. So that you might choose the ratio that is best suited to your needs, I will list and explain all the ratios that I have found in books on credit and collections and a special ratio that I devised myself. The ratios that are listed by most of the books or that credit managers have told me are the most useful, I have marked with an asterisk (*). However, some ratios, even without an asterisk, may be more important in a specific industry. You must be the judge. For convenience, ratios are listed in the order they are given in the Dun and Bradstreet *Key Business Ratios.*

I will illustrate each ratio with figures from the financial statements of Hero Manufacturing (good results) and Rotten Distribution (poor results).

*Current Ratio (Current Assets to Current Liabilities)

The current ratio (1) measures the customer's liquidity and the extent of protection for short-term creditors (you); (2) gives a general picture of the adequacy of your customer's working capital and his ability to meet day-to-day payment obligations; and (3) measures the margin of safety provided for paying current debts in the event of a reduction in the value of current assets. If receivables and inventory are valid, the current ratio is important as a specific measure of the capacity of a company to meet daily financing requirements.

To calculate the ratio, divide the total current assets by the total current liabilities as follows:

$$\text{current ratio} = \frac{\text{total current assets}}{\text{total current liabilities}}$$

EXAMPLES: Hero Mfg.   Rotten Dist.

$$\frac{\$2,049,800}{\$499,762} = 4.1 \text{ times} \qquad \frac{\$1,208,720}{\$1,091,120} = 1.11 \text{ times}$$

In the example, Hero Manufacturing has enough current assets to cover their current liabilities approximately four times. If they were forced to liquidate their current assets to pay their current liabilities they would have much more than they needed to pay off obligations. If you look at the industry ratios for iron and steel foundries (Figure 6.1a), you can see that the lowest times assets cover liabilities is 2.02; the average 2.37 times; and the highest 3.45 times. With a ratio of 4.1 times Hero is not only above the industry average, they are higher than the highest ratio recorded for the industry. Needless to say, that is good.

Rotten Distribution, on the other hand, had a very poor ratio. With only 1.11 times coverage, if nip comes to tuck they would barely be able to cover their current liabilities with the liquidation of their current assets. Rotten has a ratio that is lower than the lowest in the industry, just the opposite of Hero. For the Scrap and Waste Materials wholesale industry (Fig. 6.1), the highest current ratio is 4.1 times; average, 2.41 times; and lowest, 1.54 times. Any way you look at it, logically or by industry standards, Rotten has a bad ratio.

Net Profit on Net Sales

The net-profit-to-sales ratio is important for measuring the profitability of your customer's business. This ratio represents the net profit margin as a percentage of sales. It explains what percentage of sales the actual net profit is after taxes. Too small a profit margin may indicate ineffective management or other internal problems. Every company has as its goal the maximum realization of profit from each dollar of sales. This ratio measures a company's success in achieving that goal. The profit-to-sales ratio is calculated by dividing the net profit after taxes by the net (after returns and allowances) sales:

$$\text{net profit on net sales} = \frac{\text{net profit after tax}}{\text{net sales}}$$

EXAMPLES: Hero Mfg.   Rotten Dist.

$$\frac{\$224,800}{5,620,000} = 4.0\% \qquad \frac{\$29,400}{4,200,000} = 0.7\%$$

Four percent of Hero Manufacturing's sales go to profit after tax, whereas Rotten Distribution is making about a half of a percent (0.7 percent) net profit margin. For Hero, the industry average is 3.19 percent and the best in the industry is 4.85 percent. Hero is better than the industry average, and almost as good as the best. Rotten's industry average is 1.59 percent, and the worst is 0.8 percent. Again, Rotten does worse than the worst.

*Net Profit on Tangible Net Worth

This ratio measures the return on invested capital and gauges the possibilities of future growth. The tendency today is to look more and more to this ratio, rather than the profit-to-sales ratio, as a criterion of profitability. Generally, a profits-to-worth relationship of at least 10 percent is regarded as necessary for providing draw or dividends plus funds for future growth. Tangible net worth is net worth minus such intangibles as goodwill, patents, copyrights, trademarks, organization expenses, and treasury stock. To arrive at Hero Manufacturing's tangible net worth we have to subtract $5,000 amortized value of the organization expenses from $1,729,200 net worth, leaving $1,724,200. In the case of Rotten distribution, we must subtract $40,000 in trademarks, and $30,000 amortized value of organization expense from a net worth of $700,000, leaving $630,000. The net-profit-to-net-worth ratio is calculated by dividing net profit by net worth:

$$\text{net profit to net worth} = \frac{\text{net profit after tax}}{\text{tangible net worth}}$$

EXAMPLES: Hero Mfg.   Rotten Dist.

$$\frac{\$224,800}{1,724,200} = 13.0\% \qquad \frac{\$29,400}{630,000} = 4.67\%$$

Hero Manufacturing is returning 13 percent on net worth (investment) to its owners. This is a good return for the industry, better than the average return of 9.39 percent, and almost as good as the top industry return of 15.92 percent. Rotten Distribution's return to its owners is not as good as the industry average of 6.95 percent (the scrap industry has a lower average return than the iron and steel foundries). Rotten (again) did worse than the worst company recorded at 4.72 percent. How does Rotten Distribution survive!

Net Profits on Net Working Capital

Working capital is the cushion available to the business for carrying inventories and receivables, and for financing day-to-day operations. This ratio is useful in measuring profitability of firms whose operating funds are provided mostly by long-term borrowings, and whose permanent capital is therefore very small in relation to sales. Working capital (or net working capital) is arrived at by subtracting total current liabilities from total current assets. The net-profit-on-working-capital ratio is calculated by dividing net profit after tax by working capital:

$$\text{net profits on working capital} = \frac{\text{net profit after tax}}{\text{net working capital}}$$

EXAMPLES: Hero Mfg.   Rotten Dist.

$$\frac{\$224,800}{1,550,000} = 14.5\% \qquad \frac{\$29,400}{117,600} = 25\%$$

Hero Manufacturing has net profit as a small percentage of working capital, which indicates that it has a strong working capital position. Hero's percentage is better than the industry average of 15.4 percent, but not quite as good as the best in the industry, which is 12.08 percent. Rotten Distribution has a poor working capital position because even though net profit is low, it is still a large percentage of working capital. The worst in the industry is 24.18 percent, the average is 12.57 percent.

Net Sales to Tangible Net Worth

The net-sales-to-net-worth ratio is sometimes known as the trading ratio. It indicates the extent to which a company's sales volume is supported by invested capital (net worth). A substantially higher than average ratio indicates that the company is an overtrader, that is, a company that is attempting to stretch the invested dollar to its maximum capacity. The overtrader's financial statement shows heavy debt. When someone has heavy debt their survival will hinge on the long-term continuation of optimum internal and external conditions. The undertrader, on the other hand, has either large capital reserves or inadequate sales to support the business. The most pressing need of the undertrader is generally to bring sales up to a profitable level. The net-sales-to-net-worth ratio measures the degree to which a company has attained a balance between the extremes of undertrading and overtrading.

In other words, the ratio is a measure of the relative turnover of capital. If capital is turned over too rapidly, liabilities build up excessively. If capital is turned too slowly, funds become stagnant and profitability suffers. The net-sales-to-net-worth ratio is calculated as net sales divided by tangible net worth (net worth minus intangibles):

$$\text{net sales to tangible net worth} = \frac{\text{net sales}}{\text{tangible net worth}}$$

EXAMPLES: Hero Mfg.   Rotten Dist.

$$\frac{\$5,620,000}{1,724,200} = 3.25 \text{ times} \qquad \frac{\$4,200,000}{630,000} = 6.67 \text{ times}$$

Hero Manufacturing turned its capital over a little more than the industry average of 2.71 times. Yet they could not be considered overtrading because they came in well below the industry's biggest overtraders who turned capital 3.59 times. A quick look at Hero's large cash and security amounts and at the current ratio indicates that they have more than enough working capital to pay any foreseeable short-term obligation. Rotten Distribution turns their capital over twice as much as Hero, but they still have to go some distance before they can do as badly as the worst in the industry at 7.32 times. The industry average is 3.74 times, higher than the average in Hero's industry.

Net Sales to Net Working Capital

This ratio indicates the demands made upon working capital to support the sales volume of the company. It is like the net-sales-to-net-worth ratio except that it measures the turnover of working capital. If the ratio is too high, there is a tendency of the business to owe too much money. Turning working capital very fast necessitates dependence upon credit granted by suppliers, banks, and others to provide operating funds. In cases where this ratio is disproportionately high, there is a good indication of working capital deficiencies.

The net-sales-to-net-working-capital ratio is calculated by dividing net sales by net working capital:

$$\text{net sales to working capital} = \frac{\text{net sales}}{\text{working capital}}$$

EXAMPLES: Hero Mfg.   Rotten Dist.

$$\frac{\$5,620,000}{1,550,000} = 3.63 \text{ times} \qquad \frac{\$4,200,000}{117,600} = 35.7 \text{ times}$$

Hero Manufacturing obviously has plenty of working capital because it turns so slowly. As a matter of fact, Hero turns its working capital slower than the best in the industry (3.72 times); the industry average is 5.3 times. Rotten Distribution is 180 degrees in the opposite direction. Rotten turns its working capital over three times faster than the worst in its industry (10.61 times). Rotten turns its working capital five times more than the industry average (7.51 times). Obviously Rotten is hurting for working capital.

*Collection Period

As any credit manager can tell you, a company's credit and collections program and terms exert a direct influence on sales attainment, profits, and the need for borrowing capital. This ratio helps analyze the collectability of receivables. The average collection period should not exceed the net maturity indicated by selling terms by more than 10 to 15 days. This ratio is especially important today when accounts receivable is an increasingly major asset.

The collection period in days is determined by a two-step formula (discussed in Chapter 4). The first step is to divide the annual *credit* sales by 365 days to obtain the average daily credit sales. If all the company's sales are on credit, the credit sales equal the total net sales. But if the company does a large portion of its business on a cash basis, the cash sales must be subtracted from net sales to get credit sales. The second step in the formula is to divide accounts and notes receivable by the average daily credit sales (the result of the step 1 calculation) to get the average collection period in days.

Step 1:   average daily credit sales $= \dfrac{\text{total annual credit sales}}{365 \text{ days}}$

Step 2:   collection period in days $= \dfrac{\text{notes and accounts receivable}}{\text{average daily credit sales (from Step 1)}}$

EXAMPLES: Hero Mfg.   Rotten Dist.

Step 1: $\dfrac{\$5,620,000^*}{365 \text{ days}} = \$15,397$ $\dfrac{\$4,200,000^*}{365 \text{ days}} = \$11,507$

Step 2: $\dfrac{\$580,000}{15,397} = 37 \text{ days}$ $\dfrac{\$690,000}{11,507} = 60 \text{ days}$

Hero Manufacturing collects its receivables faster than anyone in the industry (industry best: 40 days; average: 48 days). The faster a company collects their receivables, the less likely their need for additional working capital. Rotten Distribution collects their receivables slower than anyone in the industry (slowest: 48 days) and much slower than the average (36 days). This means that Rotten is going to require more working capital than anyone else in the industry, and since, as we have seen, they have precious little working capital now, they will have to borrow or go slow on their trade obligations. *Note:* If the figures you have from your customer are not annual figures, but interim figures, you must divide credit sales by the number of days in the period (183 days for two quarters, 90 days for one quarter, and so on). Dividing by 365 days is done only if you are using annual figures.

*Net Sales to Inventory

This ratio determines the number of times the customer turns their inventory in one period. If the ratio is less than the industry average, it would indicate obsolete merchandise, poor buying, or conservative buying. A ratio higher than the industry average might indicate over-trading — using the suppliers' money to buy and sell merchandise. This ratio does not indicate an actual physical turnover of inventory, but it provides a yardstick for comparing stock-to-sales ratios of one firm to

*Note: All of Hero Manufacturing and Rotten Distribution's sales are on credit, therefore, total net sales equal credit sales.

another. Higher than average ratios also indicate a chronically over-stocked condition in which sales are being lost because of lack of adequate inventories. Lower than average ratios may mean obsolete or stagnant inventories. This could indicate that a write-off of inventory is in store for the future.

The net-sales-to-inventory ratio is computed by dividing sales for the period by the book value of the inventory, expressed as "times."

$$\text{net sales to inventory} = \frac{\text{net sales}}{\text{inventory}}$$

EXAMPLES: Hero Mfg.   Rotten Dist.

$$\frac{\$5,620,000}{330,300} = 17 \text{ times} \qquad \frac{\$4,200,000}{583,310} = 7.2 \text{ times}$$

Hero Manufacturing again demonstrates that it is one of the best credit risks in the industry. Hero is neither turning inventory too fast or too slow (fastest: 21.6; average: 10.3; slowest: 5.9). Rotten Distribution demonstrates that they have a lot of slow-moving, perhaps obsolete, inventory. Rotten turns their inventory slower than anyone in the industry (slowest: 7.1 times). It makes sense that Rotten will eventually have to write off some inventory. At any rate, it is apparent that they have inventory that is not making any money.

*Fixed Assets to Tangible Net Worth

This ratio tells you what percentage of the customer's net worth is invested in fixed assets. Ordinarily, this ratio should not exceed 100 percent for a manufacturer, and 75 percent for a wholesaler or retailer, but industries differ widely on this ratio, so check your industry's figures. A percentage beyond the maximum limits of the industry indicates that a disproportionate amount of capital is frozen in machinery and the building itself. This will limit the amount of operating funds for carrying inventories, receivables, and maintaining day-to-day cash outlays. It also means that the business will be unprepared for the hazards of unexpected developments (and every business gets its share of those) that may drain income into heavy debt payment and maintenance charges. But remember, a high percentage for this ratio does not automatically prove that fixed assets are excessive. The ratio may be distorted by inadequate net worth or recent investment in modernizing an out-of-date plant.

The fixed-assets-to-tangible-net-worth ratio is computed by dividing fixed assets by net worth and is expressed as a percentage:

$$\text{Fixed assets to tangible net worth} = \frac{\text{total fixed assets}}{\text{tangible net worth}}$$

EXAMPLES: Hero Mfg.   Rotten Dist.

$$\frac{\$833,500}{1,724,200} = 48.3\%   \qquad \frac{\$420,000}{630,000} = 66.7\%$$

Hero Manufacturing's fixed assets are a smaller percentage of their net worth than the industry average (63.4 percent). Rotten's fixed assets are much too large a percentage of net worth; a higher percentage than the worst in the industry (59.4 percent). This indicates that Rotten has too many, probably unproductive, fixed assets, which limits the amount they have for day-to-day operations.

Current Debt to Tangible Net Worth

This ratio is infrequently used. (A more frequently used ratio, total liabilities (total debt) to net worth, follows.) This ratio of current-debt-to-worth should not exceed 80 percent, and generally the higher the percentage, the more the company depends on current financing to meet operation capital requirements. The current-debt-to-tangible-net-worth ratio is computed by dividing current liabilities by tangible net worth and is expressed as a percentage:

$$\text{Current debt to tangible net worth} = \frac{\text{current liabilities}}{\text{tangible net worth}}$$

EXAMPLES: Hero Mfg.   Rotten Dist.

$$\frac{\$499,762}{1,724,200} = 29\%   \qquad \frac{\$1,091,120}{630,000} = 173.4\%$$

Hero Manufacturing has current liabilities as a percentage of tangible net worth at pretty close to the industry average (30.7 percent), which indicates that they use current liabilities no more than the industry in general. Rotten Distribution is very dependent on short-term (current liability) financing. As a matter of fact, they are more dependent on current liability financing than anyone in the industry (highest percentage: 88.3 percent).

*Total Debt (Total Liabilities) to Tangible Net Worth

Sometimes simply called the debt-to-worth ratio, this ratio measures the proportion of the owner's investment in the business compared to the creditors' investment. If the total debt exceeds the net worth, it means that the suppliers and the banks have invested more than the owner. The management of top-heavy liabilities entails strains and hazards that can become a threat to business survival. They expose the business to unexpected risks such as a sudden downturn in sales, changes in customer preferences, strikes, fires, rapid rises in business costs, and other factors. Companies that have a lower than average ratio indicate a strong ownership interest. Although this total-debt-to-worth ratio is more frequently used than the current-debt-to-worth ratio, the current ratio provides notice of more immediate danger. On the other hand, long-term debt has its own peril in that it is fixed as to maturity and more enforceable because it is supported by specifically pledged collateral.

The total-debt-to-tangible-net-worth ratio is calculated by dividing total liabilities by tangible net worth, expressed as a percentage:

$$\text{total debt to tangible net worth} = \frac{\text{total liabilities}}{\text{tangible net worth}}$$

EXAMPLES: Hero Mfg.   Rotten Dist.

$$\frac{\$1{,}470{,}000}{1{,}724{,}200} = 85.3\% \qquad \frac{\$1{,}470{,}000}{630{,}000} = 233\%$$

Hero Manufacturing has a weak percentage of total liabilities compared to the net worth, though slightly more than the industry percentage (58.8 percent). Hero's percentage is also slightly more than the highest in the industry (80 percent). Rotten Distribution exceeds the worst percentage in its industry (182.8 percent), which again points up Rotten's strong dependence on outside financing to the tune of twice its net worth.

*Inventory to Net Working Capital

This ratio provides information on your customer's ability to finance the purchase of merchandise. If an excessive percentage of net working capital is reflected in unsold inventory, difficulty may be experienced in meeting currently maturing obligations. Under normal circumstances this ratio should not exceed 80 percent, that is, your customer's inventory should total no more than four-fifths of its working capital. Because inventory is usually a very large and important element in the composition of working capital, and because it is sometimes subject to major downward value revisions, the percentage of working capital represented by inventory becomes important.

The inventory-to-net-working-capital ratio is computed by dividing inventory by working capital (current assets minus current liabilities) and is expressed as a percentage:

$$\text{inventory to net working capital} = \frac{\text{merchandise inventory}}{\text{net working capital}}$$

EXAMPLES: Hero Mfg.   Rotten Dist.

$$\frac{\$330,300}{1,550,000} = 21.3\% \qquad \frac{\$117,600}{583,310} = 496\%$$

Hero Manufacturing has a smaller percentage of its working capital tied up in inventory than anyone in the industry (smallest percentage: 31.5 percent). This indicates that Hero is doing well in managing their inventory and should have plenty of money for inventory in the foreseeable future. Rotten Distribution has too much inventory, as this ratio again shows. Rotten shows a poorer percentage than the worst in the industry (103.6 percent). Rotten's high percentage shows that the company has too much inventory or too little working capital, or, more likely, both.

Current Debt to Inventory

This ratio (not commonly used) is another indicator of the extent to which the business depends on funds from disposal of unsold inventories to meet its debts. The current-debt-to-inventory ratio is calculated by dividing the current liabilities by inventories, expressed as a percentage:

$$\text{current debt to inventory} = \frac{\text{current liabilities}}{\text{inventories}}$$

EXAMPLES: Hero Mfg.   Rotten Dist.

$$\frac{\$499,762}{330,300} = 151.3\% \qquad \frac{\$1,091,120}{583,310} = 187.1\%$$

Hero Manufacturing has its current liabilities reasonably well covered by inventories. Hero does poorer than the industry average (115.4

percent), but not as badly as the worst in the industry (177.6 percent). Rotten Distribution has almost twice as many current liabilities as inventories, which indicates a dependence on current liability financing. The industry average is 127.3 percentage, and Rotten does worse than that. But surprisingly (for Rotten), the company does better on this ratio than the worst in the industry (229.5 percent). Considering Rotten's poor performance on the other ratios, we will consider this a favorable sign.

Funded Debts to Net Working Capital

This ratio compares funded debts with net working capital to help determine whether long-term debts are in proper proportion. Funded debts are long-term obligations including mortgages, bonds, and term loans. The money for paying funded debts when they become due comes from three sources: refunding (borrowing new money to repay debt), accumulating earnings, or raising new equity capital. The probability of borrowing money or of getting new capital when the loans become due is an uncertain factor. This ratio tells to what extent the company can depend on working capital (built from accumulating earnings) to pay total funded debt. Ordinarily this ratio should not exceed 100 percent. The funded-debts-to-working-capital ratio is computed by dividing funded debts by net working capital, and is expressed as a percentage:

$$\text{funded debts to net working capital} = \frac{\text{total funding debt}}{\text{net working capital}}$$

EXAMPLES: Hero Mfg.   Rotten Dist.

$$\frac{\$822,238}{1,550,000} = 53\% \qquad \frac{\$888,880}{117,600} = 755.9\%$$

Hero Manufacturing has a higher (therefore, poorer) ratio than average (39.2 percent), but is still better than the worst in the industry (75.1 percent). This percentage indicates that Hero has enough working capital to cover all funded debt about two times, but indicates that they depend a little more on funded debt than the industry average. Rotten Distribution is really in bad shape, much worse than the poorest in the industry (107.7 percent). This indicates not only that Rotten depends on funded debt, and could not possibly pay it off from working capital, but also that when the debt comes due, unless Rotten makes a lot of profit between now and then, it can only be paid by refunding or raising new capital.

Sales to Receivables

This ratio is helpful in analyzing the quality of your customer's receivables. The smaller the receivables in relation to total sales, the more times receivables are "turned," the better the ratio is. If this ratio shows that receivables are turned a small number of times, this indicates that your customer's accounts are slow; if your customer's accounts are slow, you can generally expect your customer to be slow with you.

The sales-to-receivables ratio is computed by dividing total credit sales by accounts receivable, expressed as "times":

$$\text{sales to receivables} = \frac{\text{total credit sales}}{\text{accounts receivable}}$$

EXAMPLES: Hero Mfg.   Rotten Dist.

$$\frac{\$5,620,000}{580,000} = 9.6 \text{ times} \qquad \frac{\$4,200,000}{690,000} = 6.1 \text{ times}$$

Hero, as we already know from the collection ratio, turns their receivables very well. The ratio confirms this by showing that the receivables turn almost ten times per year (the period we are using). Rotten's receivables turn slowly, almost twice as slowly as Hero's do. This indicates that Rotten will probably run slow in their payments to their suppliers.

Tax Ratio

There is no question in collections as to which creditor always gets the first shot at a company's assets. It is not the first mortgage hold; not the bank who holds chattel mortgages on assets; not the creditor who holds accounts receivable as collateral; and not the supplier. It is the Internal Revenue Service (IRS).

The IRS gets its money *first*. And there is no lengthy court procedure required. If a company does not pay, the sheriff comes with a padlock for the front door and that is that. Nothing puts the fear of failure into the company president more than when he has to ask the IRS for a *second* extension on the company's quarterly taxes.

Usually a company will show tax liabilities on its balance sheet under the items "payroll taxes payable," "income tax payable," or merely "taxes payable." All businesses also show on their income statement an expense item called "payroll tax," or "taxes," which shows the amount of taxes it has either paid to date or is currently due. On its income statement, a company will also (usually) show the expected taxes on income (under "reserve for taxes") below the net profit before taxes figure. Remember, when any taxes are listed as a payable on the balance sheet, this means that they are either overdue or due within the next three months.

The ratio for finding out the authenticity of the payroll or income tax payable figures on the balance sheet is calculated by dividing the payroll tax expense and the reserve for income tax figures for the period by the number of quarters (three-month periods) in the period of the statement. This would be four quarters for each year. This ratio (tax ratio no. 1) shows how much money the company spends in the average quarter for payroll and income taxes. Compare the answer to the "taxes payable" entry on the balance sheet. If the payroll taxes payable are more than the average taxes per quarter, you know that the firm might be more than one quarter delinquent on its taxes. If, on the other hand, the payroll taxes payable figure is less than the average taxes paid per quarter, the company has either paid on time or has had a recent drop in salaries. This ratio is as follows:

$$\text{tax ratio no. 1} = \frac{\text{total tax costs for the period}}{\text{number of quarters in the period}}$$

EXAMPLES: Hero Mfg.   Rotten Dist.

$$\frac{\$414,740^*}{4} = \$103,685 \qquad \frac{\$84,000^*}{4} = \$21,000$$

When we look at Hero Manufacturing's taxes payable on their balance sheet, we see that the total of payroll and income tax payable is $117,310, fairly close to the $103,685 figure arrived at by tax ratio no. 1. This indicates that Hero Manufacturing is current with their taxes and there should be little concern that the IRS will step in. Rotten Distribution, however, has income tax and payroll tax payable on their balance sheet for a total of $47,600, well above the $21,000 amount calculated by the ratio. There are only two explanations for this: either Rotten is past due on their taxes or they have had a sudden increase in salary (and therefore, payroll) expense in the last quarter. The credit manager should note that usually the figure calculated by the ratio and the amount shown on the balance sheet are going to be somewhat different because of salary fluctuation during the year. But the two figures should not be significantly different.

*Note: Total tax includes payroll tax from general and officer's salaries, factory wages, and selling wages plus reserve for income tax.

To find out how long overdue the tax payments are, we use tax ratio no. 2. This ratio shows how many quarters the company is behind in their taxes. If the company is two or more quarters behind in their payments, watch out! The IRS is going to severely drain their capital soon. The second ratio, tax ratio no. 2, is calculated by dividing the payroll tax and income tax payable (from the balance sheet) by the average payroll and income taxes due per quarter (the answer to tax ratio no. 1). The answer is expressed in quarters:

$$\text{tax ratio no. 2} = \frac{\text{taxes payable}}{\text{average tax due per quarter}}$$

EXAMPLES: Hero Mfg.   Rotten Dist.

$$\frac{\$117,310^*}{103,685} = 1.1 \text{ quarters} \qquad \frac{\$47,600^*}{21,000} = 2.27 \text{ quarters}$$

Hero Manufacturing owes taxes for one quarter, so everything is all right with them. Rotten, on the other hand, is two or more quarters behind in their income and payroll taxes. Undoubtedly, Rotten will use a chunk of their working capital to pay off the IRS this next quarter. Where is the money going to come from?

The biggest problems with these ratios, as you might have guessed, is that most companies are not totally accurate as to what they owe on taxes. Some companies may be in trouble with the IRS but have not a single entry on their balance sheet showing their tax liability. When the information is available, however, it is a good idea to find out if there is going to be another creditor, stronger than you, in line for payment — the IRS.

Summary of the Rotten Distribution and Hero Manufacturing Cases

Hero Manufacturing, Inc., is strong on all the ratios, and very strong on some of them. They have a higher-than-industry-tops current ratio, which indicates that they have a very strong current asset position in relation to their current liabilities. They can pay off current liabilities four times over out of current assets. Their good performance on that ratio and most of the working capital ratios (net profit to working capital, net sales to working capital, and inventory to working capital) indicates

*Note: The taxes payable figure includes both payroll taxes payable and income taxes payable.

TABLE 6.8
Schedule of Industry and Actual Ratios for Hero Manufacturing and Rotten Distribution

RATIOS	Hero Manufacturing			Rotten Distribution		
	Industry Range	Ave.	Actual	Industry Range	Ave.	Actual
Current (times)	3.45 2.02	2.37	4.1	4.1 1.54	2.41	1.11
Net Profit to Net Sales (%)	4.86 2.07	3.19	4.0	3.37 0.8	1.59	0.54
Net Profit to Tangible Net Worth (%)	15.92 5.55	9.39	13.0	12.11 4.72	6.95	4.67
Net Profit to Working Capital (%)	33.38 12.08	15.4	14.5	24.18 8.09	12.57	25.0
Net Sales to Net Worth (times)	3.59 2.09	2.71	3.25	7.32 2.67	3.74	6.67
Net Sales to Working Capital (times)	8.13 3.72	5.3	3.63	10.61 4.39	7.51	35.7

	40 60	48	37	20 48	36	60
Collection Period (days)	40 60	48	37	20 48	36	60
Net Sales to Inventory (times)	21.6 5.9	10.3	17.0	30.0 7.1	11.5	7.2
Fixed Assets to Net Worth (%)	47.9 29.0	63.4	48.2	19.3 59.4	36.0	66.7
Current Debt to Net Worth (%)	22.6 53.8	30.7	29.0	21.3 88.3	37.2	115.9
Total Liabilities to Net Worth (%)	33.1 80.5	58.8	67.1	36.0 182.8	103.1	233.0
Inventory to Working Capital (%)	31.5 89.1	63.1	23.1	28.5 103.6	63.8	496.0
Funded Debt to Working Capital (%)	16.8 75.1	39.2	53.0	15.9 107.7	47.5	755.9
Sales to Receivable (times)	No Industry		9.6	No Industry		6.1
Tax Ratio No. 1			$103,685 Tax per quarter			$21,000 Tax per quarter
Tax Ratio No. 2			1.1 quarters due			2.29 quarters due

that they have enough working capital (current assets minus current liabilities) to cover most contingencies. Their funded debt to working capital is not as good as the other working capital ratios, indicating that they may depend a little more on debt than the industry. Hero also did well on the profitability ratios (net profit to net sales and net profit to tangible net worth), indicating that they make plenty of profits to continue working capital strength and have good liability repayment ability. Hero's collection period is better than anyone's in the industry in strength, which makes more money available to them and assures prompt payment of suppliers. The inventory ratios (net sales to inventory and inventory to working capital) show ratios below the average indicating Hero's inventory may be excessive, but nothing to worry about. The fixed-asset ratio (fixed assets to net worth) shows a better than industry utilization of fixed assets freeing more money for working capital. The tax ratios show that payment of obligations to federal and state government is prompt. All in all, Hero Manufacturing is a very good credit risk, now and into the foreseeable future.

Rotten did poorly on all the ratios. One of their most crucial problems is a shortage of working capital (demonstrated by a worse than worst-in-the-industry current ratio, net sales-to-working-capital ratio, and especially their inventory-to-working-capital ratio). Since working capital is the crucial element when considering extending credit, bad news on the working capital front should probably eliminate consideration of this company in most cases. Add to that Rotten's excessive, slow-moving inventory (net-sales-to-inventory ratio among others) and their dependence on funded debt (debt-to-worth and funded-debt-to-working-capital ratios), and you get a really bad picture. Insufficient working capital, slow-moving inventory and dependence on debt should put a squash to your extending credit to Rotten. If that is not enough, Rotten's 60-day (way over the worst in the industry) collection period should do the trick. Not enough? They are probably two quarters behind in their income tax and payroll tax payments. Rotten does have a fair net worth and could probably pay you from liquidation and they are making a profit, but if you sell to them you can expect slow payments. If you feel you must sell to Rotten, at least arrange special terms (such as trade acceptances discussed in Chapter 2).

TRENDS

Ratios give you a good picture of your customer's business today, but what about tomorrow? Ratio analysis gives you a partial look at what will be happening to your customer's business in the near future (the next quarter or so). Trend analysis takes into consideration past movements (up or down) in your customer's finances. The idea behind trend analysis is that if you can see how your customer got from there to here, you can see where they will be going in the future.

If a company has decreasing sales, for example, for every one of the past three years, it is fairly safe to say that sales can be expected to decline, or at least stay the same next year. If sales are headed upward, they will probably continue up next year. The items of the financial statements whose movements (upward or down) are crucial to the prediction of future stability of the company are: sales, net profits, current assets, fixed assets, total assets, current liabilities, total liabilities, and net worth.

Statement Comparisons

The first step in predicting the future standing of the company is to take all the old financial statements (at least two years, preferably more) as well as the current financial statements, and put them side by side. For instance, put the sales for last year in a column next to the sales for this year in another column, next to the sales for the year before last. When you put each statement in a column side by side, this is called a "spread."

When you set your customer's financial statements on a spread sheet and see them side by side you can easily see if any of the key items are increasing or decreasing. Increasing sales and profits indicate company growth and give a strong indication that growth will occur in the future. Increasing sales but *decreasing* profits indicate that a company is growing well, but is poorly managed. Falling sales and increasing profits, on the other hand, indicate good internal company management but poor marketing.

Increases in current assets could mean that more working capital is available (if current liabilities do not increase proportionately) or that there are larger amounts of accounts receivable, inventory, and/or cash. If the cause of the increase in current assets is an increase in inventory, this can be a bad sign indicating that inventory is slow moving. Increases in accounts receivables are usually good, but you should check their collection ratio to make sure that the increases are not caused by slowdowns in collections. Increases in cash are good, but this will usually be temporary. Decreases in current assets (unless there is a corresponding decrease in current liabilities) should be a cause for concern.

Increases in fixed assets often mean decreases in current assets. Any increase in fixed assets will decrease the money available for working capital, and increase the amount of debt. If the increase in fixed assets is to modernize the plant or make badly needed factory expansion, this is a good indicator of future growth. If the increase in fixed assets is caused by a purchase of a fancy new headquarters building, it is not so good since fixed assets decline in value every year because of depreciation. If the amount of fixed assets stays the same or increases, it means new assets have been added. Total asset increases or decreases are usually affected by either movement in fixed or current assets.

Current liabilities are increased by taking on more debt, accruing expenses that are past due, and by slow payment of payables. Ordinarily we would not want to see current liabilities increased unless the company had to take on more debt to expand the operation by buying more assets. If the current liabilities increase more than a corresponding increase in current assets, this gives the company less working capital. If the current liabilities increase more than the total assets increase, this usually means that the company is financing its accounts receivable or inventory. Total liability increases should be accompanied by at least a corresponding, if not larger, increase in fixed assets.

Net worth is a sensitive indicator of a company's progress. Net worth increases can be attributable to a new influx of capital, an addition of retained net profit, a profit due to the sale of some asset, or by a write-down of a liability. It is of crucial importance to know which of these factors caused the increase, but any increase in net worth for whatever reason is generally considered a hopeful sign. A decrease in net worth can be caused by a loss, too high an amount of owner's draw, or a sale of an asset for a loss. Any decline in net worth is considered a bad indicator of future performance.

Further Operations Performed on Comparative Statements

There are two methods that you can use to set up your balance sheet and profit and loss comparisons to highlight changes and trends. The two methods are a common-sized statement and percentage change per year analysis.

Instead of listing dollar amounts, a common-sized statement assigns total assets or total liabilities and worth, or total sales a value of 100 percent. You then calculate what each item represents as a percentage of sales, assets, or liabilities and worth. Changing percentages can often tell you a lot more than just the dollar amounts. Table 6.9 shows Hero Manufacturing, Inc., and Rotten Distribution Company on a common-sized statement format (see Tables 6.2, 6.3, and 6.4 for the balance sheets and profit and loss statements of these companies).

Discussion of Examples

Although the sales and net profit at Hero Manufacturing increase in dollar amount from last year to this, the net profit as a percentage of sales *decreased*. Note that Hero's figures do not include income from interest on securities because we want to show just the operating income for these comparisons. If you look at Hero's cost of sales figures you will see that their production costs went up as a percentage of sales from 71 to 76 percent, which is the primary reason that their net profit as a percentage of sales declined. Their operating expense as a percentage of sales decreased, indicating that they are doing better this year in controlling fixed operating expenses. If Hero's production costs (cost of sales) continue to increase as a percentage of sales, there could be some profit problems in the next couple of years. Taking a look at the asset common-sized we see that the largest asset as a percentage of total assets is security holdings, which account for 32 percent of total assets.

Hero is strong on their current asset position since current assets amount to fully 71 percent of total assets. We see that from last year to this year there has been a slight increase in assets for Hero, but the percentages the asset items represent remain about the same. The most obvious change from the previous year is the decline in inventories from 15 percent of total assets to 11 percent. This could mean either that last year they had excessive inventories or this year they have the right amount or not enough.

Looking at the liabilities and net worth common-sized we see that net worth is a strong 60 percent of total liabilities and worth, and total liabilities are only 40 percent. A strong current working capital position is indicated by current liabilities, which represent only 17 percent of total liabilities and worth. The largest liability item is long-term notes payable at 12 percent of the total.

Rotten Distribution indicates a declining business on the income statement common-sized. Not only are sales and profits declining in dollar volume, but profits as a percentage of sales are declining (from 3 percent last year to 1 percent this year). In addition, production costs as a

TABLE 6.9
Trend Analysis — Hero and Rotten

	Hero Manufacturing				Rotten Distribution			
	12/30/1978	%	12/30/1977	%	12/30/1978	%	12/30/1977	%
INCOME STATEMENT								
Sales	$5,620,000	100	$4,323,000	100	$4,200,000	100	$4,620,000	100
Cost of Sales	4,271,200	76	3,402,000	71	3,402,000	81	3,696,000	80
Gross Profit	1,348,800	24	1,253,670	29	798,000	19	924,000	20
Operating Expense	991,823	18	921,770	21	756,000	18	792,000	17
Net Profit (before taxes)	356,977	6	331,900	8	42,000	1	132,000	3
ASSETS+								
Total Assets	2,888,300	100	2,663,500	100	2,170,000	100	2,180,600	100
Cash	200,000	7	353,400	13	(5,000)		50,000	2
Securities	900,000	32	623,483	23	-0-		-0-	
Accounts Receivable	580,000	20	528,367	19	690,410	31	712,300	33
Inventory	330,300	11	386,000	16	583,310	27	551,300	25
Other Current	39,500	1	42,200	2	(60,000)	(3)	(61,000)	(3)

Total Current Assets	2,049,800	71	1,933,450	73	1,208,720	55	1,252,600	57
Furniture & Fixtures	75,000	3	75,000	3	12,000	1	12,000	1
Equipment	520,500	18	303,503	11	195,000	9	195,000	9
Vehicles	90,000	3	85,000	3	55,000	3	45,000	2
Building and Improvement	350,000	12	350,000	13	200,000	9	200,000	9
Less: Depreciation	(302,000)	(10)	(191,453)	(7)	(72,000)	(3)	(430,000)	(2)
Land	100,000	4	100,000	4	30,000	1	30,000	1
Total Fixed Assets	833,500	29	722,050	27	420,000	20	439,000	20
Total Other Assets	5,000		8,000	0	541,280	25	489,000	23
LIABILITIES AND NET WORTH								
Total Liabilities & Worth	2,888,300	100	2,663,500		2,170,000	100	2,180,600	100
Accounts Payable	209,490	7	129,950		512,000	24	507,800	22
Taxes Payable	117,310	4	93,250		47,600	2	91,800	4
Notes Payable	162,900	6	156,500		510,000	23	469,582	21
Other Accruals	10,062		163,400		22,520	1	19,518	1
Current Liabilities	499,762	17	543,100		1,091,120	50	1,088,700	48
Mortgages Payable	320,338	11	331,000		160,000	7	173,000	8
Notes Payable	339,000	12	285,000		218,880	10	208,300	9
Long-Term Liabilities	659,338	23	616,000		378,880	17	281,300	17
TOTAL LIABILITIES	1,159,100	40	1,159,100		1,470,000	67	1,370,000	65
Total Net Worth	1,729,200	60	1,504,400		700,000	34	810,600	35

percentage of sales are getting higher (from 80 to 81 percent) and operating expenses are increasing (from 17 to 18 percent). Rotten Distribution shows every indication of being on a downhill sleigh ride.

The assets common-sized indicate that although current assets are a good percentage of total assets (56 percent), other assets are an outrageous 25 percent of total assets. As we discussed previously, other assets are not worth much as far as productivity or assets available to creditors. Rotten has also had a decline in assets, most notably cash, from the previous year.

Looking at the liabilities and worth common-sized, we see that current liabilities are an unusually large 50 percent of the total, indicating a poor working capital position. Almost totally the opposite of Hero Manufacturing, net worth is only 34 percent of the total and liabilities are 67 percent. This indicates that the company is very debt dependent. Notice an increase in liabilities from the previous year showing that Rotten has borrowed within the last year. Last year net worth was a larger percentage of total liabilities and net worth.

Another method for comparative analysis is calculating the percentage change (up or down) that each item has undergone from year to year. For instance, Hero's sales have increased 30 percent over last year while Rotten's sales have decreased 9 percent from the previous year. Percentage increase or decrease is calculated by taking the most recent figure and dividing by the previous period minus one, as follows:

$$\text{percentage increase } (+) \text{ or decrease } (-) = \frac{\text{recent figure}}{\text{previous figure}} - 1$$

EXAMPLES: Hero Mfg.   Rotten Dist.

$$\frac{\$4,620,000}{4,323,000} - 1 = +30\% \qquad \frac{\$4,200,000}{4,620,000} - 1 = -9\%$$

It may be too time consuming to do this for every figure, but you might want to do it for key figures. Determining percentage increases or decreases for sales, inventories, and cost of sales might be a good indication of what you can expect your customer to be ordering from you in the next year if percentage increases and decreases continue. For example, if Hero's sales increase 30 percent each year, you might easily expect to have a 30 percent increase in sales to them each year.

7

Correspondence With Customers

Letters are often used in the credit and collection procedure. They offer the advantage of being relatively inexpensive, good documentary material for your customer files, and a means of personal and exact communication between you and your customers. Of the various methods of collection used by a collection department, the letter is in several respects the most important. Moreover, the letter possesses other qualities essential to collection efficiency: flexibility, timeliness, economy, and personality.

Credit and collection letters are basically of two types: credit letters establishing or rejecting accounts and collection letters designed to collect overdue accounts. When dealing with routine situations, such as acknowledging applications and approving charge accounts, the credit manager usually employs form letters or printed announcements. However, credit managers must be able to meet every situation with an appropriate letter that will serve a specific purpose and at the same time promote the interest of their company.

PRINCIPLES OF WRITING CREDIT AND COLLECTION LETTERS

Good credit and collection letters should be polite, straightforward, and concise. They should say what they mean simply and naturally. Letters reflect the efficiency and dignity of the firm they represent in their appearance. In style and form, they should vary to suit the character of the collection problem and customer. They should reflect the personal interest of the writer in the mind of the person addressed.

The following are some basic principles of writing good collection letters:

1. Always include the debtor's name and address, the date of the letter, a description of merchandise bought, the amount due, and a self-addressed return envelope (if the number of accounts are small).

2. The collection of debts is most effective when done on a person-to-person basis. Whenever possible type collection letters individually and avoid form letters. This is especially true as the debt gets older and the number of letters already sent increases. Always address the letters to a particular individual, not "Accounts Payable Department" or other general term.

3. If your company has shipped to the debtor cn the basis of a telephone order or oral reorder, omit reference to this in the letter.

4. It is a good idea to make an appeal to the customer's reputation, fair play, self-interest, or fear of the problems you may cause. These types of letters are considered "appeal" letters and will be discussed later in this chapter.

5. While maintaining a businesslike tone in your letter, create a sense of urgency about the collection. Letters mailed in rapid succession (once a week) may accomplish this.

6. Keep the attention of the debtor by using different letters with different formats, or by using different colored or different sized paper, and intersperse letters with a telegram or a telephone call. Another suggestion is that you send out letters signed by increasingly important people — your assistant, yourself, and the president of the company.

7. Send more important letters by certified mail, return receipt requested. This will assure you that the letter will be received by the right person.

8. Attempt to get the debtor to make some kind of response (telephone call or letter) so that you are dealing with the problem on a person-to-person basis. If you suggest a partial payment be made, this will usually get a response. Encourage the debtor to promise payment by a certain date; even a tentative promise of payment can create a sense of obligation. If the debtor acknowledges that the debt should be paid, then accepting the debt has been accepted without dispute.

9. Have "address correction requested" printed on the outer envelope just in case the debtor has moved.

10. Remember that the squeaky wheel is the first one to be greased. If the wheel makes an ear-piercing screech, people will drop everything they are doing and take care of it. That is, persistent follow-up has proven to be the most effective collection tool.

CREDIT LETTERS

A credit-granting letter is the most pleasant letter for both credit manager and customer. It informs a customer that their application for credit has been approved. A courteously worded, printed form is often used for this purpose. If, however, you choose to write a letter, it offers you an excellent opportunity for capitalizing on the customer's interest in your company and products. Sample Letter 7.1 is an example of this type of letter.

Letters that grant credit will probably be treated as contracts. So the credit manager must make sure that he is willing to live with everything he puts into the letter and that he can live without everything he does not put into the letter. Such a letter is not only a very nice gesture, but it could greatly help relations with your customer in the future.

Letters that refuse credit are a little more difficult. You want to inform the customer of your negative decision without loosing goodwill. A poor risk today may be a good account in the future. Composing a rejection letter is an art. The cardinal principle in writing rejection letters is: Never give applicants the impression that the rejection is a reflection on their personal character.

If you received a rejection letter similar to Sample Letter 7.2, you probably would not feel too bad about the rejection and you might even order on cash terms. That should be the credit manager's objective in a

---

SAMPLE LETTER 7.1
Credit Granting Letter

Dear Mr. Hero:

In accordance with your request of December 12, we are happy to extend to you our most favorable terms (2/10, net 30). Your order is being shipped by air express today.

We want you to know that the best delivery, prices, and quality of this first order are also to be found in all metal fabrication products we sell.

The information that we have received concerning you is completely favorable to you as a businessman and personally. We appreciate your choosing us as a supplier. As you become more familiar with our company and products, you will come to know that you can depend on us for your supply needs.

We appreciate your business, Mr. Hero. We shall do everything possible to assure that this order will be the first of many.

Sincerely,

---

rejection letter. If you are one of the first suppliers that has been approached, chances are good that the customer will go ahead and take cash terms for awhile.

COLLECTION LETTERS

Collection letters should be used with the expectation that the collections can be made with a single letter. Letters should state the case for collection clearly and convincingly. The form and content of the letter will vary according to the circumstances of the writer and the debtor. If the delinquency is the first default of a long established customer, the letter should be different in content than one to a customer that has shown consistent slowness. The content of a letter to a new customer regarding a first slow payment should be different than the content of a letter to a debtor who has completely ignored all previous pleas for payment. Generally, however, every collection letter should have certain characteristic qualities relating to the beginning, the body, the ending, and the tone of the letter.

SAMPLE LETTER 7.2
Rejecting Credit Application

Dear Mr. Whatyasay:

Thank you for sending your business statement and references so promptly. All your references spoke highly of you.

We have studied your business very carefully, and we would like to make two helpful suggestions. We do not believe that it would be to your advantage for us to fill your order on open terms. Frankly, Mr. Whatyasay, your business is somewhat undercapitalized, and for you to assume additional liabilities from us might jeopardize your prospects. If you possibly can, you should obtain additional capital. With your personal ability and good location, you should have little difficulty in doing so.

We would also like to recommend that you allow us to have your order and ship to you on cash terms. You will receive a 1 percent discount, which should help your cash flow.

We believe that you will soon be in a position to command our most favorable credit terms. We hope that our suggestions will help you. We will ship the first half of your order the moment we get your approval.

Sincerely yours,

Letter Form

The beginning of the letter should be used for making a definitive, positive statement. But be careful not to oversimplify the beginning. Oversimplified beginnings tend to become repetitious, impersonal, and, consequently, ineffectual. A remedy for this is to combine the fact about the debt with some other statements relating to an item of mutual interest to the debtor. The beginning must be one of some real interest, sincerely made, and not glib merely for the sake of creating a beginning.

The body of the letter should include all the things relevant to the situation. It may express urgency, review the original understanding of the credit terms, tell the debtor the consequences of failure to pay, or suggest that further discussion is required.

The ending states or restates the request for payment. All that needs to be said after giving the facts is what is expected of the debtor. The more specific the request, the more compelling it is.

The tone of the letter is the quality that reflects the writer's (your) attitude. The tone of sincerity is essential above all other attitudes in collection letters. The second most important tone, or attitude, is one of firmness. Fear, doubt, unwarranted suspicion, and uncertainty on the part of the letter writer suggest a tone that can antagonize the reader. Most damaging in tone is the use of such terms as: "you failed to," "be compelled to," "delinquent," "require," "we insist," and "our demand."

Part of the tone of the letter is your own attitude toward debt. No apology needs to be made for seeking settlement, so do not offer excuses for requesting payment or beg for payment. Money due should be paid without further delay.

Sample Letter 7.3 illustrates the qualities of a collection letter.

Writing effective collection letters that get the money and keep goodwill requires an understanding of human nature and the ability to apply that understanding. Most people bristle at the first implication that they have broken a promise, even when the implication is based on an obvious fact. Any suggestion of curtness on the part of a credit letter might induce the debtor to "get even" for the imagined or real indignity suffered. The debtor may delay payment even longer. Another debtor might respond to the same letter by promptly paying the bill, then closing the account.

SAMPLE LETTER 7.3
Collection Letter

Dear Mr. Potslopper:

Haven't you at some time tried to keep from looking at a friend when he has overextended his visit? We have been reluctant in the same way to notice that the calender shows that your payment for our last shipment has considerably overrun the credit period allowed for payment. Your account for $_____ is past due.

We know from our experience, however, that it is not only good manners but good business to call this to your attention. Each of us will be more at ease if a prompt payment is made.

Won't you send us your check today? Let us open the way for another 'visit' instead of prolonging this one.

Yours sincerely,

You might choose to use a series of letters to the debtor. Underlying the correspondence and determining the character of the series are the following considerations: promptness, regularity of the series, classification of debtors (Chapter 8), and a consideration of costs and profits of the situation.

A history of the account should be reviewed to acquaint yourself with the facts of the case. Personal recollections of the customer and information in the credit file should be of some help. Generally, it is necessary to make certain assumptions concerning the debtor's reasons for nonpayment. When payment is not immediately forthcoming, it is assumed that the debt has escaped the customer's attention and reminders are in order. If no explanation or payment is forthcoming, it should be assumed that the customer is unwilling to meet his obligations. At this point, the customer must be made to understand that such obligations must be met or he will suffer the consequences.

There are three stages through which the collection process runs its course: reminder, follow-up (or discussion), and compulsion (or drastic action). Reminder letters are sent only when duplicate bills or invoices fail to stimulate payment, although it is acceptable to send them as first reminders. Follow-up letters are usually appeals. Compulsion letters give the debtor an ultimatum. Some credit managers spread their collection letters over a period of as many as three months, with two or three reminders, perhaps five or six appeals, and a couple of statements that collection will be forced by law unless the account is paid.

Reminder Letters

The assumption underlying reminder letters is that nonpayment is the result of an oversight or neglect. This assumption will be true in most cases. The honest debtor possessing the money to pay will generally make a settlement on being reminded. The more serious debtors, however, will not be moved to action by a mere reminder.

Reminders are of three forms. Some consist of only one phrase or sentence, such as "past due: please remit" or "The above amount is past due and a prompt remittance will be appreciated." These reminders are sometimes made in the form of a phrase stamped on an invoice.

The second type is a more elaborate form that is printed and accompanies an invoice or statement. It is frequently printed on a card that is clipped to the statement. The following is an example: "We call your attention to the accompanying statement, which, no doubt, has escaped your attention."

Separating the statement and the reminder in this manner might make the presentation more effective. It is a good idea if the card is a different color from the statement.

The third type of reminder is a printed or lithographed form, with no introductory address or complimentary closing, containing blank spaces for the insertion of the name and address of the customer, the amount owed, and the period in which the purchase was made: "We call attention to your account for _____ (date) amounting to $_____. We hope it will have your immediate attention."

Follow-up Letters

If one or two reminders bring no response, it is time to press for payment with letters that are firmer in tone. The follow-up letters are usually the most numerous of the three stages of letters. You want to make sure you give the debtor a reasonable chance to repay before you take more drastic action and send out the compulsion letters.

For follow-up (or discussion) letters, form letters are generally not appropriate. Personally written letters in which appeals are graded in strength and tone must be employed. You (as credit manager) can assume at this point that the debtor has a reason for the delay in payments and may be in financial difficulties. You should make attempts at this point to secure a response from your customer explaining the reasons for the delay. A customer's account is overdue and you might offer to allow additional time or become more insistent and proceed to the next and last stage of the collection process.

To find out if the customer is unable to pay or simply stalling, you must write directly to the customer. Sample Letter 7.4 is a letter of inquiry, offering the debtor a chance to discuss the situation with you.

The heart of the collection letter is the appeal around which it is built. Credit managers use personal information gleaned from agency reports and previous correspondence with a debtor to determine the right appeal to use. Some information that appears to be of little value in a credit file may be of great value in an appeal letter. If a debtor, for example, is active in civic and church affairs, an appeal to the debtor's honor may bring the best and most immediate response. The appeal that you will use to motivate a debtor to make a payment must be suited to that particular debtor. The appeals that seem to work the best are those involving honor, self-interest, pride, and justice.

Appeals to honor in collection letters stress the contractual obligations of the debtor. They show respect for the debtor's integrity as a businessperson. Simplicity of expression is important in this type of appeal, (see Sample Letter 7.5).

SAMPLE LETTER 7.4
Letter of Inquiry

Dear Mr. Slipshod:

We are at a loss to understand why your account of $221.00, due since October 1, has not been paid.

If you have some compelling reason for not paying, won't you tell us about it? Please indicate your reasons in the space provided below and return this letter to us in the enclosed stamped envelope.

Sincerely,

This account has not been paid because ⎯⎯⎯⎯⎯⎯⎯⎯⎯⎯⎯⎯⎯⎯⎯

⎯⎯⎯⎯⎯⎯⎯⎯⎯⎯⎯⎯⎯⎯⎯⎯⎯⎯⎯⎯⎯⎯⎯⎯⎯⎯⎯⎯⎯⎯⎯⎯⎯⎯⎯⎯⎯

Check for $⎯⎯⎯⎯⎯ is enclosed. The account will be paid in full on or before ⎯⎯⎯⎯⎯⎯⎯⎯⎯⎯⎯⎯⎯⎯⎯⎯⎯⎯⎯⎯⎯⎯⎯⎯⎯.

SAMPLE LETTER 7.5
Appeal to Honor Letter

Dear Mr. Obe:

Eric Honnor, who has been taking your orders for us for several years, tells me that you have substantial credit business in Wolvestown. I need not remind you, then, of how difficult it is to write a reminder letter to a worthy customer who lets his account run long overdue without a word of explanation.

Won't you save me the problem of writing that letter? Your account of $192.00 has been overdue since January 25th.

Sincerely,

Appeals to self-interest should be used when the appeals to honor and justice fail. These letters may employ what will happen if the customer fails to pay the account, but they are still made in a positive and friendly tone.

Appeals to pride assume that people are motivated by self-respect and by the respect others have toward them. A subtle appeal to this characteristic is often effective. (See Sample Letter 7.7.)

Appeals to justice make the customer feel that they are not dealing fairly with you (the creditor). They point out that the bill is due for value received. They also show that the account has been carried long after it is due and that it is not fair to force the creditor to wait any longer for payment. (See Sample Letter 7.8.)

Compulsion Letters

If reminders, follow-ups, and appeals fail to get a reply, it becomes apparent that your customer will pay only if forced to. You should now offer the debtor, in one or more demand letters, the choice of paying or facing drastic action. This drastic action might include having a draft drawn against them or having the account turned over to an attorney or a

---

SAMPLE LETTER 7.6
Appeal to Self-Interest Letter

Dear Ms. Bankbuster:

Often we are asked by other wholesalers about the paying habits of our customers who might want to open an account with them, or place an unusually large order, or are behind in payments to them. We give this information freely, because we expect our friends in the trade to reciprocate, and they do.

Prompt-paying customers get a big advantage from this interchange. Their orders are shipped without delay. The wholesaler knows that he can expect his money when it is due. We like to report that a customer is "prompt pay," but to do so we must have a record of prompt pay from the customer.

A statement of your account which shows a balance of $467.00, 40 days overdue, is enclosed. Please take care of it now so that we may have the privilege of telling our friends that you are always "good pay."

Sincerely,

SAMPLE LETTER 7.7
Appeal to Pride Letter

Dear Mr. Prejudice:

We could not help holding in high esteem the standards that you had for prompt payment of your account in the past, and we want you to know that we have appreciated this.

At present, however, your account is past due in the amount of $218.00. We are reminding you of this knowing that you would not generally permit your account to remain this long in arrears.

May we have your check covering the amount stated? We are counting on your cooperation.

Sincerely,

SAMPLE LETTER 7.8
Appeal to Justice Letter

Dear Mr. Justice:

We confidently expected a remittance on your account of January 15, 1978 for $581.00 as a response to our last letter.

Frankly, we are disappointed because we cannot believe that you would intentionally impose upon us. By not remitting the payment promptly you impose upon us the difficulties involved in carrying the account longer than we had originally agreed to.

Without elaborating, you know the importance of prompt collections. We are still confident that we can count on your ability to be fair and just with us in this instance.

Very truly yours,

---

collection agency. The compulsion letter is basically an ultimatum. But do not send several letters that say, "if you do not pay by _____" and then extend the date on each letter. It serves no purpose to send idle threats repeatedly.

Before you send the ultimatum letter, however, it is sometimes advisable to send a "letter of courtesy" in which the customer is given one more opportunity either to explain neglect or make payment. An attempt may be made to secure at least partial payment and arrange for additional payments at future intervals. This type of letter will almost always bring a reply. This method is usually used by companies where the accounts carried involve relatively large sums.

Ultimately, however, the creditor must forcefully point out the customer's obligation and the consequences of nonpayment. It is advisable to first notify the customer that you will use a draft to secure repayment. If this fails, you may resort to suit or a collection agency.

The advance notice of draft is a letter announcing intention to send a draft to the customer's bank. It consists of a simple statement reviewing the action already taken and stating that unless a response is made within a certain time, a draft will be dispatched to the debtor's or some other designated bank. When using this letter (see Sample Letter 7.9), a legal opinion might be advisable because the procedure may be tricky.

If the draft is dishonored and all personal appeal letters have failed, you may want to (under special circumstances) go to the customer yourself or send a personal collector. If none of those actions are feasible, threat letters can be sent. These letters appeal to fear and are the harshest of all the collection letters (see Sample Letter 7.10). The debtor is usually

---

SAMPLE LETTER 7.9
Intention to Send a Draft

Dear Mr. Dolittle:

Your account amounting to $432.00 is now 95 days overdue, as we have pointed out in several letters.

This is as long as we feel we can carry your account. Unless we hear from you by June 10, we will assume that we have your permission to draw a draft on your company for this amount. It will be drawn through Security Bank of Elsy.

We hope that you will wish to avoid this roundabout and inconvenient method of paying, and to prevent the unfavorable reflection on your credit that this will create at your bank, by remitting to us directly before the date indicated. Please let us hear from you by return mail.

Yours truly,

---

threatened with suit unless reparation is made. It is sometimes desirable to write a rather lengthy letter in which you dwell on the seriousness of the matter.

Some manufacturers or retailers or merchants associations have form letters or printed forms that they can furnish members. These forms are supposed to have been sent by the association and read as if they were. These letters can be very effective, as is Sample Letter 7.11.

SAMPLE LETTER 7.10
Appeal to Fear Letter

Dear Mr. Drastic:

Despite the fact that you have been sent numerous notices and letters regarding the past due bill of $276.00 for December 12, 1978, we have heard nothing from you and we are at a loss to understand the situation. We feel that we have waited long enough and now urgently request your immediate attention.

We have no desire to embarrass or trouble you, but it is necessary that this account be settled at once and that you make satisfactory arrangements immediately.

Sincerely,

SAMPLE LETTER 7.11
Association-Prepared Letter

Dear Mr._____:

In preparing the files of this bureau, organized for the mutual interchange of credit information, we find that (name of company) reports an account against you which is past due.

We would suggest that you make settlement with your creditor at once so that your record may be clear in our files.

Members of the bureau will, under our rules, report to us within five (5) days as to whether or not settlement has been made.

Yours truly,

LEGAL ASPECTS OF WRITING COLLECTION LETTERS

In writing collection letters, especially during the advanced stages of delinquency when strong appeals are made, you have to be cautious about what is written. Possible legal liabilities might be involved. If the contents of the letter threaten violent reprisals, prosecutions, or publications of matters not directly related to the disputed bill, it might be possible for the customer to bring a criminal charge for extortion against the company. Whether the charge will stand depends upon statutes and case decisions. You would probably not be liable, depending upon the particular state in which the case arises and the facts of the situation, if you wrote that as a member of a certain association the past due amounts of the debtor would have to be reported after a certain date. The line of legal liability, however, is sometimes pretty thin.

If you write a demand letter, you must avoid libelous statements. Generally a libel is a written statement, sign, or picture that tends to expose an individual to hatred, contempt, or ridicule. A libelous letter that passes through the hands of a third party, such as a secretary, clerk, or stenographer (yours or the debtor's) is considered published, and as such it leaves you open to a libel suit (even if the statements are true). Look at the following two examples in Sample Letter 7.12: the first is clearly libelous, the second says the same thing without implying fraud or a moral failing.

Liability for libel is without a doubt the major risk involved in writing collection letters. If the contents tend to degrade the debtor or *hold him up to public ridicule* and thus cause injury, the sender (you) could be charged with libel. Some of the statements in the letter can be libelous per se, for instance, a charge of fraud, deception, or dishonesty. In these cases the debtor does not have to prove damages. Watch out for these types of accusations.

Although collection letters and actions could give rise to a suit for invasion of privacy, it is not likely if the collections are handled in a professional and confidential manner. Attempts to publicize the debt or to send damaging remarks to the customer's employees, family, associates, or clients would probably be viewed by the courts as an invasion of privacy. Each state has its own definition of "invasion of privacy" and requirements for winning such a suit. The credit manager should be familiar with the law in his own state before planning the last stages of their collection campaign.

Regulations and laws differ widely in each state, and it is advisable to talk to your company attorney about this situation. If you have form

---

SAMPLE LETTER 7.12
Comparison of Demand Letters

NUMBER 1

Dear Mr. Match:

We have sent you two invoice copies and six letters requesting payment since March 1 when your account of $467.00 was due. You have sent us no reply. We must assume from your lack of response that you do not intend to pay.

Your willful neglect of this debt leaves us no choice. Unless the account is paid in full by Friday, June 30, we will turn it over to the Smasher Collection Agency. The Smasher Collection Agency knows how to handle cheats, I assure you, Mr. Match.

You can save yourself the embarrassment and expense only by sending us your check for $467.00 immediately.

Sincerely,

NUMBER 2

Dear Mr. Match:

We sent you two invoice copies and six letters requesting payment since March 1 when your account of $467.00 was due. We have heard nothing from you. Mr. Match, frankly our patience is exhausted.

Unless the account is paid by Friday, June 30, we will turn it over to the Smasher Collection Agency for their attention.

If you send your check immediately, it will reach us in time to forestall this unpleasant action. Please send us your check by return mail.

Sincerely,

---

letters that you use, it might be a good idea to have the attorney check them over.

FORM LETTERS

If your company wants to use form collection letters, it is wise to prepare one or more series of letters that are applicable to various situations.

These series should follow the same order as the letters described in this chapter — reminder, follow-up, and compulsion. The major advantage of these series of form letters is that they can be written at leisure and polished until they become perfect for their uses. Another advantage is consistency. You do not need to be concerned with what letter a particular customer was sent. Since it was a form letter, you already know what it said.

One compromise between the form letter and the individual letter is to prepare hundreds of form paragraphs to fit every conceivable situation. Each paragraph would be given an identification number and put in a manual. When the writer specifies the paragraph number, a typist, using the paragraph manual, could complete the letter. This type of system would probably be a lot fun to put together, but in the long run it would not get much use. People writing the letters would have to look up the paragraph numbers to write a number "letter," then the typist would have to spend time looking them up again in order to type. It is usually easier (unless you have a large organization) just to write a letter or use preprinted form letters.

Form letters are usually numbered and indexed for easy reference. When a particular letter is sent to a debtor, the index number can be noted on the debtor's folder. Do not send a particular form letter more than once to the same debtor.

The irony of form letters is that they are generally more effective if they do not appear to be form letters. The best way to get form letters that do not look like form letters is by using a magnetic card typewriter, sometimes called a "smart typewriter" or an "auto-typist." With these machines you can put a form letter on tape, leaving space for names, addresses, amounts, and dates. The machine automatically types the rest of the letter and stops at the places where specific data is to be inserted.

Multigraphed letters can also be used for form letter correspondence. When you use these, however, the manually typed addresses and fill-ins should match the multigraphed type style and should be accurately aligned with the copy. Remember, the whole letter may become ineffective if just one phrase is used that does not apply to the debtor.

Sample Letter 7.13 is a carefully planned series of form letters. The series begins with a reminder and ends with a notice that the account will be referred to an attorney.

SAMPLE LETTER 7.13
Series of Form Collection Letters

NUMBER 1

Dear Mr. Jones:

We haven't yet received your check for our December 15 invoice (copy enclosed). If it crossed this letter in the mail, please consider this a THANK YOU instead of the friendly reminder it is intended to be.

Sincerely yours,

NUMBER 2

Dear Mr. Jones:

Our December 15 invoice to you, amounting to $89.50, is still marked unpaid. Could your check have gone astray, or have we misplaced it here? Please let us know right away if you have sent a check, or send one today.

Sincerely,

NUMBER 3

Dear Mr. Jones:

We have received nothing from you concerning the payment of our invoice of December 15, amounting to $89.50, which is now thirty days past due.

To maintain your credit standing with us, you must send us your check within the next few days. Please do it today.

Sincerely,

NUMBER 4

Dear Mr. Jones:

When you place an order with us you expect us to ship exactly what you want as soon as we possibly can. If we are unable to ship immediately, you expect us to let you know why we cannot, and when we think we can. You have every right to expect this, and we do our best to live up to your expectations.

When we ship an order on open account, as we did to you, we expect the customer to pay on or before the due date, or to let us know why he cannot pay and when he thinks he can. We expect this consideration.

SAMPLE LETTER 7.13
Series of Form Collection Letters (cont.)

It is not too late for you to restore your credit standing with us to its old position, but to do so you must send us, TODAY, your check for $89.50.

Sincerely,

NUMBER 5

Dear Mr. Jones:

When one of our customers lets an account go sixty days past due without so much as a word of explanation, it is our fixed policy to turn that account over to an agency for collection. We make no exceptions to this rule, Mr. Jones.

Your account with us — $89.50 due since January 15 — will be sixty days past due in just five more days. To avoid the embarrassment of an agency collection, you must send your check to reach us by Wednesday afternoon at five o'clock. If there is any doubt of a letter reaching us in time, WIRE YOUR PAYMENT.

Sincerely,

NUMBER 6

Dear Mr. Jones:

You will hear no more from us about the $89.50 overdue on your account since January 15.

Having had no reply to any of our numerous letters to you about the account, we must turn it over to the Absolute Collection Agency of your city. All further communications about the account will come from them.

Sincerely,

8

Dealing
With Slow Payers

Most people when they borrow money (or get supplies on credit) have every intention of paying the debt back. It is extremely rare that a businessperson will borrow money or take supplies on credit with the *intention* of never repaying. Usually something happens in the interim time between getting the supplies and paying for them that forces the businessperson, against his better judgment, to become slow in his payments.

Generally, the reasons for becoming slow are business financial problems. If you (the credit manager) have done your job well, that is, you did a full analysis on the customer's financial condition before you extended credit, your chances of encountering this problem will be rare. But unfortunately no matter how careful you are, problems will arise. Besides business financial problems there are several other reasons for a customer becoming a slow payer including oversight; bad paying habits; laziness; personal misfortune or disaster; or dissatisfaction with you, the supplier. Problems of customer oversight or dissatisfaction with orders can be easily solved and do not present a permanent problem for collections. Laziness may be turned into action by a phone call or personal visit. Financial overextension and business and personal disasters are the problems that will cause you the most difficulties.

Collections from slow payers is a most delicate process. If collections are done right they should create goodwill, retain business already on the books, and promote repeat business. Collections done poorly can cause loss of temper, animosity, and loss of business. The procedures required to maintain good collections are simple but sometimes go against human nature. Remember collectors are salespeople (aggressive, patient, and optimistic) who are selling a very difficult product: *present* payment for *past* benefits.

In the past few years, accounts receivable and collection periods have been growing at unprecedented rates. Recently, especially in the poor economic years of 1974 and 1975, business started developing an automatic tendency to let suppliers become bankers by slowing or withholding payments. If you realize that this is happening and develop techniques (to be discussed in this chapter) for combating the problems (such as staying on top of collections and billing sooner) you will be able to do well.

I do not need to tell you that collections are important to profits. But did you know that if you have bad-debt losses of only $50, and your company's net profit percentage is 5 percent, $1,000 in sales would be required to cover the losses? Table 8.1 illustrates how much in additional sales are required to offset bad-debt losses at various net profit levels. Look for your company's net profit percentage. You might be surprised.

The first step to good collection is a well-planned collection policy. Collection policy should establish the time allowed to pass before the first collection step is taken and the intervals between each stage of the collection process. Collection policy should include guidelines for when to use collection agencies. When, if ever, attorneys should be used for suits, should also be made clear by the collection policy. The amount of bad-debt losses allowable and at what stage debt should be considered "bad" and written off should be understood.

The major aspects of a collection procedure are classification of the debtor; determination of collection tools to be used; and improvement of collection efforts. Most of this chapter will be devoted to the collection tools (letters, telephoning, visits, and third parties).

In classifying customers and getting results from collections, it is best

TABLE 8.1
Sales Required to Offset Bad-Debt Losses

If Your Net Profit Is	And Your Bad-Debt Loss Is											
	$50	$100	$200	$300	$400	$500	$750	$1,000	$1,500	2,000	$2,500	$5,000
	This Amount of Sales Will be Required to Offset The Loss											
2%	2,500	5,000	10,000	15,000	20,000	25,000	37,500	50,000	75,000	100,000	125,000	250,000
3%	1,666	3,333	6,666	10,000	13,333	16,666	25,000	33,333	50,000	66,667	83,333	166,667
4%	1,250	2,500	5,000	7,500	10,000	12,500	18,750	25,000	37,500	50,000	62,500	125,000
5%	1,000	2,000	4,000	6,000	8,000	10,000	13,000	20,000	30,000	40,000	50,000	100,000
6%	833	1,666	3,333	5,000	6,666	8,333	12,500	16,667	25,000	33,333	41,667	83,333
7%	714	1,429	2,857	4,282	5,714	7,143	10,714	14,286	21,429	28,571	35,714	71,429
8%	625	1,250	2,500	3,750	5,000	6,250	9,375	12,500	18,750	25,000	31,250	62,500
9%	556	1,111	2,222	3,333	4,444	5,556	8,333	11,111	16,667	22,222	27,778	55,556
10%	500	1,000	2,000	3,000	4,000	5,000	7,500	10,000	15,000	20,000	25,000	50,000

to follow the procedure illustrated in Figure 8.1. First, you should research the customer's file, then classify the customer by past performance or by an educated guess. Next you should use your collection tools, such as letters and telephones, in the order of reminders, appeals, and compulsion, which we discussed in detail in Chapter 7. If these tools are not successful, then the credit manager must use outside collection agencies or the courts. During the entire procedure, feedback from the courts or agents should be sought.

CLASSIFICATION OF ACCOUNTS

In Chapter 2 we discussed the general classification of accounts into automatic (orders processed without checking for almost every amount); semiautomatic (orders up to a certain amount processed without checking); nonautomatic (average); and marginal categories. When accounts become past due (which could happen to any of these classifications) they fall into new categories related to the cause of their delinquency. The categories of delinquent payers are: confused, negligent, not-at-fault delinquent, seasonally delinquent, chronically slow, and can not pay. Each of these categories must be dealt with differently just as each type of account (automatic, semiautomatic, and so on) must be dealt with differently.

Confused accounts are accounts which are either unclear about what the terms are, have lost their invoices, or who do not want to pay the account "because the balance is too small to be bothered with." These types of slow payers will pay you once they understand the terms, are sent duplicate invoices, or when they are billed for a larger amount that they can tack onto the "small balance." All these accounts are basically honest, and, with the exception of the "small balance" folks, will cause little difficulty to your collection efforts. You can understand that certain accounts would rather wait until they have larger balances before they pay, but all these small balances add up.

Negligent accounts are those where the debtor has the money and the intention to pay, but needs reminding that the bill is past due. Sometimes company employees are instructed not to pay until they get a past due notice. One way to solve this problem, if you notice that a customer is doing this constantly, is to send out the past due notice early.

Not-at-fault delinquent accounts are those that have had some disaster strike. This would include natural disasters such as fire, flood, earthquake, or blizzard, as well as difficulties such as material shortages or labor troubles. If any of these disasters occur, you should do what you can to get your customer back on his feet. These are usually short-term problems and do not affect your long-term collection efforts. Instead of pressing the customer in times like these, it might be a good idea to explain that you understand the difficulties and that your company will voluntarily suspend the debt repayment required for a few months. Your customer will remember you when the troubles are over, and the future benefit to your company far outweighs the temporary loss of income.

Seasonally delinquent accounts are those who fall behind in payments when their slow season comes. When production is slow, but a company must maintain its fixed overhead costs, they may experience temporary monetary problems. If the company is well-managed, they would have made allowances for this during the fast periods, but unfortunately there is little you can do about this except wait. Just make sure if you have to carry this customer that you are not the only one not being paid.

Chronically slow accounts fall into two types: (1) the customer who has the money but makes creditors wait as a matter of policy and (2) the customer who is undercapitalized and depends on trade credit to finance operations. Customers who have the money but make you wait are a tough case because they figure that they can go to a competitor if you do not like waiting. The best way to deal with this type of customer is personally and/or speed up your past due notices. If you find that the account is undercapitalized and is using your money to keep afloat, it might be wise to review your terms or even drop the account. The type of customer who falls into this category is the chronic slow payer who promises payment, but does not keep the promise or even answer your inquiries. The marginal account that is new or on your "watch list" might also fall into this category. The other two types of customers whom most credit persons have run across in this category are the complainer who refuses to pay for any plausible reason and the dissembler who insists that the check has already been mailed when in fact it is still sitting on his desk.

Cannot pay accounts may admit that they are temporarily short of capital pending a loan or some capital injection. In fact, they may be seriously close to insolvency. These are the accounts that give the credit person the biggest headaches and may end up as bad debts. The best thing to do is to press for immediate and full or partial payment. If your efforts prove unsuccessful, consider the possibility that aid from your company and other suppliers might rescue the debtor company. Attempts should be made to bring the creditors together to work out a solution. If the company is virtually bankrupt, it is time to investigate legal action. Remember, it is always better to catch this type of situation early and do something about it, than to wait and let it sink under its own weight.

Overall, with all the different categories and types of delinquency, your collection program must be flexible. It must be designed to cover all your past dues, while at the same time conforming to your company policy. First, does your organization expect that your customers will be reasonably prompt or is a certain leniency extended? When is the proper time for you to begin pressing for payment? One day after the invoice becomes past due or a week? two weeks? a month? Usually the longer the paying period terms, the longer you will delay your dunning process. If your company requires payment in 10 days after shipment, you may want to send the first reminder more quickly than a company with 60-day terms.

COLLECTION TOOLS

Monthly Statements

Sending monthly statements to customers used to be a much more popular collection method than it is today. Monthly statements include all amounts owing, both past and current, for a particular customer.

Many credit and collection books and articles argue against ever using this method. They point out that there is a great deal of extra expense and work involved in purchasing, printing, and processing the forms; envelope stuffing; mailing costs; and time.

Some companies send statements to all accounts and other companies send them only to those who have expressed a need for them or to selected past due accounts. I think that every account that wants to receive monthly statements (assuming that your company has the capacity to process them) should be sent the statements.

Telephone Calls

A letter has the disadvantages of being time-consuming and one-sided. Telephone calls can overcome both these disadvantages.

At one time when stamps, paper, and labor were relatively cheap, telephone calls were rarely used because of their cost. Now the telephone has become a more common collection tool, especially for serious collection problems. The telephone offers the advantages of speed and certainty that your inquiry gets to the right person. Also you can demand specific action on the telephone and find out the answer immediately. And, most important, talking in person to the debtor makes it difficult to deny the debt.

On a geographical basis, if the customer is either local or reasonably adjacent, a telephone call may be the cheapest means of contact. WATS-line service brings even the most remote customer into a cost range competitive with the letter.

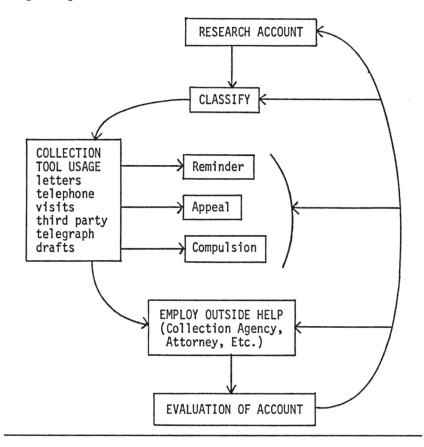

FIGURE 8.1
Collection Procedure

Traditionally, the customer is more conditioned to expect a letter or two about an unpaid or modestly overdue bill than to being called on the telephone. A telephone call early in the game might have the advantage of surprise or it might, on the other hand, upset the customer who is used to getting notices before phone calls. You will have to use your own judgment on this.

A commonly encountered telephone weakness is that of rehearsing the entire conversation with the debtor before the call is placed. Like so many incidents in life, many times the script must be discarded, and the memorized answer forgotten. The customer has a tendency to divert the conversation to a subject entirely unexpected.

To become an effective telephone collector you must develop confidence in your financial knowledge and negotiating skills. Tact, diplomacy, and sometimes bluntness are required to manage telephone collecting successfully. Use of threats should be avoided. A shouting match between you and your customer solves nothing.

Sometimes you might run into the situation where you telephone a customer four or five times over a period of a few days and get no response. This is not as bad as you might think. It indicates that the customer is uncomfortable making alibis or promises that will not be kept. There is good reason for exasperation in such a situation, but it is best to refrain from showing it.

If avoidance of your calls continues for more than three or four days, the matter requires a different tact. Calls should then be directed to some other officer or principal of the business. They will usually be obliged to give you the answer to your problem or explain why the party you have been calling without contact has not responded.

Credit and Financial Management magazine published an article called "The Telephone as a Collection Tool." The following are some interesting excerpts from that article:

> Phone-Power [is a] three step telephone collection process that preaches improved customer relations instead of the customary "get tough" collections policy.
>
> The formula is a simple one: pre-call planning plus some reverse psychology during the collection call. It can put more money in the till . . . plus the added bonus of a good rapport between business and customer.
>
> The beauty of Phone-power is that it's cheaper than letter — and in the majority of cases, far more effective, says Jack Fox of New Jersey Bell, the company that markets the collection concept.
>
> The problem with the cycle letters (reminders, appeals, compulsion)

says Mr. Fox, "is that by the time a company issues a 120-day letter, the value of the overdue dollar has shrunk to only 54 cents."

"In many cases, very little preparation goes into planning of collection calls," Mr. Fox says. "And unless you know the right questions to ask, and how to counter customer's excuses it can be very difficult to make a call of this nature."

[The] three-step phone call (process) emphasizes pre-call planning, the arrangement of an equitable payment plan with the customer, and most importantly, a thank you when the bill is paid.

[When calling] the collector identifies himself and his firm and states the reason for the call — then he pauses for six seconds.

That pause can really put the collector at an advantage — the customer feels compelled to explain himself.

If the customer offers the excuse that he is unable to pay the bill, the collector's next step . . . is to coordinate an equitable payment plan with the client.

If the customer hasn't paid his bill according to the specified arrangements, the collector calls and tries to work out another set of terms.

However, if the customer has paid according to the terms of the agreement, Phone-Power specialists suggest collectors call and say thanks.[1]

As you can see by the article, phoning is not just a slap-dash affair; you must educate your people (and yourself) in the proper use of the telephone. There are four steps to a successful telephone collection: proper identification, defining purpose, reaching an agreement, and the conclusion.

Identification is the stage where the caller identifies himself to the person he is talking to. Contact should be made with the person who signed the order contract, or the person who is responsible for the order. Identify yourself immediately. If the customer does not voluntarily indicate when payment will be made, state the reason (purpose) for your call in a direct manner. Do not sound antagonistic, but do not apologize. Every phone call should result in an agreement between you and the customer as to when payment will be made. If the suggested date given by the customer is reasonable, no further conversation is required. Be firm in establishing an acceptable payment date if the customer seems to be vague or unrealistic. Conclude every call by repeating the agreed-upon payment date so there will be no misunderstanding. Confirmation of agreement in writing is also suggested.

[1]"The Telephone as a Collection Tool," *Credit and Financial Management*, January, 1975, p. 27.

Telegrams

Telegrams are effective collection tools because they demand the recipient's attention. Telegram language can be blunt without offending. People expect short, clipped phrasing in telegrams. Telegrams are best used when the collection effort reaches the urgent phase and prompt action is required. However, use of telegrams early in the collection cycle often prompts the action you want. Western Union has preprinted forms that make the use of telegrams easier.

There are three types of mailgrams: terminal originated, computer originated, and voice originated. Terminal-originated messages are recommended for the sender who has less than 250 messages to deliver at any one time, or a single address message. They are sent from a Telex or TWX. Computer-originated messages are recommended for the delivery of messages in excess of 250. The messages are sent by magnetic tape to one of Western Union's computer centers. The most universal method of sending mailgrams is by calling one of Western Union's centralized telephone bureaus. At the bureau, the call is answered within three rings any hour, day or night. The operator takes the message and it is transmitted to the central computer, and from there to the appropriate post office.

Generally, most credit managers would rather limit their use of telegrams to the very small buyer with limited credit exposure of less than $125, up to perhaps $750. With the larger account if all other collection means have been unproductive, a sealed mailgram sent to the president or comptroller of the company may be a prelude to putting the account up for collection or taking legal action. The wire usually represents the final effort to reach a resolution.

The Personal Visit

Personal visits by credit agents with the slow-paying customer should usually be reserved for very serious or large collection problems because of the cost involved. The personal effort is sure to speed the collection requirements in one direction or another: toward settlement or toward a more serious legal action. The personal visit offers all the advantages of a telephone call plus the advantages of face-to-face discussion. Despite the costs, the personal visit usually *brings the best result of all the methods of collections.*

When you meet with the principals and see their plant and operations, you can better communicate with and understand the customer's problems. Principals are usually proud of their organization and regardless of its financial shortcomings, delighted to personally conduct you around the premises.

By seeing the customer's operation and learning about its financial problems, you might find areas where you can be of service to the customer. If, for example, receivables difficulties are primarily responsible for the cash flow problems, you can draft a credit and collection program for your customer that is more realistic than the one currently being used. Unwise buying and inadequate inventory control may be responsible for a weak financial condition. You may be able to help your customer with pointers on how to correct such improper practices. Some credit managers I have known have even gone so far as to help the company find some bank, commercial, or government financing.

Before the first visit it is a good idea to decide what objectives you will have for the meeting. Can you work out a compromise on the customer's payments that are past due? If so, what kind of compromise can you accept? The most important thing is to make a list of the objectives that you want from the customer. This negotiating list should include reasonable items that you feel you have the right to demand of the customer. If the customer has not paid after all those letters and phone calls, it is a little unrealistic for you to think that they are going to pay the full amount in cash just because you are there in person. But you can expect to agree on a payment schedule, change the debt to a note, or change the current terms of payment. Let your company's needs and the customer's needs be the determining factor on what demands you make, but here is a list of typical first visit demands:

1. Personal guarantees by the principals that the debt will be repaid.
2. Restoration of the account to a current (paid-up) position within three to six months (preferably three months).
3. The submission of monthly (or quarterly) financial statements to your company.
4. Restrictions on present and future payments including setting up COD, cash-in-advance, or draft terms (discussed in Chapter 2 and given in more detail shortly).
5. Immediate refunding of any unearned cash discounts that the company has taken in the past and a cessation of such deductions in the future.
6. Severance of the customer relationship entirely.
7. Referral of the balance of the account to attorneys or collection agencies.

The importance of these objectives will vary according to a given situation, but generally the first two — guarantees and bringing the account current — will probably be the most important. The other objectives are also desirable but may be used as concessions to assure attainment of the first two. Submission of financial statements and immediate refund of unearned cash discounts are a couple of important factors. The remaining three objectives should be considered enforcers to be used only if there is indifference on the part of the customer to the first objective. Basically the idea is to have enough objectives that you will at least get something that your company desires. After a certain point in late collections, negotiation is the only answer.

By getting guarantees from the customer, your company will have more capital supporting your claims. Moreover, personal guarantees give you access to personal assets that most people are reluctant to loose. The objective of restoration of the account to current status is obviously very important, but the time limit may be extended. Initially, however, it is best to insist on the three-month deadline as a "maximum" allowable time. If concessions of equal value are made by the customer, an additional grace period can be considered. On this point, as on other points, you (the credit manager) have to be reasonable, because a program based on wishful thinking is worthless. The customer has to have the financial wherewithal to perform.

Regular availability of the financial statements and remedying the practice of taking unearned cash discounts are also important to you. The customer's reaction to being asked to prepare and submit monthly statements may be one of anguish because of the cost and inconvenience. Yielding to the customer by allowing submission of quarterly or semiannual figures is one way of gaining acceptance of some other point of greater importance. The amount owed on unearned discounts is usually a minor amount. It is dwarfed by the magnitude of the other matters involved in the negotiations. If assurances can be given that the client will not take unearned discounts in the future, the repayment of the amount owned can be used as leverage to exact more important benefits.

The other three objectives — severance of the customer relationship, legal referral, and restriction of account terms — are intended to be peripheral and face-saving concessions for the customer if the other objectives are met. They are last resort measures to be implemented if the customer fails to be reasonable.

Should your customer fail to perform fully within the clearly designed program agreed upon in the first meeting, a second trip might be required. At this time the old objectives should be gone over, and new objectives should be added:

1. Imposition of a credit limit.
2. Converting the balance owing to personally guaranteed notes payable with interest.
3. Requiring future purchases be made on a trade acceptance basis.
4. Requiring that the customer maintain a restrictive financial ratio such as a 2 to 1 current ratio, officer's salaries be decreased, or dividends be discontinued.

Remember you always have the alternatives of sending the account to collections, cashing in on the personal guarantees, or taking legal action. How long you want to keep setting up programs that the customer either can not or will not abide by is a matter of policy and patience.

Your Sales Representative

There is much debate in credit circles as to the use of sales representatives in collecting accounts. Some maintain that sales representatives should not collect accounts because not only does it cut into sales time but sales and collections are at odds with each other. Others point out, quite correctly, that no one knows an account better than the sales representative (at least on a personal basis) and it is therefore easier for him to collect.

Those companies that subscribe to the exclusive use of sales people as collectors point out several reasons for this. They feel that the salesperson's relationship with the customer allows the salesperson to capitalize on any friendship and influence that has already been established. Since a salesperson might in the future become a manager, working with collections will help round his experience. (Since a representative calls on the customers regularly, collections can be given on-the-spot attention.)

Some companies consider collections as purely within the realm of the credit department. They maintain that the sales representative's effectiveness in generating new orders will be impaired by acting as collector. Enthusiasm will be dampened by diverting attention from selling to collecting. Furthermore, the credit manager has all the facts of the account easily available and can shape the collection approach to be consistent with these facts. Credit managers are professionals and in the area of financial problems, customers may tend to confide in them rather than the salesperson.

The best approach, however, is somewhere between the two extremes of all sales representative collections or all credit department collections — a team effort. The most effective results can be reached by using the strengths of both the credit department and the sales department.

We have already talked about how the sales representative and the credit manager might go on personal visits to the customer together. Another approach is to let the first collection contact be made by the credit department on the established risk account. The more highly regarded account (financially speaking) may first be approached by a salesperson. Should any account situation deteriorate into a crisis, sales and credit departments should maintain close communication when deciding each successive collection step.

An important way that the credit department can maximize the sales department effectiveness in collections is to keep them acquainted with any major change in the customer's status. Reciprocally, the sales representative may, through personal visits and observations, pass on vital facts or impressions that may have a present or future bearing on collections. In this way, the salesperson can give the credit manager valuable months of lead time, and the credit manager can use this time to shape a credit and collection policy for the account.

Drafts and Notes

A draft is considered a *sight draft* (the most commonly used) when it is drawn up by the creditor ordering the debtor's bank to pay a certain sum of money out of the debtor's account to the creditor whenever the draft is delivered to the debtor's bank. A *time draft* is similar except that the amount is to be paid only on the date specified on the draft. To be valid, the draft has to be signed by the debtor.

One method frequently used by credit managers as a means of collecting past-due accounts is a series of postdated checks. Only the debtor can sign checks against his account. There is no way the creditor can "create" valid checks. Postdated checks are considered to be promises to pay. They will provide a special incentive for the customer to pay because nonpayment will damage the customer's credit standing with the bank.

If you can get your delinquent customer to sign a promissory note, you will improve your chances of collection considerably. A promissory note is a promise to pay a definite sum on a definite date. It can be issued to the creditor or to "Bearer." Signing of a promissory note means that the customer has acknowledged the debt, a very useful fact if in the future you must seek legal recourse. Furthermore, it is a psychological weapon you may employ if the customer fails to live up to his agreement. Also, the existence of a note is a stronger motivation for the debtor to pay your bill sooner than all his other overdue debts. The disadvantages of a note is that, if the customer's financial situation deteriorates, you cannot press for payment until the due date written on the note. Promissory notes can usually be sold or transferred to others.

The right to charge interest should be clearly set forth from the customer's first request for credit. At the very least a notice of interest should appear on each invoice. To protect the right to collect interest, the right should be contractual, putting it in writing early in the relationship at least implies acceptance of the interest provisions by the debtor when he accepts the credit offered.

Service Charges

Imposing a service charge on overdue accounts is one way of decreasing the risk of slow-paying accounts. The service charge is imposed by the seller against unpaid customer balances that have been delinquent for an unreasonable period of time. The amount of the service charge and the time allowed before it is imposed will vary from company to company, but the most common is a 1 percent service charge if the account is over 30 days delinquent. In other words, if the normal terms are 30 days and the customer still has not paid after 60 days, the supplier will charge the account 1 percent on the unpaid balance. A case of a $1,000 balance billed is illustrated in Table 8.2.

As shown in Table 8.2, a customer who receives a $1,000 shipment from a supplier does not have to pay an additional service charge if the bill is paid during the normal period of 30-day terms. The customer still is not charged if the balance is unpaid within 60 days, 30 days delinquent. However, when the account becomes over 30 days delinquent (61 days or more since the goods were shipped and billed) a 1 percent service charge is added to the balance. The new balance ($1,010) is now owed, and if that amount is not paid by a 61-day delinquency (91 days since shipped), another 1 percent of the balance (or $10.10) is added as a charge.

TABLE 8.2
Service Charges for a Slow Paying Account

Balance Owed	Number of Days Since Shipped	1% Service Charge Added
$1,000.00	30 days	No charge
$1,000.00	60 days	No charge
$1,010.00	61 days	$10.00
$1,010,00	90 days	No additional charge
$1,020.00	91 days	$10.10

If you are going to use a service charge, I suggest you not impose it if your customer does not pay within the 30-day period. Allow at least another 30 days. For one reason or another, otherwise prompt payers may be a few days late after the initial 30 days, but seldom will a customer be over 60 days late due to an oversight.

Holding Pending Orders for Leverage

A credit manager has three options if an overdue account presents a new order. The order can be accepted, it can be rejected, or it can be held pending settlement of the overdue account.

Accepting the order can be construed by the customer as either an act of cooperation and goodwill or a sign of weakness. If approval is thought of as an act of toleration by the supplier, the customer may divert payables money to the more demanding creditors. To avoid this impression, the credit manager should write a letter to the customer saying that he is aware of the past-due situation but is making a temporary concession to the customer based on the assumption that the debt will quickly be repaid. If you can impress the customer that this is a gesture of faith, the situation will not be misconstrued.

The second alternative is outright rejection of the order, returning it to the customer with a demand that the past-due balances be repaid. This will appear as an ultimatum to the customer, therefore the approach should only be used when you are convinced that the customer's financial situation is beyond remedy. This action could also be taken when slowness is so bad that the account is clearly unprofitable and future relations would only produce additional losses.

The last, and perhaps the best, of the three alternatives is to hold up orders temporarily pending reasonable payment of past-due balances by the customer. This would point out to the buyer-debtor that terms of sales have not been complied with and that normal relations can be restored without strain if the account is brought to a current status. Be careful to notify the customer immediately that you are holding the order.

TECHNIQUES FOR INCREASING COLLECTIONS

When arguing about the most effective collection tool (besides the personal visit), credit managers tend to line up on the side of the telephone call or the letter. But if you are going to choose just the telephone call or just the letter you may have missed the point of this chapter. The most effective collection tool is a mix of *all* the collection tools (letters, telephone calls, visits, sales representatives, holding orders, monthly statements, drafts, and telegrams). The different tools should be used in different circumstances, but it is a good idea to use some kind of mix in almost every case. Obviously, everyone should get a letter for a reminder, but when you use the telephone, it is a good idea to follow it with a letter. Telegrams can sometimes be more effective than telephoning. Any use of collection tools can be effective if properly applied and sequenced in an intelligent manner. If you do use a mix of techniques, they must be put in proper sequence. In too many cases a strong telephone call, for example, is followed by a weak letter, or vice versa.

How much time and how many letters and phone calls can you afford before you seek the assistance of a collection agency? Collection agencies are usually considered to be a last resort, but how do you know when you have reached that point? It is a mistake to wait until it is too late for even a collection agency to help you.

Review your collection letters. Do they follow a sequence? Do you have several series of letters so that it is possible to alternate them to avoid sending the same letters to chronic delinquent accounts? When you tell your customer that you will refer their account to a collection agency or a credit bureau, do you do it? It is a mistake to threaten something unless you intend to follow through. Writing good collection letters to fit various types of delinquency is a job for an expert. Sequence and timing are crucial in obtaining satisfactory results. Are you or is someone in your department an excellent letter writer? This is not so important for individual letters or reminder letters, but if you need a series of letters or several series of letters and you are not sure of your competence, get outside help. The National Association of Credit Managers (NACM) has publications that feature an excellent portfolio of collection letters.

Most credit managers sooner or later come to realize that a customer who failed to pay on the due date, and made no reply to a reminder has not accidentally overlooked the obligation. The reason that the balance due has not been paid is because there were not sufficient funds to pay it. The supplier-creditor who consistently asks for money due, is the one who usually collects. The adage "the more you collect, the less you have to collect" is true. If you give all your accounts businesslike attention, your customers will soon understand your attitude and pay as agreed. (If they do let accounts slide, they will not let your payments slide.)

A businesslike collection policy is preventive medicine for the "delinquency disease." If a company has some money, but not enough to pay off everyone, they will pay some suppliers on time and other suppliers late. Some debts would not be paid at all if they can manage it. To collect money you must ask for it (and ask often). Each consecutive demand for money should be stronger than the last.

Whether your company is a large one or a small one, it is essential that you not only have a usable collection system, but that you know what it costs you. The collection system accomplishes what you are trying to accomplish. The following are some questions that you can ask yourself to help measure the efficiency and cost of your collection program.

1. What percentage of total payments are generated by the first letter, the second letter, and so on? How many letters are sent before the cost exceeds the net return?
2. How many contacts and telephone calls do each of your employees make each day? How many contacts or calls per hour are made?
3. What is the average cost of each telephone call, visit, telegram, or letter, including dollar expenditure and time costs?
4. What is the cost of each dollar collected by the various methods? Which of the collection tools brings in the most money?
5. How do you handle a promise to pay? Is there follow-up? Are most promises to pay genuine or ineffectual?

6. How many of the collection accounts are problems because of improper shipments received?

Do not advertise your dunning letters. Try to avoid the stereotype window envelope. Keep all letters short and to the point. Do not send apologetic collection letters. It is unnecessary to apologize to a customer when you are asking for your money.

Educate your customers from the beginning as to the importance of meeting their obligations. Do not let a promise to pay become history. It is important to follow-up all promises to pay with the appropriate letter or phone call if payment is not received as agreed.

Before you telephone, write a letter, or go on a personal visit, research the customer's account. Know the date of sale, when the last payment was made, the amount paid, and any history of slow payment the customer has shown.

When using letters it is sometimes a good idea to inject a second party letter (from an association, for example) into your collection series. These letters have proven to be 40 percent effective when used in the proper place.

The older an account gets the harder it is to collect. Therefore, you should be realistic about your collections. If you can not collect the account after five months of letter writing, telephoning, and visits, it is time to talk to a collection agency.

In short, take a good, hard, realistic look at your collection program and see if it is working as it should. Figure out the costs and effectiveness of all the tools. Then think about it!

9

Collections After The Final Notice

There are fewer business failures today as a percentage of total businesses than there were a few years ago. However, the average dollar liability per failure is higher than ever before. The most crucial thing to keep in mind when dealing with delinquent accounts is that you must make some effort to compromise with the debtor. If a business goes under, your chances of getting back most of your money are slim.

Assignment of the delinquent account to a collection agency is your first step. This is usually a relatively successful move unless your customer is really in financial difficulty. If the customer is in financial trouble, there are four possible courses of action for him to take: (1) try for voluntary settlement with creditors (the cheapest method for all concerned); (2) assign business assets for the benefit of the creditors; (3) file for Chapter XI or Chapter X bankruptcy; (4) be forced into involuntary bankruptcy by the creditors if debts are too severe to make any settlements.

A voluntary settlement might be arranged without attorneys, and incurs no court costs or receiver's cost (which is 2 percent off the top in California). In short, voluntary settlements are cheaper than court judgments. Court judgments occur only if the creditor sues to collect the debt under a breach of contract action. Bankruptcy, the other usual court proceeding, can produce a variety of orders and requirements. Voluntary settlements can give the customer an extension of time or allow the sale of collateral to come up with the money. The creditor (you) can make suggestions as to how to improve the debtor's business and if your suggestions are followed, you can work together; if not, you can come down on the debtor. Another possibility is to suggest that the company take on a management consultant to run the business and report to you or a group of creditors. Usually a whole group of creditors will be called together to work out suggestions for an out-of-court settlement. This would include most of the small creditors and all the large creditors. The more serious the customer's financial problems, the more likely that a large number of creditors would be involved in any out-of-court settlements. Generally speaking, if the owner is good in business, the purpose of this type of settlement is to keep him in business.

The second type of settlement mentioned is the assignment of the debtor's assets by the debtor to the creditors. From the debtor's standpoint, however, such an assignment can be hazardous because if the assets do not bring the full amount of the debt, the debtor is responsible for the balance. For this reason rarely will an individual or partnership make an assignment unless they are assured that no creditor will later insist on payment. This method is properly an out-of-court settlement and will be discussed later in this chapter.

Bankruptcy is the most expensive of the settlements for everyone concerned. Chapter XI and Chapter X bankruptcies are "involuntary" bankruptcies in that the court, not the debtor, controls the action. When the petition for a Chapter X is filed a referee will issue an order freezing liabilities. Chapter XI (the reorganization bankruptcy) is mostly for publicly-held corporations. There are two important differences between an out-of-court settlement and a bankruptcy. First, in a bankruptcy (Chapter XI) the matter comes under the jurisdiction of the courts and the debtor is protected by the judicial umbrella of the bankruptcy act. The debtor is not protected in an out-of-court settlement. Second, in a bankruptcy, it is necessary to have only 51 percent of the creditors involved, not all the creditors, which is generally the case in out-of-court settlements. In a bankruptcy, the receiver runs the business. Each creditor must show proof of the claims within a certain period of time.

When a company is so deeply in debt that claims against it cannot possibly be settled in an orderly manner, the creditors may request that the debtor be considered bankrupt. If the creditors request the bankruptcy, instead of the debtor, it is called an *involuntary bankruptcy*.

COLLECTION AGENCIES

After all collection efforts by your company have failed, it is advisable to place the account with a collection agency. The last letter or phone call should notify the delinquent debtor that this step will be taken if no remittance is received within a specified period (usually 10 days).

Although a collection agency usually can do no more than you could, the efforts of a collection agency historically have produced results when other efforts have failed. The debtor, if able, usually prefers not to have a reputation of having to pay a collection agency and may pay in full or make some other settlement. Handling by the collection people

---

STATEMENT

INVOICE	DATE	AMOUNT
TOTAL		

WARNING
READ CAREFULLY   N⁰ 20276

Date...................................., 19........

To..

Address..

It is the purpose of this notice to inform you, as a matter of courtesy, of our intention to place your account with the CREDIT MANAGERS ASSOCIATION OF SOUTHERN CALIFORNIA for collection unless your remittance is in our hands on or before...................................

This can be avoided if payment is made on or before the above date, but you must ACT WITHOUT DELAY.

The amount due is $...........................

                                    (Creditor)

                                    (Address)
By...

Credit Managers Association of Southern California • 2300 W. Olympic Blvd., Los Angeles, California 90006 • Telephone (213) 381-2661

FIGURE 9.1(a)
Free Demand Form

STATEMENT

INVOICE	DATE	AMOUNT
TOTAL		

(If above space is not sufficient, please attach duplicate itemized statement or other evidence of charges.)

Special Instructions

Mail This Copy Today

to

**CREDIT MANAGERS ASSOCIATION
OF SOUTHERN CALIFORNIA**

N⁰ 20276

2300 WEST OLYMPIC BLVD.   LOS ANGELES, CALIF. 90006

Mail at the same time you notify the debtor so that remittance may be identified and forwarded to you if received.

Date.................................., 19........

To...

Address...

We have this day mailed Credit Managers Association of Southern California Free (Direct) Demand Notices to the above.

We hereby place with and assign to Credit Managers Association of Southern California our claim against the above in the amount indicated below. Unless notified prior to the close of business on............................ that debtor has remitted in full, you are authorized to proceed at once to effect collection of the account, your current rates applying. No charges are to be made on remittances received on or before the above date.

The amount due $...

....
(Creditor)

....
(Address)

By...

TODAY — Mail this copy to Credit Managers Association of Southern California

FIGURE 9.1(b)
Free Demand Form

relieves the credit manager of the burden of collecting certain past-due accounts that could easily take up too much time. These accounts may present problems that an impartial collection agency, drawing on its experience with a wide variety of difficult debtors, can solve with fewer problems than the credit manager could.

All collection agencies allow a "free demand period." This is a period, not to exceed 10 days, in which no charge is made to you if the customer pays within that time. Some agencies ask that you mail out the free demand forms yourself (see Figs. 9.1a and 9.1b). Other agencies send out the free demand forms themselves on receipt of your claim. You must, however, specify free demand, and bear in mind that you can not ask the agency for free demand only. You must use the rest of their services as well.

There are many worthwhile collection agencies in this country. All of them offer similar services for an established fee (commission rates are uniform and set by law).

After the free demand, the agency goes through various stages. They may begin with a letter or phone call to the debtor and later a personal visit from an agency representative. A small agency will probably have to skip this last stage of personal visits for out-of-town claims unless they have reciprocal agreements with agencies in those towns.

If the agency cannot get results through its own efforts, it will then turn the case over to an attorney in the same geographical area as the customer's business, if they have approval from you to do this. If the agency does not have approval from you, the claim will be returned as uncollectable.

When looking for a collection agency, make sure it fits your requirements. If you have accounts in several parts of the country, you will want to use a company that is nationwide or has reciprocal agreements with agencies in many areas. An agency should be courteous, firm, progressive, persistent, and practical. It should subscribe to the principles of the American Bar Association but not be engaged in the practice of law. You should be sure that the money your agency collects is turned over to you as soon as there is assurance that the debtor's check has cleared.

Collection agencies are either private agencies that operate as individual companies, or they may be associated with trade groups. Even though private agencies may be the most effective, those associated with trade groups have the advantage of transmitting reports of slow-paying accounts to other suppliers, thereby causing the debtor to think twice about it. The disadvantage with trade group collection agencies is that there is the possibility that reports might cause a "run" of suits against the debtor.

One trade-associated collection agency having special appeal to the credit manager is the commercial collection department of the National Association of Credit Management, (NACM). NACM operates approximately seventy individual collection bureaus nationwide. Since each bureau is owned and administered by its members, primary consideration is given to member interests rather than profits. The commercial collection department of NACM has the advantage of being nationwide and of having a good reputation.

Collection Agency Rates

The commercial collection department of the Credit Managers Association of Los Angeles (office of NACM) had the following rates during the last quarter of 1976:

25% on the first $1,000
20% on excess of $1,000
50% on accounts under $50.00
$25.00 minimum charge on accounts from $50.00 to $125.00

Other conditions stipulated that accounts less than $15.00 are not handled, and if merchandise is returned as settlements, 50 percent of the regular rates apply. In the event that a suit is necessary, and authorized by you, the attorney's fee generally runs an additional 10 percent of the rates shown.

Attorneys as Collectors

On some claims, it may be wiser to go directly to a lawyer specializing in collections. A lawyer will not give you a free demand period and the fee will most certainly be higher than agencies. But an experienced attorney can get to the debtor immediately. Even if your customer is in a precarious situation, your attorney can sometimes get enough of a payment to make his services and fee worthwhile. Lawyers do not usually accept a small claim.

Use of an attorney is a good method for two reasons. An attorney, especially a local one, will be able to investigate the case personally. An attorney also understands what pressures can be brought to bear to induce payments. Because the account knows that the attorney will bring suit if payment is not made, the customer will be more strongly motivated than if approached by a collection agency.

VOLUNTARY SETTLEMENTS

The advantage of voluntary settlements is that they are straightforward and proceed in a traditional manner. As the name suggests, no courts are involved, and agreements are strictly between the creditors and the debtor.

This type of agreement has no legal effect except to the extent that the creditors choose to go along with the arrangement. Being a voluntary process and voluntary agreement, the debtor and creditor can function however they agree.

The procedure is rather straightforward and simple. As the flow chart in Figure 9.2 shows, most of the activities of the settlement are handled by a committee appointed by the general group of creditors.

First, all the creditors are called together by either one of the creditors or the debtor. When all the creditors get together, they appoint a committee that draws the details of the settlement. The committee's suggestions do not have to be accepted by all the creditors, but to make it compelling to the debtor, at least 90 percent should agree with the settlement plan.

The committee in most cases appoints an accountant and an attorney to investigate the debtor company and file the compromise agreement. They also appoint a secretary who corresponds with all the other debtors. The appointees (accountant and attorney) make reports to the committee on the condition of the debtor and the committee negotiates with the debtor for a settlement plan. When a settlement plan is decided on, it is submitted to the general creditors who are urged to adopt it, but may reject it if they choose.

The voluntary settlement is the most effective and inexpensive method for providing the creditors with the maximum possible return of their money. Voluntary settlements are not limited to cash payments, but

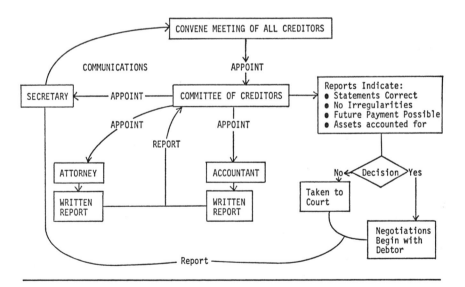

FIGURE 9.2
Voluntary Settlement Procedure

are also utilized in situations where the debtor provides payments over a period of time. Sometimes the plan for repayment agreed upon can be utilized in Chapter XI proceedings for bankruptcy, if necessary. The creditors committee may continue to function and supervise regular financial reports to ensure that installment payments are made. The accountant appointed by the committee will usually be paid by the debtor so that an independent report will be provided to the committee.

The voluntary settlement should not require a period of time longer than 45 to 60 days from the first meeting when the general creditors appoint a committee.

Appointment and Duties of the Creditors Committee

When the general group of all the creditors of a debtor company meet, they will appoint a creditors committee to do the work of negotiating the settlement and appraising the debtor company. The committee generally consists of representatives of the largest creditors, but this is not required.

The committee selects an independent accountant and lawyer to investigate the reasons why the debtor is in financial difficulty. An audit and investigation will be conducted by the accountant verifying that the assets of the company have been accounted for and he will prepare a report for the committee showing the financial condition of the debtor and income and balance sheet financial statements for the last quarter. The accountant will also show that there have been no preferences given to creditors, which would be voidable under the Bankruptcy Act.

This accountant's report is essential to any out-of-court settlement. The auditor (accountant) chosen should always be independent of the debtor's company for obvious reasons. In addition to the financial report, the accountant should ascertain the validity of any prior financial statements given to the creditors by the debtor.

The lawyer for the committee will also conduct an investigation of: all liens against the property of the debtor; the filings and the documents that purport to create security interests claimed by creditors; the capitalization of the firm; and repayments of liens and payments of antecedent indebtedness to suppliers and trade creditors to determine whether some have legal preferences on assets.

The reports and findings of the accountant and attorney will be submitted to the committee as soon as possible. The accountant's report will contain a balance sheet and an income statement and other additional information on the financial condition of the debtor. The income statement is necessary for the committee to estimate whether or not the debtor is able to pay based on present financial condition and anticipated future profit (based on payment history). The accountant also reports on whether or not all assets have been accounted for. The lawyer's report will list the secured claims and the documents supporting them.

If the company meets certain crucial criteria, the committee will begin to negotiate with the debtor for settlement or extension. The criteria that the company must meet are as follows:

1. There are no irregularities in the conduct of the business of the debtor.
2. The prior financial statements given to the trade have been accurate.
3. All assets have been accounted for.
4. The debtor has given no legal preferences to any one of the trade creditors (for example, special arrangements such as preferential payment in case of default).
5. There is a reasonable expectation that the debtor can rehabilitate the business by repaying most of the debt.

If the debtor's business cannot meet all these crucial criteria, the committee might suggest referring the matter to the courts.

Creditors Committee Negotiations

If the debtor meets the criteria mentioned above as determined by the accountant and attorney's report, the committee will proceed to negotiate between the creditors and debtor. At this point, the attorney and accountant have made their suggestions and the people who have the money at stake — the creditors and the debtor — negotiate. Negotiations may be completed in one meeting but often require more time. It is not unusual today to find two or three meetings required before the final settlement can be negotiated. Meetings usually last two or three hours. Time required, however, may be much longer.

All resolutions, with the minutes of the meeting, if possible, should also be discussed in the letters to creditors. These letters of explanation are necessary in an out-of-court settlement because for the settlement to work it is required that all the creditors cooperate. The debtor does not have the protection of a court that would be available under Chapter XI bankruptcy, therefore the creditors must be informed that the assets are not being dissipated. The secretary to the committee will have the duty of reporting all the proceedings to the general creditors.

The Negotiated Agreement and Report to the General Creditors

After negotiation of a plan by the committee has been completed, the attorney formulates the plan into a legal agreement. The agreement may provide for any settlement negotiated between the committee and debtor, but they generally include the following:

1. The amount and method that the debtor will pay the unsecured creditors.
2. The time when payment will be made.
3. Which claims will be excepted from the plan.
4. Which claims will be paid.
5. Which claims (if any) will receive special treatment and what that special treatment will be.
6. The amount of money from a source outside of the debtor's assets that will be placed in escrow as a good-faith deposit.
7. The number and amount of acceptances required to be given to the debtor on closing.
8. The conditions under which the above deposit is forfeited.
9. The amount of administration expenses of the settlement and who will pay them.

Remember, it is the creditors committee that negotiates the plan and the creditors committee cannot bind the other general unsecured creditors. The creditors committee simply makes a recommendation to other creditors after describing their investigation of the debtor, the negotiations, and the plan that is most favorable to the creditors. The plan will realize more for the creditors than if the debtor liquidates. The plan must be accepted by the creditors between the time it is negotiated and the time the first payments are to begin. The request for other creditors' acceptance of the plan will be carried out by the committee and its members, and especially the committee secretary. The secretary in a letter will report the findings of the committee to the entire general body of creditors. The letter will contain the details of the plan and recommend that the plan be accepted. The approval, depending on the number of creditors and the industry, will require between 30 and 45 days.

Debtor Deposits and Acceptance of the Plan

Because the debtor will be operating during the entire period of fact finding, negotiations, and acceptance of the plan, the creditors will generally receive a good-faith deposit put in escrow by the debtor. The debtor places in escrow outside funds that are at risk and will be forfeited if the creditors in a significant number accept the plan but the debtor rejects the plan.

Normally, creditors can guarantee that only 90 percent to 95 percent of the total creditors will accept the plan as negotiated. This percentage relates to the dollar amount of claims as opposed to the number of claims. For example, if the total amount of debt is $100,000, the creditors will obtain acceptances of $90,000 to $95,000. The agreement is written in such a way that only about 90 percent acceptance of the general creditors is required, historically, however, between 96 and 97 percent acceptances are usually obtained. In other words, 3 to 4 percent of the debt (in dollars) will be to general creditors who will not accept the plan and will hold out for something better.

Unless the creditors committee is able to furnish to the debtor the guaranteed amount of acceptances (90 percent plus), the debtor does not forfeit the deposit. If the required amount of acceptances are furnished and the debtor fails to honor the agreement, the deposit will be forfeited and creditors may proceed to liquidate the debtor.

Usually out-of-court settlements that have been negotiated in good faith may be accomplished in 45 to 60 days. The general creditors usually accept the recommendation of the appointed creditors committee, whose activity is communicated to them by the committee secretary.

Expenses of Out-of-Court Settlements

Expenses in connection with out-of-court settlements are considerably less than can be expected in a bankruptcy proceeding. The expenses are primarily the attorney, accountant, and secretary fees for the creditors committee. There is no fee paid to members of a creditors committee. Sometimes the travel expenses of members are paid, but this is not usually the case.

When a settlement is expressed as a *gross settlement* the administrative expenses will be deducted from the money paid to the creditors by the debtor. In this case, expenses of administration will be described in the letter soliciting acceptances sent to the general creditors by the committee secretary. The expenses of administration are usually 7.5 percent of the amount each creditor claims. For example, if a 50 percent gross settlement was offered to creditors, expenses of 7.5 percent might be deducted from the distribution of money, leaving a net amount of 42.5 percent going to each creditor.

In all cases of voluntary settlements, the administrative expenses are passed on by the committee. After they get the bills from their appointees (accountant, attorney, and secretary), the committee will fix the amount of expenses to the general creditors. In other words, the committee does not set arbitrary fees, but merely passes on actual fees to the general body.

Extension and Subordination Agreements in Out-of-Court Settlements

Usually voluntary settlements involve: (1) the extension of the time the debtor has to repay the debt and (2) a subordination of certain (usually the larger) creditors' claims to allow the extension of new credit during the interim period. Extension and subordination arrangements have been, for the most part, extremely successful because they provide both creditors and the debtor all the protection that any other type of proceeding can provide.

The rights of the parties involved are governed by the terms of the subordination agreement, not by the general principles of law.

A subordination is the postponement of the collection of a claim to allow another claim to be paid in full before payment of the subordinated claim. For example, the debtor owes Magnalump Systems a certain amount of money but Magnalump agrees to subordinate any claim to the debtor's assets to anyone who will let the debtor have credit. Zap Systems gives the debtor credit. The debtor runs into trouble and files Chapter XI Bankruptcy. Zap Systems' claim must be paid *in full* before Magnalump Systems receives a dime because Magnalump has subordinated their claims to Zap Systems.

Usually it is the large credit granters (the ones to whom the debtor owes the great majority of trade payables) who become the ones to plan and carry out the extension or subordinations. Since the large creditors have the greatest risk, they would be the most likely to concede that an extension or an extension and subordination of their claims is required to allow the debtor a chance at rehabilitation. These large suppliers usually will be on the creditors committee and will play an important role in determining extension allowances under a plan.

If the main suppliers and/or the creditors committee determine that the financial condition of the debtor requires time to recover, then an extension arrangement is usually suggested. In these situations the main suppliers will be looking for a 100 percent payout over a period of time. The debtor might need the time to liquidate a heavy inventory, collect receivables, or get through a troublesome season in which merchandise must be held for a period of time until there is a market for it. The debtor usually needs additional credit to operate during this time.

Because the vital element in rehabilitation is the continued flow of credit to the debtor, it may be necessary for the major suppliers to subordinate their claims to new credit granted to the debtor during this period. The motivation for subordination is to recover the full amount of the debt in the long run and also to keep a good customer relationship.

Nobody is going to be willing to extend the subordinate without a certain amount of control, however. The debtor may require constant supervision both by an accountant selected by the suppliers and by the suppliers themselves. Usually these controls are expressed in a formal agreement drawn up by an attorney.

The agreement must provide a creditors committee who will have powers to exercise certain controls. Clauses in the agreement are usually included to allow for substitution of the members of the committee and specifications that the committee shall not be liable for any acts except willful and malicious malfeasance. The agreement should grant the committee power to terminate the extension and liquidate the business of the debtor when they determine the necessity for doing so. The accountant retained by the committee to monitor the debtor should be paid by the debtor.

The principals of the debtor company should also subordinate their claims to the payment in full of not only new credit but also the payment in full of the extended claims. There should be limitations on capital investments and no dividends should be allowed until all extended claims are paid in full. Other items that should be regulated in the debtor company are:

1. *Sales* should be regulated by the committee's accountant to protect against the selling of merchandise below cost out of the ordinary course of business.

2. *Purchases* are controlled to prevent unnecessary build-up of an inventory that would retain the debtor in a tight financial position. This build-up would prevent accumulation of cash to pay the creditors.
3. *Inventories* should be slowly liquidated (not at distressed prices) with a resulting build-up of cash with which to pay creditors.
4. *Salaries* of officers and new help should be kept as low as possible.

The agreement will also have a stop-loss provision allowing for the automatic cessation of the extension followed by liquidation. The stop-loss provision would automatically cause termination when the debtor company accumulates losses above a certain amount. When a level of losses is reached in the debtor company the committee should have the discretion to terminate the extension.

If the extension arrangement has to be terminated, this does not modify the subordination of claims as to credit that was granted between the beginning date of the extension and the date of the termination. For this reason it is necessary that the agreement provide for a termination date after which the creditors will be notified that there will no longer be any subordination.

BANKRUPTCY

Although bankruptcy is a drawn-out legal procedure, it is relatively easy to understand the process. The flow chart in Figure 9.3 illustrates the bankruptcy process, which is an expanded version of the voluntary settlement. The difference is that under the Bankruptcy Act, the reorganization or payment plan must be approved by a court after the creditors committee makes the suggestion and trustees, sometimes a receiver, may be appointed. The main difference legally between the out-of-court settlement and the court settlement is that the debtor is taken under the wing of the court and only a majority (more than 50 percent) of the creditors have to approve the plan (in voluntary settlements, 90 percent or more must approve the plan). It should be noted that information presented here on bankruptcy is for general information. Specific questions and situations should be referred to the company lawyer.

Examining the flow chart we see that the debtor files a petition for

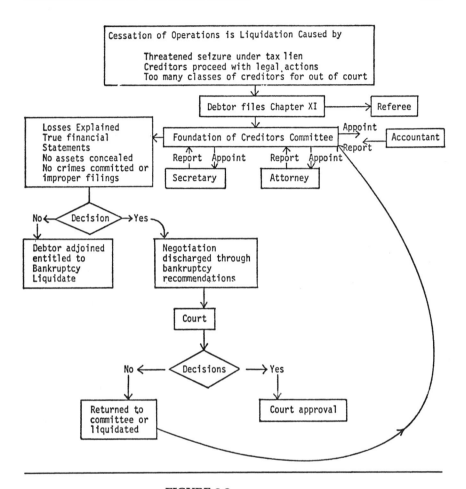

FIGURE 9.3
Bankruptcy Procedure

Chapter XI Bankruptcy to the court. The court appoints trustees (but not always) and convenes a general meeting of the creditors to elect a creditors committee. The creditors committee appoints a secretary, accountant, and attorney. The creditors committee negotiates with the debtor to design a plan to meet payments. When the creditors committee and the debtor have arrived at a plan, the plan is then given to the court for approval. If the court approves the plan, it is then implemented. If no reasonable repayment plan can be arrived at, the company will be ad-judged bankrupt and the assets will be liquidated for the benefit of the creditors.

The major features of the Chapter XI Bankruptcy Act are summarized as follows:

1. The debtor files an original petition stating insolvency or in-ability to pay bills as they come due. Provisions of the arrange-ment that will be proposed to creditors including amounts owed are also stated.
2. A bankruptcy judge is appointed.
3. Shortly after the petition is filed, a meeting of the creditors is called at which time a judge or referee rules on the claims of the creditors and receives written acceptances of the creditors. Also at the meeting, upon receiving acceptances, the referee will designate a receiver or trustee to be held responsible for distributing money of the debtor for monthly debts.
4. Arrangements are made for extensions and operations of the debtor.
5. A creditors committee is appointed by the general creditors to examine the debtor's affairs, negotiate with the debtor, and collect and file acceptances of the proposed arrangement.
6. The court confirms the agreement if it is satisfied that the provisions of the law are complied with, the plan is feasible, and the debtor has performed all the duties required by the act.

Duties of the Bankrupt

The duties of the bankrupt include attending the first meeting of cred-itors and all meetings necessary; examining papers and all proof of claims; executing transfers of property; preparing property schedules; submitting to examination concerning conduct of the business; and preparing a detailed inventory.

When to File a Petition for Chapter XI

When there is a threat of a complete cessation of operations and an involuntary liquidation would be detrimental, a Chapter XI bankruptcy is filed by a debtor. The debtor usually files when a seizure under a

Federal Tax Lien is threatened, in order to prevent the threatened seizure. The petition might also be filed when an out-of-court settlement is agreed upon but some creditors proceed with legal actions and attachments that make the out-of-court settlement difficult.

A petition under Chapter XI of the Bankruptcy Act can only be filed by a debtor. It is not a proceeding that creditors can institute. The arrangement under the Bankruptcy Act allows the debtor an opportunity to continue operations under the protection of the court. It provides the debtor sufficient time to negotiate with the creditors. At the same time, creditors will have the opportunity of examining the affairs of the debtor and approve or disapprove the plan.

Secure Creditors and Chapter XI

As it has already been pointed out, the Chapter XI proceedings cannot result in a modification of the contractual agreement between the secured creditors and the debtor. A secured creditor cannot be compelled to adjust a claim with a debtor or accept a settlement or be required to extend the contractual arrangements between them and the debtor. There is an exception to this, however. Generally, the plan of a debtor cannot affect a secured creditor, but a secured creditor may be enjoined from reclaiming security, an act that would defeat the debtor's chances of rehabilitation during the proceedings.

Here is a typical situation. A manufacturer finds himself in financial trouble and files a petition. The manufacturer has several machines vital to his operations that are subject to valid security agreements. The debtor is paying a certain amount monthly on these productive machines to the secured creditor. If the debtor is delinquent in the payments at the time of filing, the question arises, should the secured creditor be entitled to reclaim these machines or is the debtor entitled to relief from these payments? There is no agreement on this point and it is up to the judge to rule.

The Creditors Committee

Chapter XI allows for a formation of a creditors committee and provides for a method for official recognition of the committee. The Bankruptcy Act also considers the possibility that a creditors committee has been formed before the filing. The committee is allowed to retain representatives such as a secretary to the committee, accountants, and attorneys. The Bankruptcy Act allows for compensation to be paid to the committee (unlike out-of-court settlements) for their services. If a plan is confirmed, the members of the committee are entitled to be compensated, as well as the appointees of the committee, with the approval of the court.

The great advantage of Chapter XI is that all creditors are bound by the majority vote in number and amount of claims, as we mentioned previously. If over 50 percent of the creditors vote for a plan, all other creditors are bound by the conditions of that plan.

If a debtor's plan is confirmed providing for the settlement of the debt for less than 100 percent of the amount of claims, the balance is discharged. As a matter of fact, the ability of the debtor to be discharged from debt is one of the most important results that the debtor is seeking when filing for bankruptcy.

Some acts by the debtor, even with the acceptance of the plan by creditors, would prohibit the plan from being confirmed by the court. The acts that would disqualify the debtor from confirmation of the plan include inability to explain losses satisfactorily, failure to maintain books and records· and acquisition of debt by means of false financial statements. Other prohibitory acts of the debtor are filing false schedules with the court and commissions of crimes relating to the administration of the bankruptcy proceeding. A single creditor can object to the confirmation of a plan if the creditor can show that the debtor is not entitled to the confirmation because of the commission of one of these acts.

The Court and Disputes — Recommendations

Even though the creditors accept a plan, the court may find that the plan of the debtor is not feasible and cannot be successfully carried out. The proceeding requires a finding by the referee that the plan is feasible. The committee and the debtor must prove to the court that the plan is feasible.

Another advantage of a Chapter XI proceeding over an out-of-court settlement is the provision for the court to litigate claims. In order to share or receive payment under a plan, a creditor must file a claim with the court (discussed later in this chapter). The claim must be prepared in a sufficiently detailed manner to provide the debtor with information to determine whether or not the amount of the claim is proper. The debtor, too, is required to file schedules showing the assets of the company and the amount of indebtedness to each creditor. If the debtor regards the claim of the creditor to be excessive or disputed, the debtor may litigate the claim in the summary proceedings available under the Bankruptcy Act. This is a very advantageous and inexpensive method of resolving disputes between debtors and creditors. A summary hearing before a referee in bankruptcy does not require all the formal rules of evidence. Additionally, the referee can decide issues of fact without a jury. The referee may shorten the proceedings or require them to be litigated in a quicker fashion than normal trials. These disputes can usually be dealt with in a matter of days or a few weeks.

The jurisdiction of the court in a Chapter XI proceeding is extensive, covering the entire United States, and the process can be started anywhere in the country. This extensive jurisdiction together with the summary type of litigation proceedings gives the debtor an advantageous position. Where no lien is proper, the debtor is able by means of the summary proceedings to compel the creditor to release the property improperly liened. There are many cases where substantial amounts of assets are held by creditors with improper liens and without the court proceedings, the debtor would suffer.

Indemnity for Creditors

If the creditors committee decides that the debtor's chances of rehabilitation are slim, the committee can apply to the court for an order directing that the debtor post indemnity. This will usually insure that the debtor must liquidate the business. The purpose of indemnity is to insure the creditors against losses that might occur from the debtor's business operations during the bankruptcy proceedings by requiring that the debtor make a deposit of money. This indemnity deposit must come from funds outside the debtor's assets.

Since no one is willing to act as surety and risk sizable sums of money on the chance that the debtor will be successful in operating during the proceedings, a deposit is unlikely. For example, if the anticipated losses for a period of time from filing to settlement (perhaps three months or more) are $30,000, the indemnity has to be placed at that amount. The amount would be deposited before the debtor even has a chance to meet with creditors to negotiate a plan. In most cases, because of the depressed financial condition of the debtor and the fact that the money must come from outside sources, the debtor will be unable to raise the amount either through friends or bonding companies. This will result in an adjudication of bankruptcy.

DEBTOR OPERATIONS DURING CHAPTER XI PROCEEDINGS

When a petition under Chapter XI is filed, the debtor may apply for permission to remain in possession and operate a business as debtor-in-possession (DIP). The creditors can also apply for the appointment of a receiver though this is seldom done. If the debtor is honest, it is best that the debtor continue to operate the business. A receiver is essential only in those cases where there is some question as to the honesty of the debtor. The DIP is an officer of the court and must account to the court, the same as any other fiduciary. The debtor is best qualified to run the business and the receiver, usually an attorney, has no qualifications to run the debtor's business.

Financial Reporting

During the proceedings the DIP must file regular monthly reports showing the results of the operations of the business. In this way, the court is provided with sufficient information to determine whether or not indemnity should be posted or whether or not the losses occurring during the proceedings will make the plan impractical. The referee will usually have informal meetings with the debtor and committee after every report is received. In addition to these informal hearings there are regular hearings before a referee where the court will be advised of the progress of the proceedings and negotiations. As soon as the plan is developed, it will be put into a draft and filed with the court.

One of the vital rights of a creditors committee in a Chapter XI proceedings is to have an independent audit conducted to determine the reason for the losses and financial condition of the debtor. The committee should insist on an independent auditor, and usually does. Often the argument is advanced by the debtor or court that the expense of an audit is an unnecessary one. Even though it is an expense, it is an essential one for the committee in order that accurate information is received.

Extending Credit to a DIP or Receiver

Often a creditor is requested to extend credit to a debtor-in-possession in a Chapter XI proceeding. Credit extended to a DIP is regarded as an administrative expense of the proceedings. That does not mean, however, that the administration claim will be paid. The fact that credit extended during a Chapter XI proceeding will be granted the status of an administration claim does not ensure that there will be sufficient funds to pay the claim. The extension of credit to a DIP or receiver requires a thorough credit investigation on the part of the credit manager. The most crucial question to ask yourself (as credit manager) in the credit evaluation is: "Will there be enough money to pay this extension of credit as an administrative expense?"

The credit manager's investigation should include an investigation of information collected by the creditors committee (if there was one) before and after the filing of the petition. The credit manager should also receive copies of reports filed by the DIP with the court.

If a committee was formed prior to the Chapter XI proceeding, you can talk to the committee and its appointees to see if there is any chance that the debtor can validate a plan arrived at in the proceeding. You should find out if other members of the committee are extending credit and if not, why. If a debtor files a petition without a creditors' meeting in advance, either you or one of your representatives should attend the first and subsequent meetings.

The debtor-in-possession is like any other business enterprise, and if it is making a profit or breaking even during the proceedings, the chances are that credit will be granted. Shorter terms are possible in this type of case unless there are good reasons to grant normal terms.

CLAIMS IN CHAPTER XI BANKRUPTCY

Administration Claims

If no plan is confirmed in Chapter XI and the debtor is adjudicated bankrupt, administration expenses of the superceding bankruptcy have a higher status than the administration expenses of the Chapter XI proceedings. When a straight bankruptcy ensues, the following expenses will have priority over the administration expenses of the preceding Chapter XI proceedings: the referee's salary and expense fund, the trustee's commissions, the fees of the trustee's accountant and attorney, the auctioneer's expenses and commissions from the sale of assets, the expenses for the occupation of the bankrupt's premises prior to property liquidation, and storage expenses. The other priority expenses are bond premiums of the trustee, expenses of recording and distributing transcripts of the various meetings, and certain incidental expenses of the trustee during the proceedings.

More often than not, administration expenses of the Chapter XI proceedings are not paid in full. Because the expenses in connection with the superceding bankruptcy proceeding have priority, there is usually only a prorated dividend made to administration claimants of the Chapter XI proceedings.

Priority in Settlement of Claims

According to the Bankruptcy Act, revenue derived from the sale of the bankrupt's assets is distributed according to the following priority:

1. The costs and expenses of administering the bankruptcy proceeding (discussed previously)
2. Employee wages
3. Taxes
4. Rent and other obligations that might have priority under the law
5. Creditors, according to the following preferences:
   a. Transfers of any of the property of a debtor to or for the benefit of a creditor or on account of an antecedent debt
   b. A lien obtainable by legal and equitable proceedings
   c. Certain classes of preferred stockholders if the bankrupt is a corporation
   d. Unsecured creditors

Creditors' voidable liens and transfers and how they work in bankruptcy will be discussed more thoroughly in the following section. One of the powers of the bankruptcy court is to determine whether a preference has been given to a creditor. It should be noted that jurisdiction is granted to the bankruptcy court if proof of claim is filed in the Chapter XI proceeding.

FILING A PROOF OF CLAIM

In order to get your money under a Chapter XI plan, you (the credit manager) must file a claim. Within the last several years, a number of amendments have been added to the Bankruptcy Act (especially the revisions of 1973) with respect to the time when proofs of claim must be filed. Under the present law you have to file proof of claim even if the debtor has listed your claim in the debt schedules that have been filed with the court. The present law provides that a claim must be filed up to within 30 days after confirmation of the plan. Unfortunately, if you wait to file your claim until after the plan confirmation, only that sum that is listed in the schedules of the debtor as the amount of the claim will be allowed you. If the amount of money listed on the debtor's schedules is different than the amount you have claimed, your chances of collecting are virtually eliminated. The best idea is to file the proof of claim *before* the confirmation of the plan, preferably at the first meeting. If you file a proof of claim before plan confirmation and there is a dispute as to the amount, there can be litigation and resolution of the dispute by the referee of the bankruptcy court.

In order for a creditor to vote for or against a reorganization plan proposed by the debtor and the creditors committee, a proof of claim must be on file with the court at the time of the vote. Where proof of claim is on file, it is counted as a "no" vote unless a signed acceptance to the plan is on file. When no proof of claim is on file, the obligation owing to the creditor is not included in the calculation. The right of the creditor to recover the correct amount of the debt owed him can only be protected by filing a proof of claim. Moreover, if a claim is not filed, the creditor gets no vote in deciding on the reorganization plan.

In cases where the plan is filed together with the Chapter XI petition, a vote on the acceptance of the plan may be held at the first meeting of the creditors. It is conceivable that within 30 days after a petition is filed a vote will be taken on the acceptance or rejection of the plan.

Sometimes a debtor, anticipating that a large number of creditors may reject the plan, will use this quick claim filing and voting as a strategy to get the plan through before the other creditors "knew what hit 'em." Here is how it works. A debtor will negotiate a plan with several creditors whom he knows will accept the plan. The debtor then proceeds to file the plan and the petition simultaneously. The notice of the first creditors' meeting, notice of the filing, and the plan will all be sent to creditors at the same time. It is not necessary for creditors to file a claim at the first creditors' meeting. However, the debtor can arrange to have those creditors who accept the plan file proofs of claim and acceptances at the first meeting of creditors. In these cases, only the claims actually filed at time of the first meeting can be counted for the purpose of determining the acceptance of the plan. It is possible that even though there are 100 creditors, ten proofs of claim and ten acceptances filed at the first meeting can make the plan deemed acceptable by the court. This is because those companies who have not filed their claim do not get a vote. So the ten people with a vote make the decision for the ninety who have not filed.

The debtor cannot prevent other creditors from filing claims at the first meeting, but there is a distinct lethargy prevailing among creditors in having representation at the first creditors' meeting, much less filing claims. Therefore a plan could be accepted under the debtor strategy mentioned even though there have been no real negotiations. You can see that a debtor may be able to put over a plan that is not acceptable to the majority of the creditors.

LIQUIDATIONS

In liquidation situations basically two things happen: (1) the creditors foreclose on or otherwise take possession of the debtors' assets and (2) the assets are sold, either to one buyer (bulk sale) or many (auction). Liquidation is expensive, not only because the assets sold rarely bring their true value, but because of the costs associated with the sale such as attorney's fees and auctioneer's fees. There are three types of liquidation procedures: (1) bulk sales (see Section 6 of the Uniform Commercial Code), (2) assignment for the benefit of the creditors, and (3) bankruptcy liquidations.

The flow-chart in Figure 9.4 illustrates the liquidation procedure. If reorganization is not possible, the debtor may decide to sell the business "in bulk" (the whole shooting match — assets and all) to a third party or to assign the assets "for benefit of the creditors." If there is a bankruptcy proceeding, either voluntary or involuntary, the trustee of the court may choose to sell the assets at auction. In any case, the creditors committee will be consulted directly or indirectly and it may assign professionals, such as an attorney or accountant, to investigate. The assets are either sold at auction or to another single party "in bulk." The proceeds of the sale, after administrative expenses and preferential payments, go to the creditors committee and are distributed to the general creditors.

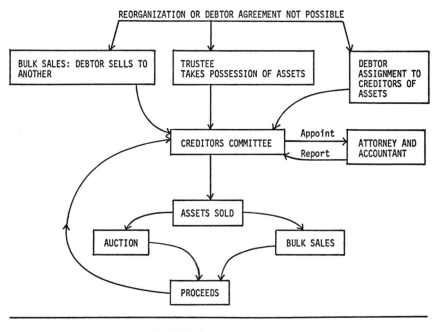

FIGURE 9.4
Liquidation Procedure

Bulk Sales as an Out-of-Court Settlement

Bulk sales are often utilized as a method of out-of-court settlement or liquidation. If it is an out-of-court settlement, the debtor seeks out a purchaser for the business; if it is used as a method of liquidation, the creditors seek a buyer. Either way it has the same result — the business assets are sold and the dollar amount received for them is only a small amount of the value. This is generally considered a poor method of settling creditors' claims.

A proposed bulk sale negotiated solely by the debtor may be consummated without the negotiation and advance approval of the creditors committee as long as the debtor has notified all the creditors. The debtor is required to notify creditors of a bulk sale under Article 6 of the Uniform Commercial Code, but does not need their approval. Bulk sales may, with some difficulty, be legally stayed. Therefore, if you as a credit manager receive a bulk sale notice unaccompanied by a letter from a creditors committee, you should take some action as soon as possible.

If a creditors committee investigates the sale before it happens, your chances of getting more money as a creditor will be better.

The procedure of settlement is usually that a fixed dollar amount is paid into one fund from which all creditors share on a pro rata basis.

There is usually a psychological panic surrounding a bulk sale because everything must be done on a rush basis, including the audit, the audit report, negotiations, and meetings. Only after the sale is there sufficient time for creditors to file their claims.

The obligation of the creditors committee or distributor of funds under a bulk sale method is far greater than in any other method of settlement. The creditors committee must make the final determination as to what claims are to be paid and when the fund is to be distributed to creditors on a pro rata basis. Timing is important. If the fund is distributed too early, a tax claim may remain unpaid after distribution of the funds and there arises a serious question as to who is liable for the tax. If there are claims greatly in excess of what was originally scheduled on the debtor's books, there is no practical method for settling. The creditors committee must evaluate each claim to determine whether to allow it or not. This saddles the creditors committee with more responsibility than it should have under normal circumstances.

As you can easily see, the bulk sales method makes fairness very difficult. This method should be avoided if at all possible. Even when the creditors committee is arranging the sale of a debtor's assets "in bulk," the probability of getting more than a few pennies on the dollar is low. But sometimes it is desirable as it avoids a lengthy and expensive method by selling assets on a piecemeal basis.

Liquidation Under the Assignment Method

A general assignment for the benefit of creditors is a voluntary proceeding to liquidate a debtor, initiated by the debtor. There cannot be an involuntary assignment proceeding. The general assignment, a document setting forth an assignment of assets to creditors, must be executed by the debtor and delivered to an assignee. Every state in the United States has statutes relating to assignments, but unfortunately there is little uniformity. General assignments are frequently used as a method of liquidation and this is preferable to bankruptcy when there are no irregularities. If there are no irregularities in the assets of the debtor according to a creditors committee investigation, the expenses of a bankruptcy proceeding are not warranted.

In a classical assignment proceeding, a debtor in financial trouble consults an attorney who suggests that the debtor take some extraordinary steps with the creditors. If there appears to be no pressing need for a Chapter XI proceeding, the attorney calls together the creditors in a meeting. At the meeting a committee is formed and the debtor, through the attorney, advises that there has not been enough time for the attorney to develop a settlement plan to offer to the creditors. The creditors make their investigation and then they get back together with the debtor to negotiate an extension or settlement. If the creditors and the debtor cannot agree to a settlement, the debtor will indicate to the creditors that they should liquidate the business.

The creditors committee is then left with the question of the type of liquidation proceeding to be utilized. If there are no irregularities in the debtor's assets or assignments, the company is comparatively simple to liquidate and bankruptcy proceedings are not needed for litigation. The committee will appoint someone to supervise the liquidation of the company and sell the assets, reduce the assets to cash, or make a distribution. Like the bankruptcy trustee, the assignee must examine all of the claims filed against the debtor and judge which ones are proper. The assignee must object to excessive claims and review them carefully.

Federal tax claims have priority over all other claims in an assignment proceeding. They must be paid before other tax claims (city or state). Priority claims in each separate state of the United States will depend on the local law of that state. Practically every state grants a priority to wage claimants although the dollar amount granted is sometimes limited.

The expenses of an assignment should be considerably less than those of a bankruptcy proceeding. There is no receiver, attorney, or accountant for the receiver. The attorney for the debtor (assignor) is allowed only a nominal fee for the preparation of the assignment. There is no referee's salary and expense fund, and administratively there will be fewer reports than in bankruptcy.

The assignee appointed by the creditors must file a final accounting in most states. The assignee will request the court to settle the accounting — that is, to approve it so that a distribution of the funds can be made. In the unlikely event that all monies are not properly accounted for in this filing, there is recourse against the bond that is usually filed by the creditors at the inception of the proceedings. The assignee is in every sense a fiduciary (holds funds in trust) for the creditors. He must be in strict compliance with all laws, statutory and common, governing fiduciaries.

When the court reviews the final accounting of the assignee and accepts it, an order approving the accounting will be entered. This will allow the assignee to make a distribution of the funds in accordance with the schedules attached to the accounting as approved. The court also reviews fees charged by the assignee, and the assignee's attorney and accountant. The court can reduce these fees if it judges them to be too expensive.

Friendly Assignments

General assignment for the benefit of creditors is a voluntary act on the part of the debtor. It is not instituted by the creditors. It is a liquidation chosen by the debtor. Therefore, all creditors should determine whether a general assignment for the benefit of creditors is a creditor-controlled assignment or a "friendly assignment." A friendly assignment is when a debtor's attorney advises that a general assignment for the benefit of creditors should be made to a friend of the attorney and the attorney will become counsel for the assignee. The owners of the debtor company can then start a new company or get jobs and the attorney can proceed to liquidate the business and distribute payment to creditors.

Needless to say, in this type of circumstance creditors will suffer because there is no investigation and the attorney handling the liquidation has a conflict. Duty to his own client is greater than duty to the creditors. It is, therefore, advisable for the creditors to take action against this type of arrangement.

The Bankruptcy Act provides that the making of a general assignment for the benefit of creditors is an act of bankruptcy allowing creditors to file a petition against the assignor (the attorney acting for the debtor). The involuntary petition in bankruptcy must be filed within four months of making the general assignment. This is the remedy for friendly assignments. It should be utilized whenever an assignment is taken without regard to creditors.

Liquidation in Bankruptcy

Liquidation is possible under all chapters of the Bankruptcy Act. Under Chapter XI, if there is an ultimate adjudication (judgment) of bankruptcy because of a failure to negotiate a plan, the choice of the method of liquidation is *not* available to creditors.

Involuntary bankruptcy is when a debtor has more than twelve creditors, three or more of whom file a petition against the debtor. In other words, one or two creditors cannot file an involuntary petition in bankruptcy — there must be at least three.

Involuntary Petitions for Bankruptcy

An involuntary petition cannot be filed simply because the debtor company is unable to pay its debts. One of the following conditions must exist where the debtor has:

1. Concealed or removed part of its property with the intent to hinder, delay, or defraud his creditors.
2. Made a preferential transfer as defined in Section 60 of the Bankruptcy Act.
3. Permitted any creditor to obtain a lien upon any of his (the debtor's) property while insolvent, and which were not discharged within 30 days after the lien was filed or within 5 days before any sale of those assets.
4. Made a general assignment for the benefit of creditors.
5. Permitted the appointment of a receiver or trustee to take charge of the assets while insolvent.
6. Admitted in writing an inability to pay debts and a willingness to be adjudged bankrupt.

The first two situations mentioned above are technical points requiring legal analysis. If it appears that the debtor is attempting to defraud creditors by concealing assets or removing them, an attorney should be consulted immediately.

The third act of bankruptcy mentioned above speaks of a lien on property obtained through legal proceedings. If an action is instituted against a debtor using attachment and the lien is not discharged within 30 days or 5 days before the sale of assets is scheduled, an involuntary petition can be filed. If a debtor company is unable to pay its rent and the landlord seizes the property within the premises of the debtor, this lien can be a grounds for filing an involuntary petition.

When a creditor finds that general assignment for the benefit of creditors has been made without a general meeting of the creditors (the friendly assignment mentioned previously), an involuntary petition can be filed.

If creditors request the appointment of a receiver by the state courts, other creditors may determine if an involuntary petition should be filed. In this case, the filing of a petition might be required if the creditors judge they are better off with a liquidation rather than a receiver.

Assignment of a Trustee

Shortly after the adjudication of bankruptcy (whether a result of a failure or a Chapter XI proceeding or the institution, voluntarily or involuntarily, of a bankruptcy proceeding), a meeting of creditors will be held. The committee will elect a trustee.

The trustee, as distinguished from the referee, is the person who will execute the functions of liquidation of debtor's assets. The trustee will do so within limitations prescribed by the Bankruptcy Act and must report regularly to the referee. If the proceeding started as a Chapter XI, the trustee will normally be elected at the first meeting of creditors. The trustee is elected during the first meeting so that if there is a resulting adjudication of bankruptcy, the trustee can immediately take possession of the assets. In the Chapter XI proceeding this trustee is referred to as a stand-by trustee. Only those creditors who have filed proof of a claim can vote at the creditors meeting for the election of a trustee.

Sale of Assets and Distribution of Funds

Sale of assets by the trustee must be according to procedures provided for in the Bankruptcy Act. An appraisal of assets is made by an appraiser appointed by the referee in the bankruptcy. That appraisal is not open to inspection prior to the sale. All sales are approved by the referee. The sales have to be equal to at least 75 percent of the appraised value or they will not be approved in most instances. The auctioneer appointed by the referee usually telephones the referee with the bids that are received at the auction. The referee approves or rejects the sale offer.

After the sale, the proceeds are distributed to the creditors after expenses. You can reasonably expect that it will be at least a year and a half before any distribution is made to the creditors of these proceeds. No one knows in advance how long it will be before the distribution will be made. A bankruptcy must last at least six months so everyone has a chance to file proofs of claims, but it usually takes much longer. It is not uncommon for a bankruptcy liquidation and distribution to take at least a year, and you can pretty well expect it to take a year and a half.

There are many things that can delay the closing of a bankruptcy. The trustee must examine not only the assets but all claims, especially those who claim they have preference under Section 67 of the Bankruptcy Act (discussed previously). These examinations take excessive periods of time because all examinations have to be approved by the referee. The referee is limited by calendar commitments in the court and is not usually able to allow lengthy continuous examinations. These examinations may have to be scheduled over a period of weeks and sometimes months.

The trustee usually has to examine hundreds of claims, which is a long and tedious task. The proceedings are also delayed by the institution of actions brought by the trustee to recover preferences and to set aside conveyances. In any kind of legal proceeding there are usually delays because of the crowded condition of courts in general.

Bankruptcy Liquidation Expenses

Expenses of a bankruptcy liquidation include:

Fees for the attorneys and accountants of the trustee.
Trustee's commission.
Referee's salary and expenses.
Transcript expenses.
Bond premiums for the trustee's bond.
Rent of the bankrupt's premises until the premises are vacated. (It is usually better to auction equipment on the premises because it is hooked up and the buyer can see if it works.)
Storage of books and records.
Receiver's fees (if applicable) and the fees of the appointed attorney.
Expenses for the preservation of the estate.

The general creditor is the last one to receive any distribution in a bankruptcy. Before the general creditors are paid, administration claims for a prior Chapter XI proceeding (if applicable), taxes and wages, and priority claims are paid.

Final Creditors Meeting

All creditors receive a final meeting notice to be held before the referee in the bankruptcy. The final notice includes a statement about the amount of money on hand and indicates the allowances requested that require approval by the referee. Any creditor may attend the last meeting of creditors and be heard on any of the matters. You, as a creditor, may object to any of the allowances requested. However, as a matter of course, referees will usually award less than the fee requested.

At the final meeting of creditors, the court will make a determination as to fees and distribution. It will usually take about 60 days after the final meeting of creditors before the distribution is actually sent. Checks received from bankruptcy trustees should be deposited right away. After a certain period of time if the check is not deposited, the account of the trustee is closed and the money deposited with the clerk of the court. This will create an additional problem for a creditor who will then have to apply to the clerk for payment, which is time-consuming.

SUMMARY

Bankruptcy, reorganization, and liquidation involving trustees, referees, committees, accountants, and attorneys can get pretty complicated. So let me take a customer of yours, Rotten Distribution Company, through the stages of bad debt, reorganization, and bankruptcy, so you can get a feeling for what happens.

Rotten Distribution has been late on their payments for several months, and you have gone through all your letters and had a personal meeting with John Rotten, the owner. It has become obvious to you that the company has been terribly mismanaged since old man Ezekiel Rotten died a few years ago and left the company to his irresponsible son, John. You have heard talk among the other creditors that they are having trouble, too.

You send the account to a collection agency. After three months, the agency admits that they can not get the money and suggests that you take the claim to an attorney. You give the case to an attorney recommended by the collection agency. Meanwhile, you get a note from one of Rotten's big suppliers suggesting that a creditors meeting be held.

At the meeting you elect a committee of creditors and request that they make an investigation. The debtor, John Rotten, is at the meeting and he agrees that he will negotiate with the creditors when a plan is devised.

The creditors committee appoints an accountant to do an audit of Rotten Distribution and an attorney to handle any required filings.

In about a month you get a letter from the creditors committee with a copy of the accountant's report. During this period of time, you have given the creditors committee a complete itemization of the money that Rotten Distribution owes your company. The letter sent to you by the committee also gives you a brief outline of the plan they will negotiate with the debtor and a schedule of what the debtor's book shows that you are owed. The amount in Rotten's books agrees with your amount.

In another month you get a letter from the committee telling you that the debtor company, Rotten Distribution, cannot come to agreement on the proposed plan and has instituted bankruptcy under Chapter XI of the Bankruptcy Act.

After you file your claim with the court and several creditors meetings have been convened, the creditors committee sends you the plan designed by the debtor and negotiated with the committee for reorganization. The plan has been approved by the referee of the bankruptcy and you are asked to verify the amount that will be allowed for your debt and the terms.

Before you agree to the plan of reorganization, you get news from one of the creditors, who is a friend of yours, and a letter from the bankruptcy referee that John Rotten has decided that he no longer wants to run the company and has given the court a written statement. The statement testifies in writing that Rotten Distribution is willing to be judged bankrupt. Liquidation proceedings will be the order of the next creditors meeting.

At the meeting the trustee who was originally elected in the first creditors meeting of the Chapter XI bankruptcy says that he intends to auction off the assets using A. B. Z. Auctioneers for a date later that month.

After the auction you get an accounting of the money raised, the administrative, tax, and preferred expenses along with the amount you can expect to receive. The amount that you can expect to receive is only about 20 percent of the amount owed.

Three months later, a year and two months after the first creditors meeting was called to salvage Rotten Distribution, you get your check.

10

Avoiding
Legal Hassles

The best way to avoid legal hassles, future insolvency, and bankruptcy brought about by the customer's failure to pay debts, is to "be prepared" like the Boy Scouts. There are certain precautions you can make to assure yourself of a reasonable recovery of your loss. Some preparation techniques you can use are: credit insurance; personal guarantees and subordination agreements; good sales contracts and contractural liens; and arbitration. All these techniques will be discussed in this chapter.

As a credit manager, you should be aware of your major legal avenue in these cases — utilizing the *Uniform Commercial Code* (UCC). Since this law is the creditor's main source of security, we shall discuss it first.

THE UNIFORM COMMERCIAL CODE

The Uniform Commercial Code is not a United States (federal) law. It is an "ideal" law written by lawyers, scholars, and commercial people.

Each state has adopted its own version of the UCC. While these versions are quite similar, they usually differ significantly in details. The businessperson cannot ignore the differences because rights and obligations in this area are determined by details.

The Uniform Commercial Code concerns any transaction involving sale of commercial goods for money or notes. It also describes the nature of security for any commercial financial transaction. This law is probably best known for the article that specifies the requirements of securing assets of a buyer or borrower, but it has several sections covering other financial transactions. Ordinarily, the state-adopted Uniform Commercial Code contains the following ten articles:

1. General provisions
2. Sales
3. Commercial paper
4. Bank deposits and collections
5. Letters of credit
6. Bulk transfers
7. Warehouse receipts, bills of lading, and other proof-of-title documents
8. Investment securities
9. Secured transactions
10. Effective date and repealer

The following discussion is general. Each credit manager should learn about the specific Uniform Commercial Code in his state.

Secured Transactions

The most important article of the Uniform Commercial Code to you as a credit manager is undoubtedly the article covering secured transactions. Before the code, the creditor had to use different security devices for different types of assets as a factor's lien covered inventory and a chattel mortgage covered fixed assets. Under the present code a *security agreement* covers *all* assets.

The security agreement provides for a second interest in a particular asset or assets and gives specific details of the transaction (who, when, and what). The security agreement can be used to secure future as well as present debt. Provisions for the repayment of the creditor are defined and the collateral on which a lien is given is listed.

In instances where a security agreement exists covering all the inventory of your customer, you might be hesitant to ship the account. The merchandise you sell to your customer may become subject to the lien of the existing creditor. To avoid this kind of embarrassing possibility, you can file a *financing agreement,* which represents public notice of your right to the shipped goods and you can notify the existing secured creditor of your transaction. The financing agreement is like a security agreement (though usually shorter in length) that is filed with the state. As a matter of fact, in most states you can file a security agreement and it automatically becomes a financing agreement.

In some types of secured transactions, the signing of a security agreement without filing it with the state will give you adequate and complete protection. But for most transactions you will have to file a financial agreement (or statement) to "perfect" (make legal) your secured interest. Generally, a security agreement is not a matter of public record. You have to file it as a financing statement before it becomes public.

A financing statement (or agreement) is a brief document that will not contain as much information about the secured transaction as will the security agreement. It need only contain the following:

1. Names, addresses, and signatures of the debtor and the creditor.
2. A brief description of the collateral identified in the security agreement.
3. A statement as to whether the proceeds and the products of the collateral are covered.

A security agreement may list as collateral specific items of equipment, but the financing statement, which is the public record of the transaction, may simply describe the collateral as "specified equipment" or just "equipment."

Once a financing statement is filed, it is effective for a maximum of five years even though no maturity date is shown. A continuation statement can be filed before the expiration of the first filing extending the interest of the secured party (creditor) for another five years or less.

Reclaiming Goods Shipped to Customer

Section 2–702 of the Uniform Commercial Code is also important to the credit manager. This section has the regulations regarding the right of the seller (creditor) to reclaim goods shipped to a customer. There are two important rules in this section.

The first rule is that a seller may reclaim goods received by a buyer if the seller asks for their return within 10 *days* after delivery to the buyer. For example, if you shipped goods to a customer on January 1 who received them on January 4, you have 10 days, or until January 14 to reclaim the goods. Notice that it is not the date of the shipment to the buyer that is important but the date the buyer *receives* the goods. If the buyer is requested in this 10-day period to return the goods and refuses to do so, the seller has the right to institute a reclamation proceeding or action to complete the goods' return.

Another part of Section 2–702 is more complicated and is somewhat difficult to explain. If a buyer misrepresents solvency to the seller (saying he is solvent when, in fact, he is not) in writing within three months before delivery of the goods, the seller can reclaim the goods without regard to the 10-day period previously mentioned. That is, the seller does not need to make the demand for the return of the goods within 10 days after the buyer receives delivery. Misrepresentation of solvency, however, requires proof by the seller that the buyer was insolvent at the time the buyer made the misrepresentation. This will usually require extensive and difficult accounting to demonstrate exactly when the buyer became insolvent. Despite the difficulty, you should remember this fact in case of expected future difficulty. It could give you one jump ahead of everyone else and it may mean that you get 100 percent of your money instead of 20 percent after bankruptcy.

CREDIT INSURANCE

Commercial credit insurance protects jobbers, wholesalers, manufacturers, and certain service industries against large, damaging credit losses. It also provides collection services and credit advice. Credit insurance is provided by two companies: (1) American Credit Indemnity and (2) London Guarantee and Accident Company.

A credit insurance policy provides protection against credit losses due to both insolvency and nonpayment of debtors. The policy amount is based on the policyholder's sales volume (for example, 5 percent of annual sales volume) and size of credit business.

Each policy usually has a deductible amount subtracted from the aggregate credit loss and not from each individual bad debt. The deductible is stated as both a minimum amount and as a percentage of the projected annual sales volume. For instance, assume that the deductible is set at .3 percent of total sales volume or $30,000 minimum, whichever is more, on a projected sales volume of $10 million dollars. If the sales are more than $10 million, the deductible is 3/10 of 1 percent ($33,000 on $11 million, $45,000 on $15 million). If the sales are less than the $10 million projected, the $30,000 minimum deductible applies ($30,000 for sales of $9 million or $8 million or $7 million).

Regular coverage is provided on your customers' orders according to their credit rating with a mercantile reporting agency (usually Dun and Bradstreet). Each policy has a table attached to it that lists the Dun and Bradstreet rating and the maximum that will be covered on a particular customer so rated Table 10.1 is an example of a credit rating table. Looking at Table 10.1 you will notice a rating, then a dollar amount right after it under the "gross amount covered" column. For example, a customer rated BB1 is allowed orders up to $50,000. A customer rated EE2, however, cannot be covered for any one order in excess of $5,000. Customers that are not covered by the table of ratings (those with no

TABLE 10.1
Credit Rating Table

Column One			Column Two		
Rating		Gross Amount Covered	Rating		Gross Amount Covered
5A, 4A, 3A	1	$100,000	5A, 4A, 3A	2	$25,000
2A	1	50,000	2A	2	25,000
1A	1	50,000	1A	2	25,000
BA	1	50,000	BA	2	25,000
BB	1	50,000	BB	2	25,000
CB	1	50,000	CB	2	25,000
CC	1	30,000	CC	2	15,000
DC	1	25,000	DC	2	12,500
DD	1	20,000	DD	2	10,000
EE	1	10,000	EE	2	5,000
FF	1	5,000	FF	2	3,000
GG	1	2,500	GG	2	1,500
HH	1	1,500	HH	2	750

rating) are subject to the insurer's approval. A credit limit is established for each account in this category and all the accounts are named in the policy.

The cost or premium for a credit insurance policy will vary for each insured based on such items as sales volume and risk. Usually it is a fraction of 1 percent of gross sales volume.

PERSONAL GUARANTEE

There is considerable debate as to whether a personal guarantee is really valuable. A personal guarantee is a written statement that if the company cannot make payment to the creditor, the owner (or person signing the guarantee) will guarantee the amount with his own personal assets (for example, house or savings). The people who say a guarantee is of no use argue that if the company goes insolvent, the principal stockholders may go the same way, and follow the company into bankruptcy, making the guarantee useless. This is true many times; however, there is always the possibility that each case will be the exception to the rule — that the principal stockholders retain solvency even though the company does not. More importantly, the guarantee of a principal stockholder has a persuasive psychological value. A guarantee, however, may be by someone other than the principal stockholder. If the company is moving toward insolvency, the owner might want to make sure that the creditor with the guarantee is paid first so as to keep himself off the hook. Always in the back of the owner's mind is the possibility of starting life anew even though the company goes under. If the guarantee had no other value than this, it would be worthwhile to have it.

It is easy to see that there is a greater possibility of being paid from the corporate assets, as funds are available, when you hold a personal guarantee. Even if you, as the creditor, have to accept a settlement on a guarantee, this will be considerably more than you would have received from liquidation alone. With a guarantee you collect from the company and also the guarantor. If you still think guarantees are not a good idea, ask yourself this question, "If guarantees are not always a good idea, why do banks and several secured creditors insist on them?"

Guarantees received from other corporations are important when there are affiliated corporations, parents, and subsidiaries. Guarantees must not be hastily prepared and executed. Many guarantees prepared that way have been ruled by the courts as unenforcable for a number of reasons. Not only should the documents be drawn up properly but they must be properly executed. For instance, corporate guarantees need a resolution of the board of directors. But corporate resolutions by themselves do not constitute a legal guarantee. You should consult an attorney either to draw up a guarantee or to review guarantees drawn up by the customer.

Guarantee Provisions

Certain basic provisions should be contained in a guarantee including the following:

1. The guarantee should be unconditional and state that it is a "continuing guarantee." However, any words intended to cover more than one transaction are sufficient. It is especially important for the guarantee to be continuous if several transactions will be involved.
2. The agreement must be signed by the party making the guarantee.
3. The liability of the person signing the guarantee (debtor) should be unconditional and not subject to counterclaim, claim of set-off, or defense.
4. The liability of the person signing the guarantee (guarantor) should include any extension that the creditor with the guarantee may allow or any settlement between creditor and guarantor.
5. The guarantor should pay all obligations that the creditor incurs when trying to enforce the guarantee (attorneys' and court costs).
6. All payments owed and guaranteed should be paid on time regardless of bankruptcy or similar insolvency actions.
7. The guarantor should acknowledge that the amount he will owe to the creditor will be the amount shown on the creditor's books in the name of the original debtor and that amount shown there is correct. This is a good feature because if the guarantee has to be taken to court, the creditor can just use his books as proof without having to prove the delivery and acceptance of goods. Remember the guarantor is liable only when the original debtor does not pay his own debts. Until then the guarantor owes the creditor nothing.
8. The guarantor should waive trial by jury.

9. The guarantee should contain a provision saying that the laws of a specified state should apply to avoid problems involving multistate transactions.

10. Where possible, the guarantee should state that the owners' claims to any company assets will be subordinated to the creditor.

Remember, a guarantee only allows the creditor claim on assets. A subordination agreement allows claim on assets *before* the owner's claim.

SALES CONTRACTS AND CONTRACTUAL LIENS

Many companies have sales contracts only for large orders that take some period of time to fill. However, a sales contract is a very valuable tool to use to avoid legal hassles and to get the upper hand if any proceedings are instituted against the buyer. Whether you obtain a signed contract or not, the buyer (your customer) should receive a summary of the sale terms (payment due and so on) in writing. By putting together all your sale terms in writing and convincing the buyer to sign the terms, you have a sales contract.

The terms of the contract are vital in the relationship between you and the buyer. The questions of when payment arises, acceleration of payment, changing the terms, and others should be covered. The following are some important provisions that you might like to have in your sales contract.

1. A provision that allows you to apply any money you receive from the customer to any debt balances. This would mean that payment could be applied against any invoices that may be outstanding for the longest period of time or even against invoices where unauthorized deductions were taken.

2. A provision that allows you (the seller) to change the credit terms and require cash-in-advance, if deemed necessary, and to charge a service charge on the unpaid balance. If terms of the contract are 30 days and the customer is slow paying, this provision would give the seller the option of changing the terms to 10 days or cash-in-advance.

3. A provision that requires either a signature or acceptance of the goods shipped as confirmation of the contract. It is, of course,

best to get a signature, but if you cannot get the contract signed, you will still have legal recourse using this provision.

4. In instances where the buyer of the goods has another corporation or person pay the invoices, a provision should state that both parties sign the contract. That is, both parties, buyer and payer, are designated as the buyer.
5. An arbitration provision should be written into the contract, allowing disputed claims to be bound by third-party decisions.
6. A provision that will grant a "contractual lien" on all goods produced for the buyer and still in the possession of the seller. This provision allows a lien on all the buyer's goods ordered, whether paid for or not, to secure all indebtedness of the buyer to the seller "under this or any other contract."
7. The right to charge interest on past due accounts.

Contractual Liens

Contractual liens are difficult to understand using definitions, but can be easily explained by example. Suppose the buyer, Rotten Distribution, orders 200,000 transistors from your company to be delivered at the rate of 20,000 per month for a ten-month period. Rotten takes delivery on and pays for 120,000 transistors over a period of six months. Rotten also pays for 10,000 more transistors in advance. But in the seventh, eighth, ninth, and tenth months, Rotten does not take delivery on the rest (80,000) of the transistors. At this point Rotten Distribution becomes insolvent. Since Rotten does not take the other 80,000 transistors, even though they paid for 10,000 of them, you (the seller) have suffered damage. These damages constitute a claim against Rotten Distribution. The contractual lien allows you to have a lien on *all* the transistors still in your possession, even though 10,000 of them are already paid for. This provision of the sales contract grants a lien by the buyer to the seller on goods that have been paid for but are still in the seller's possession.

The *contractual lien* is, as the name suggests, a lien by contract. This is not to be confused with a seller's lien. The seller's lien is a common-law right of the seller and is available without a contract. In the seller's lien situation, the seller has the right only to those goods in his possession that have not been paid for. In a seller's lien situation, if we use the illustration of Rotten Distribution above, the buyer would have the right to the 10,000 transistors that were paid for but not delivered. In this case of Rotten Distribution, because of the contractual lien, you can keep the goods in your possession whether they were paid for or not.

The Seller's Lien

The seller's lien involves a situation where goods that are ordered but unpaid for and still in the seller's possession may be retained when the buyer becomes insolvent. If a customer becomes insolvent, their trustee in bankruptcy cannot require a seller to deliver goods simply because a contract to deliver them exists. You, as the seller, have the right to demand payment for the goods before they are delivered.

Another right of the seller generally classified under the seller's lien is the right to stop goods in transit. This is not in actuality a seller's lien, but a separate and distinct right called *stoppage in transit*. The seller has the right to stop goods before they are delivered to the buyer when it has become clear that the buyer will be unable to pay for the goods. It is important that you have a good reason for this action. If you sell FOB, shipping point title passes when the carrier takes possession, and the buyer can sue if you stop in transit for a nonvalid cause.

You have the right to a seller's lien or stoppage in transit whether you have it in the contract or not. But in order to be able to keep goods paid for but not delivered, you need to institute a contractual lien in your contract.

ARBITRATION AND ADJUSTMENT BUREAUS

Arbitration and adjustment bureau services are usually two different things. Arbitration is the act of having a third party settle a dispute between seller and buyer. The services of adjustment bureaus are used to supervise extensions, out-of-court settlements, and assignments for the benefits of creditors between many creditors and the debtor. They are similar in that they both are third-party factors in judgments or payments between creditor and debtor.

Arbitration

We discussed earlier the importance of including in your sales contract a provision that would allow for arbitration by a third party in case of dispute between you (the seller) and your customer (the buyer). Disputes arising out of late delivery, merchandise, or quality can be resolved through arbitration before a panel of businesspersons familiar with this type of dispute. It is usually more helpful to the seller to have a hearing before business people than a jury or judge who do not fully understand the transaction involved.

A panel of arbitrators from the American Arbitration Association are all selected from business people who have had experience in the kinds of problems that will be brought to arbitration. This is not so in the jury systems. Arbitration can usually be performed long before a jury trial because the crowded court situation today causes delay, sometimes long delays.

Remember, in order to have arbitration, a separate arbitration provision must be in the sales contract and, generally, the contract must be a signed one.

Arbitration awards can be confirmed by a court and the confirmation will result in a judgment in favor of the party receiving the award. That resulting judgment will have the same legal effect as one obtained in court.

Adjustment Bureaus

Credit managers throughout the country use the services of adjustment bureaus whenever there is a serious problem between creditors and a debtor. Most adjustment bureaus are part of the National Association of Credit Management (NACM).

The function of an adjustment bureau is to supervise extensions and compromise arrangements between trade creditors and a debtor. If bankruptcy is inevitable, the bureau supervises the liquidation of the debtor's business assets for the benefit of creditors without the debtor having to declare bankruptcy.

Adjustment bureaus supervise meetings of creditors and a debtor, assist in development of extension and compromise plans, and, in case of liquidation, sell and distribute the debtor's assets.

Services of the adjustment bureau are made available to a distressed debtor through the following methods:

1. The debtor may come to the adjustment bureau voluntarily and seek assistance.
2. The debtor may first discuss the financial problem with an attorney or accountant, who may then bring the debtor to the adjustment bureau.
3. The debtor may discuss the problem with a major creditor, a member of NACM, and the creditor may refer the matter to the adjustment bureau.

4. A member of NACM may ask the local adjustment bureau to contact a debtor-customer, who is known to be in financial difficulty, for the purpose of calling a meeting of creditors.

The facilities of adjustment bureaus are usually available, without charge, for the calling of a creditors meeting to discuss the financial problems of the debtor. If the creditors choose to use the services of the bureau, a fee is charged. The amount of the administration fee is usually very reasonable and is based on a sliding scale: the percentage figure decreases for larger estates. The administration fee is usually paid by the debtor in extension or compromise settlement arrangements.

11

Foreign
Credit Decisions

The percentage of bad-debt losses in foreign trade is actually lower than that experienced in domestic credit transactions, according to the NACM records. Roland J. V. Faucher of Security Pacific Bank's international banking division explained it to me: "Most export credit managers are pretty sophisticated. They know the local laws and customs. More important, they know their customer very well. The export managers we deal with do an incredible amount of traveling."

But it is really more than just sophistication that keeps the loss ratio low (only about 0.75 percent according to Faucher, compared to from 5.9 percent to 13.0 percent for domestic credit transactions). International shipping of goods has all kinds of safety measures built into the transaction: insurance, goods paid on delivery, sophisticated financing arrangements (notes and drafts), and a number of cautious third parties (shippers, bankers, insurers).

For new customers, exporting companies usually require that the goods be paid for *before* they are picked up from the port. Goods that are shipped are many times insured, not only for damage, but also against the possibility of the importer going under because of financial difficulty or political uncertainty. Shipments of goods can be assigned to the foreign bank so that the title to the goods is in their name and they are responsible for payment or return shipment. Banks are usually involved in these transactions, both here and in the foreign country to which you are shipping. Express companies will not turn over goods to the purchasing company (importer) until they are sure it has title to the goods (bill of lading). All this adds up to a transaction that is much more secure than any domestic transaction will ever be.

The growth in foreign trade has been enormous in the past few years. There was very little foreign trade with socialist iron curtain countries until just within the past decade. Cuba was embargoed for fifteen years before trade resumed in 1977. The new affluence and creditworthiness of third world countries (especially those with oil) have given American exporters a greater demand for export goods than any other time in history. It is now inevitable that if a small business gets to the medium-sized business category, it will probably be engaging in some international trade.

In this chapter we will cover several important basic factors to understanding foreign credit transactions including:

1. International shipping, insurance, and market problems
2. Judging risk and making credit decisions
3. International financing with letters of credit and bankers' acceptances
4. International collections
5. International trade regulations (Uniform Customs and Practice for Documentary Credits)

INTERNATIONAL SHIPPING

Products are marketed to foreign markets by either direct or indirect means. Most manufacturers with relatively large overseas markets prefer to conduct their own export division. This is direct marketing. Other, usually smaller, businesses sell their products abroad through an export agency (export broker or commission house). This is the indirect method.

Direct exporting requires a sales force and other support such as people involved in collections, shipping, and accounting. Maintaining an organization overseas eliminates the need to pay a broker or middle-man as is required with direct exporting.

Unlike freight forwarders, who are paid a percentage of shipping costs for shipping goods, export brokers are paid a percentage of *profits* realized from the sale of goods. The most important function of the export agency is the assumption of the credit and exchange risks. Export agencies can perform all export operations including packaging, ship-ping, distribution, and overseas sales. The export agent usually takes care of details involving the manufacturer's shipment, but not always.

A company looking for an export agent to handle international ship-ping should choose one who (1) is quick to process documents, (2) is financially stable, (3) has extensive overseas offices, and (4) has a lot of experience. Roland Faucher of Security Pacific said that it would be a good idea to ask freight forwarders and banks for suggestions since they are involved in international trade daily.

Currency Exchange

In domestic credit transactions, of course, there is no problem with currency; everyone transacts their business and pays in U.S. dollars. Other countries have their own currency (over fifty monetary systems are used in everyday foreign transactions), and they all fluctuate in value against the dollar. For this reason almost all foreign shipments from the United States are required to be paid for in U.S. dollars.

The purchaser usually pays its bank in local currency (for example, Italian lira) and that foreign bank transfers funds to your U.S. bank in dollars. It is always possible that if the foreign buyer has been billed in U.S. dollars and the local currency (the lira) devalues, the (Italian) buyer may want to delay payment until the exchange rates are more favorable. In fact, this rarely happens because most companies involved in foreign transactions are sophisticated enough to know that this devaluation (or appreciation) is just a risk of doing business. The occasions when a devaluation is most likely to cause delay is when the devaluation is a large and unexpected one (for instance, the enormous devaluation of the Mexican peso and English pound against the U.S. dollar in 1977).

To assure stability in currency values in response to new govern-ments, disasters, and problematic internal affairs, the International Monetary Fund was set up. The IMF, as it is sometimes called, has about eighty members, each of whom subscribes to a certain amount of gold or currency to provide a huge reserve to promote exchange stability. If a member of the fund wants to improve its exchange position, the member "buys" the currency of other nations at rates lower than par value. It uses this money to relieve payment difficulties. When the rates of exchange improve, the member "repurchases" its own money from the IMF over a three- to five-year period.

The Export-Import Bank of the United States — Loans and Insurance

The Export-Import Bank (Eximbank) is the principal United States agency in international trade. Its purpose is to support and encourage international trade by private U.S. enterprises. The Eximbank supports trade primarily through insurance and loans.

Eximbank frequently loans money to foreign countries (about $5 million minimum per transaction) and businesses for the purpose of purchasing U.S. material and equipment. The bank also provides guarantees for exporters and may purchase the notes and acceptances received by an exporter from a foreign buyer. The Eximbank has four types of loans:

1. Emergency loans to maintain the stability of trade and exchange relations with other countries
2. Development loans (through DISCS) to support construction projects for large public and private enterprises overseas
3. Small exporter loans to U.S. manufacturers to assist in completing equipment sales abroad
4. Commodity loans to assist in the sale of agricultural products abroad (for example, some of our wheat sales to Russia)

Two types of insurance are available to the exporter to insure foreign shipments. One type, the major one, is available from the Eximbank. The other type of insurance is available from large insurance companies such as Continental Casualty Company in the United States.

The Eximbank insures foreign credit transactions against political risk and loss due to war. Coverages are for losses due to expropriation, prevention by law of importation of goods after they are shipped, and war or civil strife beginning after shipment. Also covered are losses due to cancellation of the buyer's import license after shipment, and the inability to exchange foreign currency for U.S. dollars. The Eximbank indemnifies exporters for 90 percent of the value of the goods lost.

Coverage is usually for 90 days at the rate of twenty-five cents for every $100 of coverage up to 30 days and increasing slightly after that. The coverage offered by the Export-Import Bank does not protect the exporter against commercial losses suffered because of the importer's failure to pay.

Other Insurance

Insurance to cover the exporter against commercial losses suffered because of the importer's failure to pay is offered in the United States by Continental Casualty Company. They insure shipments for up to 85 percent of loss due to insolvency of the buyer or its failure to pay within nine months of the due date. The policy could cover goods and sales of subsidiary companies located in foreign countries.

Insurance for damages of goods in transit because of shipping abuses or losses due to theft is available routinely from several insurers, but you should talk to the express company who is handling your shipping before you take out this insurance.

Time and Distance

Most foreign credit transactions involve large distances, which means that the seller has to "carry" the merchandise while it is being shipped and sometimes for an extended period (30 to 90 days) after the merchandise is in the foreign port. Since inventory that is in transit or in ports but not paid for does not generate money, the exporter has to take into consideration greater costs of inventory and longer receivable periods than its domestic counterpart.

Payments can be speeded up, of course, if they are shipped by air, but this is an unrealistic prospect for most products such as grain, cotton, minerals, or wood. Generally the exporter has to use bank financing to promote cash flow during the interim period between shipment of the goods and payment by the buyer.

JUDGING RISK AND MAKING CREDIT DECISIONS IN FOREIGN TRADE

In international trade credit, practices are generally very conservative. But because of the long distances and usually large amounts of goods involved, even small mistakes can be very expensive. In international business, the credit manager (or export manager) is usually as interested in the economic condition of the importer's country as the resources of the importer. Banks and agencies that report on importers usually include pertinent remarks about the country as a matter of course.

Probably the best sources of credit information about a perspective customer is the international division of the U.S. bank you deal with. Most large international banks have an international credit management service department which, for a fee, will make inquiries in foreign countries about your customer. The bank may already know about this customer from its own experience, or it may make inquiries at foreign banks (especially the ones it deals with), and also use special credit reporting information services. If your company has a small number of foreign customers, this service is undoubtedly the best for you.

If you have a large number of foreign customers, Dun and Bradstreet has credit reporting facilities in nineteen countries. International credit reports, which are similar to the more familiar domestic D & B reports, are available from the Dun and Bradstreet New York headquarters and from their overseas offices.

Members of the National Association of Credit Management have a foreign credit service through the FCIB-NACM Corporation. The service (formerly called Foreign Credit Interchange Bureau) provides trade records of foreign buyers to American producers. The report is similar to the domestic interchange report (Chapter 3). Members who send in ledger information rate their experience with particular accounts as "high," "good," "satisfactory," "unsatisfactory," or "undesirable." FCIB-NACM also offers periodic bulletins, consulting services, and discussion groups and lectures.

The most important factor in assuring good credit is to know as much as you possibly can about the foreign buyer personally. If foreign sales are for large amounts, it is very important that the credit manager or a representative visit the company. A lot of travel time is logged by credit managers involved in international credit transactions.

Typical Credit Patterns

Very seldom does international selling begin with open account terms. Before open account terms can be considered, several shipments have to produce satisfactory results and the exporter has to have considerable trust in the foreign buyer.

The typical credit pattern for foreign sales is to use signed draft letters of credit first, then usance (or time) letters of credit, and then, if the company is particularly strong and has shown good payment ability, open account terms can be arranged.

Figure 11.1 shows the typical international payment arrangement. This arrangement is for both sight draft (the buyer pays a foreign bank *before* the goods are picked up) and time draft (the buyer pays the money a specified period *after* the goods are picked up) letters of credit.

The transaction proceeds in the following manner:

1. The exporter (Hero Manufacturing) gives the title to the shipped goods (bill of lading) to its U.S. bank and assigns the goods to a freight forwarder to ship to the foreign country.
2. The U.S. bank cables or sends the title to the goods to its foreign correspondent bank and the freight forwarder delivers the goods to the foreign port.
3. The purchasing company (Purco) gives the money to the foreign bank and the foreign bank gives it the bill of lading. If the letter of credit used is a time draft, Purco gives the bank a promise to pay and the bank gives it title. Purco will pay off the amount in 30 to 90 days, depending on the time allowed by the draft. If the letter of credit is a sight draft that the purchaser gives the seller (Hero), money will be immediately sent to the U.S. With a time draft, the money is sent when paid.

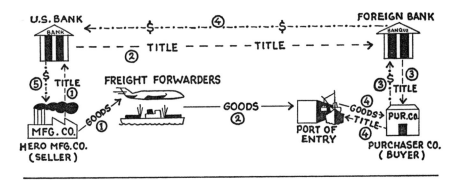

FIGURE 11.1
Typical International Payment Arrangement

4. The importer, Purco, goes to the port of entry, gives the freight forwarder, the bill of lading (title) and the freight forwarders give Purco the goods.
5. The U.S. bank pays the exporter, Hero Manufacturing, the amount due them. In the case of a time draft, the U.S. bank may issue Hero Manufacturing a banker's acceptance due when the time draft is supposed to be paid. Hero Manufacturing may discount (cash in for less than the face amount) this acceptance if it needs the money before the purchaser, Purco, pays the foreign bank.

The process for an open account (see Fig. 11.2) is different. It is similar to a domestic open account, but extra shipping time is required. In Figure 11.2, Hero Manufacturing sends the goods by a freight forwarder and mails or cables the title (bill of lading) to the purchaser, Purco, in a foreign country. The freight forwarders deliver the goods to the port of entry and Purco takes them the title and receives the goods. Thirty days later (or whatever the terms are), Purco mails the money due (or sends it through its bank) to Hero Manufacturing back in the United States.

INTERNATIONAL FINANCING

Marketing and selling merchandise in a foreign country involves a long period of time. For example, a shipment from the United States to the Far East cannot be completed in less than six weeks, and it might take the

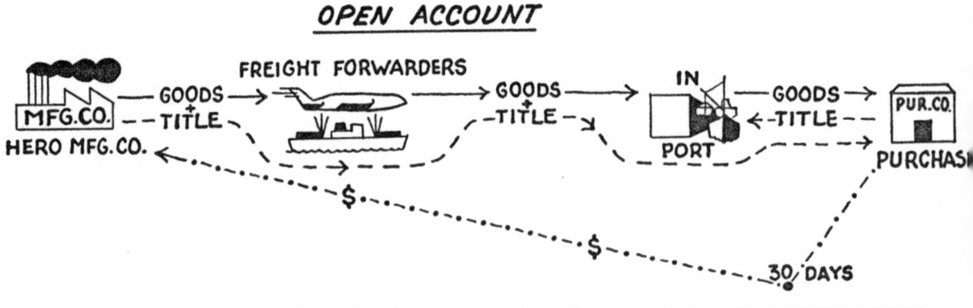

FIGURE 11.2
Open Account Process

same length of time for payment to be received. That means three months minimum is required to complete the transaction. The seller, or exporter, may not have the cash flow required to finance such a lengthy transaction, or the exporter may not want to tie up capital for such a long period of time. Therefore, the exporter generally relies on bank financing through letters of credit. Distance of the customer from the exporter, differences in laws and customs, and the difficulties of securing adequate credit information on countries abroad are also reasons that an exporter may choose to use letters of credit. Since the exporter would like to insure receipt of payment for its goods before the goods leave their own country, the exporter will also ask the buyer to go to the correspondent foreign bank and arrange a commercial letter of credit.

LETTERS OF CREDIT

There are few hard and fast rules for letters of credit. Almost every letter of credit is different in terms, and every action taken must be done on the merits and circumstances of the particular case. Besides the time period, however, export letters of credit fall into a few basic categories: revocable, unconfirmed irrevocable, irrevocable, and correspondent's irrevocable.

Revocable credits are credits, or more properly "advances," issued by a bank abroad on behalf of its customer (the importer) processed through a U.S. bank in favor of the exporter (or beneficiary). This "advice" or process may be amended or cancelled at any time and this may be done with or without notification of the exporter. Revocable credits are merely to assist the shipper in preparing and presenting the necessary documents. It gives no assurances that the draft and documents will be honored when presented to the advising bank (exporter's bank) or the correspondent bank (see Sample Letter 11.1).

An irrevocable credit constitutes the undertaking of the issuing bank to pay, if the credit provides for payment, and to purchase, without recourse to those holding the credit, drafts drawn by the beneficiary on the applicant for the credit.

When an issuing bank authorizes or requests another bank to confirm its irrevocable credit and the other bank does so, the confirmation constitutes a commitment of payment by both banks. The other confirming bank guarantees to pay against the draft, to accept drafts if the credit provides for acceptance by the confirming bank, and to purchase, without recourse, drafts drawn on the beneficiary.

SAMPLE LETTER 11.1
Revocable Credit Letter

CABLE ADDRESS

TRUST COMPANY
· NEW YORK, N. Y.,

ADVICE OF AUTHORITY TO PAY

CORRESPONDENT'S NO._____
_____OF_____
OUR NUMBER_____

(BENEF)

GENTLEMEN:

        WE INFORM YOU THAT   (O/B)

HAVE AUTHORIZED US TO HONOR YOUR DRAFTS FOR ACCOUNT OF_____

FOR A SUM OR SUMS IN U.S. DOLLARS NOT EXCEEDING A TOTAL OF_____

ON US, AT_____ TO BE ACCOMPANIED BY:

        (THIS IS A SAMPLE OF AN ADVICE OF AUTHORITY TO PAY – THIS
        CONVEYS NO ENGAGEMENT ON OUR CORRESPONDENT OR ON OUR PART.)

ALL DRAFTS SO DRAWN MUST BE MARKED "DRAWN UNDER   TRUST COMPANY
ADVICE NO._____".

DRAFTS SO DRAWN, WITH DOCUMENTS AS SPECIFIED, MUST BE PRESENTED AT OUR
OFFICE NOT LATER THAN_____.

THE AUTHORITY GIVEN TO US IS SUBJECT TO REVOCATION OR MODIFICATION AT ANY
TIME WITHOUT NOTICE TO YOU.

THIS AUTHORITY IS SUBJECT TO THE UNIFORM CUSTOMS AND PRACTICE FOR DOCUMENTARY
CREDITS (1962 REVISION), INTERNATIONAL CHAMBER OF COMMERCE BROCHURE NO. 222.

THIS ADVICE CONVEYS NO ENGAGEMENT ON OUR PART OR ON THE PART OF THE ABOVE
MENTIONED CORRESPONDENT AND IS SIMPLY FOR YOUR GUIDANCE IN PREPARING AND
PRESENTING DRAFTS AND DOCUMENTS.

                                VERY TRULY YOURS,

This credit/advice is subject to the Uniform Customs and Practice
for Documentary Credits (1962 Revision), International Chamber of
Commerce Brochure No. 222.

1388

PER PRO

SPECIMEN

All irrevocable credits can be neither amended nor cancelled without the agreements of *all* the parties to the transaction (exporter, importer, and the banks).

When an issuing bank instructs another bank by cable to advise a credit, and intends the mail confirmation to be the only operative credit instrument, the cable must state that the credit will be effective only upon receipt of such mail confirmation. Unless a cable states this or states "details to follow," the cable will be deemed to be the operative instrument. The issuing bank in that case need not send the mail confirmation to the advising bank.

Unconfirmed irrevocable credits are letters of credit issued by a foreign bank on behalf of its customer in favor of the exporter and "advised" (processed) through a U.S. bank. They contain an irrevocable obligation on the part of the foreign bank to honor the exporter's drafts and documents, provided they meet with the terms of the credit. This letter of credit cannot be cancelled or amended in any manner without the consent of the exporter (see Sample Letter 11.2).

Correspondent's irrevocable credit is a letter of credit issued by a foreign bank on behalf of its customer in favor of the exporter and advised through a U.S. bank to honor the beneficiary's drafts and documents. In addition, some other well-known U.S. bank adds its confirmation to the credit, obligating itself in the same manner as the foreign bank. The letter of credit must have the consent of the exporter to be amended or cancelled. It must have a fixed expiration date (see Sample Letter 11.3).

With *import* letters of credit (as opposed to the export letters of credit mentioned above) the same terms apply, but it is the U.S. bank that issues the letters for its customers here in favor of exporters from overseas. Said another way, the letters of credit are issued by a U.S. bank for its customer in favor of an exporter in a foreign country, usually located near and advised through one of the U.S. bank's correspondents abroad. See Sample Letters 11.4 and 11.5.

All letters of credit are issued: (1) in favor of a definite named beneficiary; (2) for a fixed and determinable amount; (3) in a form clearly stating how payment is to be made and under what circumstances; and (4) with a definite expiration date. Drafts are payable in a certain time, such as 30, 60, or 90 days after presentation (sight) or even longer."Sight" drafts are payable whenever presented. Eligible time drafts or usance drafts may be drawn with a maturity up to nine months (see Fig. 11.3).

Most letters of credit are cancelled when the total amount specified

SAMPLE LETTER 11.2
Irrevocable Import Letter of Credit

CABLE ADDRESS

TRUST COMPANY
• NEW YORK, N. Y.,

•

IRREVOCABLE CREDIT NO.

•

☐ Forwarded through   ☐ Copy sent to

•

•

Gentlemen:

We hereby authorize you to value on us,

for account of

for a sum or sums in U. S. Dollars not exceeding a total of

by your drafts at
accompanied by:

Partial shipments   permitted.
Bills of lading must be dated not later than

Drafts must be negotiated or presented to the drawee not later than

Insurance to be effected by
All negotiation charges are for your account.
    All drafts must be marked "Drawn under   Trust Company Credit No.   ," and all draw-
ings negotiated under this credit must be endorsed on the reverse hereof by the party so negotiating. If any draft is
not negotiated, this credit and all documents as specified must accompany the draft.
    This credit is subject to the Uniform Customs and Practice for Documentary Credits (1962 Revision), International
Chamber of Commerce Brochure No. 222.
    We hereby agree with you and negotiating banks or bankers that drafts drawn under and in compliance with the
terms of this credit shall be duly honored on due presentation to the drawee.

                                            Very truly yours,

F 3332
ABC 6-63
(10-63)

SAMPLE LETTER 11.3
Correspondent's Irrevocable Credit Letter

CABLE ADDRESS

TRUST COMPANY
· NEW YORK, N. Y.,

Correspondent's No.
Letter—Cable of
Our Number

ADVICE OF CORRESPONDENT'S
IRREVOCABLE STRAIGHT CREDIT

MAIL
TO

Gentlemen:

We are instructed by

to inform you that they have opened their irrevocable credit in your favor for account of

for a sum or sums in U. S. dollars not exceeding a total of

available by your drafts on us, at
to be accompanied by:

All drafts so drawn must be marked "Drawn under   Trust Company Advice No.   ."
This credit is subject to the Uniform Customs and Practice for Documentary Credits (1962 Revision), International Chamber of Commerce Brochure No. 222.

The above mentioned correspondent engages with you that all drafts drawn under and in compliance with the terms of this advice will be duly honored on delivery of documents as specified, if duly presented at this office on or before

THIS LETTER IS SOLELY AN ADVICE OF CREDIT OPENED BY THE ABOVE MENTIONED CORRESPONDENT AND CONVEYS NO ENGAGEMENT BY US.

F. 2629
ABC 7-65
(7-65)

SAMPLE LETTER 11.4
Revolving Revocable Credit Letter

CABLE ADDRESS   **TRUST COMPANY**
                                 • NEW YORK, N. Y.,

_____(DATE)_____-

REVOLVING REVOCABLE CREDIT
NUMBER_____

   (BENEF.)   FORWARDED THROUGH

GENTLEMEN:

      WE HAVE OPENED A REVOLVING REVOCABLE CREDIT IN YOUR FAVOR FOR
ACCOUNT OF_____FOR NOT EXCEEDING
                                           _____PER CALENDAR
WEEK NON CUMULATIVE, AVAILABLE ONLY AT THE OFFICE OF_____
_____BY YOUR CLEAN SIGHT DRAFTS DRAWN
IN DUPLICATE ON   TRUST COMPANY, NEW YORK.

           DRAFTS DRAWN UNDER THIS CREDIT MUST BE
           MARKED "DRAWN UNDER   TRUST COMPANY,
           NEW YORK, REVOLVING REVOCABLE CREDIT NUMBER
           _____DATED_____.

THIS IS A REVOLVING REVOCABLE CREDIT AVAILABLE UNTIL REVOKED AND
IS SUBJECT TO MODIFICATION OR CANCELLATION AT ANY TIME BY US.

IT IS UNDERSTOOD THAT ANY DRAFTS NEGOTIATED BY_____
_____, PRIOR TO RECEIPT OF OUR NOTICE OF MODIFICATION
OR CANCELLATION WILL BE HONORED BY US IF DRAWN IN ACCORDANCE WITH
THE TERMS OF THIS CREDIT.

                              VERY TRULY YOURS,

                              PER PRO.

This credit/advice is subject to the Uniform Customs and Practice
for Documentary Credits (1962 Revision), International Chamber of
Commerce Brochure No. 222.

1388

SPECIMEN

SAMPLE LETTER 11.5
I.C.C. Standardized Letter of Credit Form

ORIGINAL

CABLE ADDRESS

TRUST COMPANY
• NEW YORK, N. Y.

Cable Confirmation of Irrevocable Letter of Credit	Credit Number
	of issuing bank	of advising bank

DATE

——— **Advising Bank** ———

Applicant

——— **Beneficiary** ———

Amount

Latest date for negotiation

This is a confirmation of our cable of today requesting you to advise the beneficiary

That we have opened our Irrevocable Credit in their favor having the following terms:
"We hereby authorize you to value on   Trust Company
your drafts at   marked 'Drawn under   Trust Company Credit No.
accompanied by the following documents:

Covering

Shipment from	Partial Shipments	permitted
to	Transhipments	permitted

Special conditions:

All negotiation charges are for your account.
We suggest negotiating bank forward us all documents in one mailing.

| The amount of each draft negotiated, with the date of negotiation, must be endorsed on the reverse of the advice of this credit by the negotiating bank. If any draft is not negotiated the advice of this credit and all documents as specified must accompany the draft. We hereby agree with you and negotiating banks or bankers that drafts drawn under and in compliance with the terms of this credit shall be duly honored on due presentation." TRUST COMPANY | **INDICATION TO THE ADVISING BANK**

NOTE — THIS CONFIRMATION IS NOT ITSELF THE CREDIT AND ALL DRAWINGS MUST BE AGAINST YOUR ADVICE OF OUR CABLE AND NOT AGAINST THIS CONFIRMATION. |

Authorized Signature — Issuing Bank

SPECIMEN

F2713 E (4-70)

This credit is subject to the Uniform Customs and Practice for Documentary Credits (1962 Revision), International Chamber of Commerce Brochure No. 222.

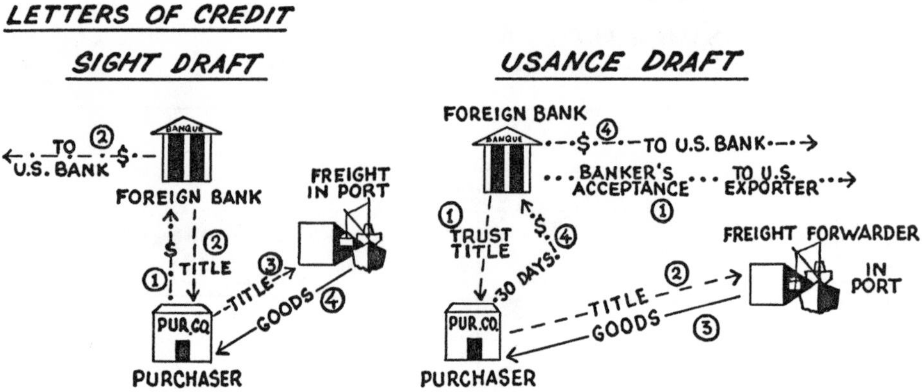

LETTERS OF CREDIT

SIGHT DRAFT

USANCE DRAFT

FIGURE 11.3
Usance and Sight Drafts

has been paid. However, they may be issued or amended so that they are renewable and available again to the exporter. Letters of credit can be issued in dollars or in any foreign currency. If they are issued in dollars, they are made payable at the office of the correspondent U.S. bank, and if in foreign currency, they are payable at the correspondent bank in the appropriate foreign country. International banks maintain accounts in foreign currencies with many foreign correspondent banks. Letters of credit are ordinarily for the named exporter and cannot be transferred to a third party.

Advantages of Letters of Credit

Letters of credit have the following advantages:

1. The burden of financing a transaction is borne by the bank and not the merchant. Neither the seller nor the buyer must extend credit, a function performed by the buyer's bank.
2. For the most part the exporter is not required to determine the credit worthiness of the buyer.
3. The exporter knows that if they have an irrevocable letter of credit they will receive cash or the equivalent upon delivery of the merchandise and at the end of the time period allocated.

4. The importer is required to make payment only when specified documents of title are received, and the exporter is required to deliver the proper documents.

How the Letter of Credit Works

In the case of an import letter of credit, after a sales contract is signed between the seller (foreign exporter) and buyer (American importer), the buyer goes to a U.S. bank and requests a letter of credit to be paid to the foreign exporter. The U.S. importer fills out an application for the amount, terms of payment, nature and quantity of merchandise, documents required, expiration date, and so on. When the U.S. bank then issues a letter of credit, it is extending credit to its customer (the U.S. importer) and must get approval to cover the risk. After approval, the letter of credit is forwarded to the beneficiary (foreign exporter) either directly or through a foreign correspondent.

After the shipment of the merchandise, the beneficiary makes out a draft on the issuing U.S. bank for the selling price and costs of shipment and presents it to its (foreign) bank together with the required shipping documents. The shipping documents include the bill of lading issued by the freight forwarder (which represents the title to the goods), an insurance policy or certificate, and invoices showing how the amount of the draft is arrived at. If the foreign bank (the exporter's bank) is satisfied that the terms of the letter of credit have been fulfilled, it buys the letter of credit from the exporter.

The foreign bank forwards the draft and documents to the U.S. bank for payment. If the documents are satisfactory and conform to the terms of the agreement, the U.S. bank pays the draft to the foreign bank. Then, the account of the U.S. importer is debited and the documents are handed over to the importer.

If the importer does not wish to pay the money owed on the draft immediately, the bank refinances the letter of credit on an acceptance basis. In the case of an acceptance, the customer gives the bank a draft promising to pay the bank in 30, 60, or 90 days for the amount of the letter of credit (the discounted amount of the acceptance) plus interest. If the letter of credit is refinanced in this manner or if the bank loans the importer the money, the shipping documents are not delivered to the customer. Instead the importer gets a trust receipt, the effect of which is that the title to the merchandise remains with the accepting bank.

Immediate payment to the exporter by the foreign bank is only the case with a sight draft. If the letter of credit is a usance (time) draft, the U.S. bank holds the draft or returns it to the foreign bank's U.S. correspondent bank until maturity. The U.S. bank then releases the merchandise to the U.S. importer on a trust receipt. When the usance letter of credit matures, the U.S. bank pays the foreign bank and collects its money from the U.S. importer, its customer. If the foreign exporter wants his money before the period of letter of credit maturity is due, his foreign bank can request that the U.S. bank discount the accepted draft (discussed in more detail shortly).

The export letter of credit follows the same procedures that we just discussed except that the exporter is a U.S. company selling goods to a foreign buyer who is then the importer. In this case if you were the U.S. firm you would be on the receiving end of the letter of credit that is issued by a foreign bank. This is the situation illustrated in Figure 11.1. In this case your bank would be notified by the foreign bank that the importer was being issued a letter of credit by that bank. If the foreign bank requests that your bank add to their confirmation to the foreign bank's irrevocable letter of credit, they issue a confirmed irrevocable credit.

If the letter of credit is issued calling for an acceptance draft from the foreign bank, the foreign bank marks the letter of credit accepted and returns the acceptance draft (banker's acceptance) to the U.S. exporter. The exporter can discount this draft at the foreign bank or any U.S. bank. When the exporter discounts the acceptance, he receives less than the face amount (total amount of the bill of lading). If the exporter takes an acceptance, he forwards all the shipping documents to the foreign (U.S. bank), pays it, and obtains reimbursement from the foreign bank in the customary way.

Documents and Definitions for Letters of Credit

Special care is always exercised in handling drafts and documents. It is the paying bank's responsibility to determine before paying or accepting that the papers presented are in strict accordance with the terms of the letter of credit or they might be refused by a customer or correspondent bank. Documents are usually checked by two different people at a bank. Otherwise, the banks may find themselves the owners of the merchandise, which might be perishable, difficult to dispose of, or worth less than the amount paid out. In other words, if they buy it, it is theirs.

Some of the documents that are important to the transaction, besides the letter of credit, is the bill of lading, the invoice, and the insurance papers.

The *bill of lading* is a unique document that we have mentioned previously in this chapter. The bill of lading is actually three documents in one: a title document, a contract for delivery, and a receipt for the goods from the freight forwarder to the exporter. It is a document issued by the captain, agent, or owner of a vessel (or transportation company) showing written evidence for the conveyance of merchandise by whatever means to its destination (the bill specifies how the conveyance is to occur).

There are two types of *invoices*, the *commercial invoice*, the one we are most familiar with, and the *consular invoice* which is only seen in international trade, and then only rarely. The commercial invoice is a document (sales slip) made out by the seller of the goods and addressed to the buyer, which gives a description of the goods, price, charges, and other details. This is the invoice every credit manager or businessperson is familiar with. The other type of invoice used in international trade is the *consular invoice*, so called because it is a detailed statement on a form provided by the consul of the country of the goods' destination. This statement describes the character of the merchandise shipped and is a certification of that country's consul. The consul invoice is seldom used and is usually for specified restricted goods such as munitions.

The *insurance* documents are fairly standardized and only rarely required by the letter of credit as a condition of paying the credit.

There are a few words used in connection with letters of credit (and other financial instruments) that might require some explanation.

CAD *(cash against documents)* means the same thing as documents against payments (D/P) defined below.

Consignment shipments are goods that are assigned to (put in the name of) the foreign bank. This is an extra precaution the seller makes to insure payment. When the shipment is consigned it means that the bank is responsible for payment for the goods if they are picked up. When shipments of goods are consigned to the bank, the bank is careful that the transaction results in payment, but this may increase the time required by a bank to consummate the deal. Consignment of goods is only used for sight draft letters of credit and does not apply to usance drafts.

D/A (documents against acceptance) means that the attached documents (usually this means title) will be released to the drawee only on acceptance of the draft.

D/P (document against payment) is an indication on a draft that the documents that are attached to the draft can be released only with payment in *certified funds* (cold cash).

Drawee is the party on whom the draft is drawn (the importer).

Drawer is the one who signs, or draws a draft (the exporter).

Endorsement is the signature on the reverse of a negotiable instrument (letter of credit or acceptance) made to transfer the rights of the instrument from one person or institution to another. It is a contract between the person in possession (the holder) of the instrument and all the parties who are affected by the transaction. The holder of the letter of credit orders the people affected by the transaction to satisfy the terms of the contract for whomever he has endorsed it to.

Payee is the party to whom a draft or any negotiable instrument is made payable.

Banker's Acceptance

A banker's acceptance is a draft, on the face of which has been acknowledged in writing the unconditional obligation of the bank upon which it is drawn to make full payment on that date. Acceptance of a draft is accomplished by writing the word "accepted" across the face of it, followed by the date, and the signature of the person or bank who is accepting it (acceptor). The Federal Reserve Bank defines a banker's acceptance this way: "A Banker's Acceptance is a time bill of exchange (frequently called a time draft) drawn on and accepted by a banking institution. By accepting the draft the bank signifies its commitment to pay the face amount at maturity to anyone who presents it for payment at that time."

In creating acceptances, a bank is lending its name, or in other words, its credit and not its money. The basic aspect of a banker's acceptance is that the credit of a bank is substituted for or added to that of the individual or firm. Since purchasers of acceptance look primarily to the name of the accepting bank, better known banks are in a preferred position for creating acceptances. Bankers' acceptances are used for both international and domestic trade, but primarily for international trade. In January 1974, of $9,101 million in bankers' acceptances outstanding, only about 24 percent were domestic, and 76 percent were international.

Figure 11.4 illustrates the process in a banker's acceptance transaction. The U.S. exporter, Hero Manufacturing, sells goods to the foreign importer, Purco, on a letter of credit that requires a banker's acceptance, or document against acceptance (D/A). The foreign bank agrees to the transaction. Then, the procedure is as follows:

1. The foreign bank executes a banker's acceptance in favor of Hero Manufacturing for a 30-day maturity and sends it to Hero. At the same time, Purco, the importer, agrees to pay the foreign bank in a 30-day period and the foreign (or issuing) bank gives Purco a trust receipt to pick up the goods in port.
2. If Hero Manufacturing chooses, they can now take the banker's acceptance and discount it at their U.S. bank for less than the face amount.
3. Otherwise, if Hero Manufacturing holds the banker's acceptance until maturity (30 days), Hero can take the acceptance to the U.S. bank and get the full face amount of the transaction.
4. After 30 days Purco pays the foreign bank and receives title to the goods.

Most acceptances arise under import or export transactions, either under a usance (time) letter of credit or by refinancing at the request of the buyer. A typical example would be a letter of credit opened by a

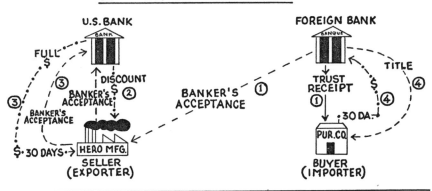

FIGURE 11.4
Banker's Acceptance Transaction

bank in Japan for the shipment of cotton from the United States to Japan. The letter of credit provides for the U.S. company (beneficiary) to draw its draft on a U.S. bank payable at a stated time, or after a particular date. When the letter of credit is presented along with the necessary documents, it is accepted and the beneficiary becomes the owner of a banker's acceptance. The acceptance can be held until maturity and presented for payment at that time or it may be discounted immediately, which is very common. The beneficiary (U.S. company) pays the cost of discounting because it receives less than the face amount of the banker's acceptance. Note that the letter of credit obligation has been met by the bank's acceptance of the beneficiary's draft and that the acceptance is now an obligation separate and apart from the letter of credit transaction.

Let us take the example of the U.S. cotton exporter (whom we shall call U.S. Cotton) to explain the flexibility of bankers' acceptances. U.S. Cotton sells for export either on a sight or time draft letter of credit basis and includes a price factor in their quote for the cost of discounting the time draft if the sale is on that basis. With these cotton sales on a time draft basis the buyer is financed through the use of acceptances. The buyer is not required to pay until the maturity of the acceptance. On the other hand, if the cotton had been sold on open account terms or time draft terms to the foreign buyer to be paid at the end of 60 days, a bank could finance U.S. Cotton, the seller, by accepting a U.S. Cotton note. If the cotton was bought on sight terms and the foreign buyer borrowed the cost from its bank in the importing country, a U.S. bank could refinance that loan by accepting the draft of the foreign buyer's (importer's) bank. Conversely, if the foreign buyer had not borrowed the cost from its bank, a U.S. bank might accept the foreign buyer's draft at the request of and under the responsibility of the buyer's bank.

A bank performs three distinct functions in connection with acceptances:

1. It creates them by accepting drafts drawn on them.
2. It discounts them, both its own and those of other banks when requested to do so by its customer or by the beneficiaries of its letters of credit.
3. It sells and purchases acceptances as part of its treasury money operations and for its customers who use these instruments for short-term investments. (Bankers' acceptances are sometimes traded on a public market for investment purposes.)

There is a commission charge for accepting a draft, which is a bank's fee for the use of its name. The importer who wants his seller (exporter) to have an acceptance pays this commission. If the holder of an acceptance wants funds before maturity of the acceptance, there is also a discount charge that is a charge for money. The exporter who receives the banker's acceptance pays this indirectly by taking less than the face amount of the acceptance when he discounts it.

INTERNATIONAL COLLECTIONS

Basically the same principles that apply to domestic collections apply to foreign credit transactions as far as assessing risk and collection letters and procedures are concerned. The biggest difference is that foreign collections of delinquent account debts are compounded by the ordinary problems of foreign trade — distance, language, and legal systems. Furthermore, exporting firms are more likely to assign the account to a collection agency than to their domestic counterparts. The reason is that the foreign collection agencies are a little different than the domestic ones. The foreign collection agencies, besides meeting with or writing to the account, will undertake to resell disputed goods or ship them back if they cannot find a buyer.

Manufacturers who are engaged in indirect exporting (using an export agent) frequently have an arrangement with the export agency to collect them. This is particularly true when the export agency is paid for its services by receiving commissions on profits and from sales, since "no profit — no commission."

Many foreign attorneys specialize in collection work for American firms. Banks that handle a great deal of export work and large export firms can usually recommend lawyers and collection agents in foreign countries.

Figure 11.5 shows how foreign collections work when a collection agency or lawyer is used. If the exporter with the delinquent account (Hero Manufacturing) cannot collect on the account and merely protesting the account will not guarantee collection, a foreign collection agency (attorney or agency) is hired. Then, the procedure is as follows:

1. Hero Manufacturing grants the foreign agency its power of attorney for the account, which allows the collection agent to proceed legally and to receive the title for the goods from the bank. If the transaction was not on open account, and a

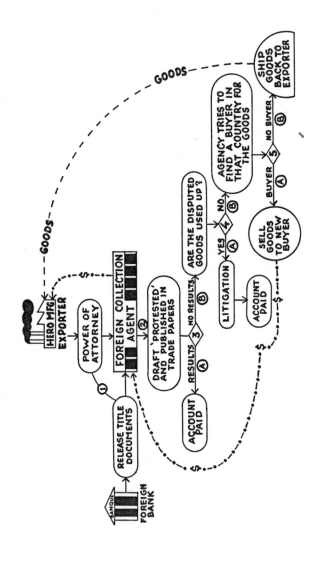

FIGURE 11.5
Foreign Collections

foreign bank is involved because a time draft was arranged, the foreign bank grants the title to the collection agent who has Hero's power of attorney. If the transaction was on open account, the bank, of course, will not be involved. Furthermore, if the foreign bank had issued a banker's acceptance for the transaction, then collection would *not* be necessary because the foreign bank has already guaranteed payment.

2. When the foreign collection agent has title and power of attorney it advertises in the trade papers that the account is delinquent and that the draft or arrangement has been protested. A protest is a notarized statement that such-and-such an account has not paid on time and owes money to Hero Manufacturing, the U.S. exporter. In foreign countries, having your account protested is a pretty serious affair and is considered extremely bad for the debtor company. In most cases this protest alone will be sufficient to get collections. Hero Manufacturing could have protested the account themselves and not hired the collection agent if they knew that it would bring results.

3. If the protest produces results, the account is paid to the collection agent and the agent forwards the money, less their fees, to the exporter, Hero Manufacturing. If the protest produces no results, the collection agent must determine if the goods from the transaction have been used. It is possible that the goods have not been used and the collection agent can reclaim them.

4. If the disputed goods are used up, then the collection agent will take the case to court and litigate for a dollar settlement. If a cash settlement is reached, the collection agent is paid the money, which it then forwards to Hero, after they have paid for their fees and court costs. If the goods are not used up, then the collection agent will try to find a buyer in that country for the goods.

5. If the collection agent finds a buyer for the goods, the goods are sold and the money is given to the collection agent who forwards it to Hero, after they take out their fees. If, on the other hand, the collection agent cannot find a buyer for the goods, the goods are shipped back to Hero Manufacturing, who must pay shipping charges and fees (a reduced amount) to the collection agency.

As we mentioned earlier in the chapter, collection problems are usually rare. As Roland Faucher told me, "Some buyers are slow, but the great majority of foreign buyers pay. It is very rare to have a dishonored draft. Right now we have about 1,200 accounts and only 15 of them are being protested." Faucher did notice one consistency in the protested accounts, however. "The more the dollar volume of the transaction, the more likely it is that they won't pay."

INTERNATIONAL TRADE REGULATIONS

Just as we have the Uniform Commercial Code in the United States (Chapter 10), international financial transactions are governed by a code. The international code is called the Uniform Customs and Practice for Documentary Credits (UCPDC), last revised in October of 1975. The code is put together by the International Chamber of Commerce, 38 Cours Albert–1 75008, Paris, France and is supported by the United Nations Commission on International Trade Law. This international code applies to both free world and socialist countries. The UCPDC is especially important if you are financing your trade with letters of credit or acceptances. It should be noted that although the UCPDC is generally followed and was prepared by the International Chamber of Commerce, it does not have any legal effect.

General Definitions

The terms *documentary credit*(s) and *credit*(s) mean any arrangement whereby a bank (the issuing bank), acting at the request of its customer (the credit applicant), draws up a bill of exchange (letter of credit or draft of acceptance). The person to whom the payment of the credit is to be made (usually the exporter) is called the *beneficiary*.

Credits are, by their nature, separate transactions from the sales or other contracts on which they may be based. Banks are in no way concerned with or bound by such contracts. Credit instructions and the credits themselves must be complete and precise.

Authorization for a bank to negotiate under a credit occurs either by (1) the bank being specifically nominated in the credit, or (2) by the credit being freely negotiable by any bank.

Liabilities and Responsibilities

Banks must examine all documents with reasonable care to determine that they appear to be in accordance with the terms and conditions of the credit.

In documentary credit operations, all parties concerned deal in *documents* and not in goods. Payment, acceptance, or negotiation against documents that appear to be in accordance with the terms and conditions of the credit bind the party giving the authorization to take up the documents and reimburse the bank that has affected the payment, acceptance, or negotiation.

If the bank, upon receipt of the documents, claims that the documents are not in accordance with the terms and conditions of the credit, notice to that effect must be given by cable to the bank from which the documents have been received (the remitting bank). The notice must state that the documents are being held at the disposal of the remitting bank or that they are being returned to that bank.

Banks assume no liability or responsibility for (1) the form, sufficiency, or accuracy of any documents; (2) the description, quality, condition, value, or existence of the goods represented by the credit; (3) the acts and/or omissions, solvency, or performance of the seller, freight forwarders, or insurers; (4) the consequences arising from delay and/or loss in transit of any messages, letters, or documents; (5) errors in translation or interpretation of technical terms and may transmit credit terms without translation; and (6) consequences arising out of the interruption of their business by acts of God, riots, civil commotions, or other causes beyond their control.

The applicant for the credit shall be liable to indemnify the banks against all obligations and responsibilities imposed by foreign laws and usages.

Documents

All instructions to issue, confirm, or advise a credit must state precisely the documents against which payment, acceptance, or negotiation is to be made.

The date of the bill of lading will be taken in each case to be the date of shipment or dispatch or taking in charge of the goods. If words clearly indicating payment or prepayment of freight appear by stamp on shipping documents, they will be accepted as constituting evidence of payment of freight. If "freight pre-payable" or "freight to be prepaid" or similar wording appears on shipping documents, it will not be accepted as constituting evidence of the prepayment of freight. Words such as "pre-payable" or "to be paid" do not indicate that payment has definitely been made.

A clean shipping document is one that bears no superimposed clause or notation that expressly declares a defective condition of the goods and/or packaging. Banks will refuse shipping documents that bear "damage" notations unless the credit expressly states the notations that will be accepted.

Unless specifically authorized in the credit, bills of lading of the following nature will be *rejected* by the bank:

1. Issued by forwarding agents.
2. Issued under and subject to the conditions of a charter-party. party.
3. Covering shipment by sailing vessels.

Bills of lading of the following nature will be *accepted:*

1. "Through" bills of lading issued by shipping companies or their agents even though they cover several modes of transport.
2. Short-form bills of lading (bills of lading issued by shipping companies that indicate some or all of the conditions of carriage by reference to a source document other than the bill of lading).
3. Those issued by shipping companies covering unitized cargoes, such as those on pallets or in containers.
4. Those indicating that the goods are loaded on board a named vessel or shipped on a named vessel.

A *combined transport document* is one that provides for a combined transport by at least two different modes of transport. Combined transport documents will be accepted by the banks if there is no form of document specified. If the combined transport includes transport by sea the document will be accepted although it does not indicate that the goods are on board a named vessel.

Where a credit calls for an attestation or certification of weight in the case of transport other than by sea, banks will accept a weight stamp or declaration of weight superimposed on the shipping document by the carrier.

Insurance documents must be as specified in the credit and must be issued and/or signed by insurance companies or their agents. Banks will refuse insurance documents presented that bear a date later than the date of shipment. The insurance document must be expressed in the same currency as the credit.

Commercial invoices must be made out in the name of the applicant for the credit and the description of the goods and their value in the invoice must correspond to the description and value of the credit.

Miscellaneous Provisions

All credits, whether revocable or irrevocable, must stipulate an expiration date for the presentation of documents for payment, acceptance, or negotiation. Where the credit stipulates a latest date for shipment, shipping documents dated later than that stipulated date will not be accepted.

In addition to the expiration date, credits must also stipulate a specified period of time after the date of the issuance of the bills of lading during which presentation of documents for payment must be made. If no such period of time is stipulated in the credit, banks will refuse documents presented to them later than 21 days after the date of issuance of the bills of lading or other shipping documents.

A transferable credit is a credit under which the beneficiary instructs the bank, which will make the payment, to make the credit available in whole or in part to one or more third parties. Bank charges for transfers are to be paid by the firm's beneficiary. A credit may be transferred only if it is expressly designated as transferable by the issuing bank and can be transferred only once. Fractions of a transferable credit (not exceeding the total amount of the credit) can be transferred separately.

WHAT TO LOOK FOR WHEN CHOOSING INTERNATIONAL BANKERS OR SHIPPERS

When you are looking for a bank to help you with international transactions, you should first try your own bank. If they have an international department, they will give you the best service; if not, they will be able to recommend a bank that does have a good international department.

Some other things that you should look for in banks are:

How many correspondents does the bank have in foreign countries? The more correspondents the better.

How fast is the service of the bank in transferring your letters of credit? (Roland Faucher of Security Pacific Bank told me that the bank should take a *maximum* of forty-eight hours for this task and that the average should be twenty-four hours). Many large banks have an extra work shift so that transactions can be handled quickly.

Does the bank have a long history of international finance or did they just get into it in the last five years? The more experience the better.

Does the bank trace and report promptly? *Tracing* is when your bank contacts the foreign bank after a period of time and gets an update on the status of the credit.

Does the bank pay your drafts and acceptances promptly?

Another way to find the best banks may be to ask freight forwarders for suggestions. Generally, freight forwarders spend a great deal of time dealing with banks and they know the good ones, especially the prompt ones, very well. Other firms in the export-import business may also be good sources for information about banks.

Speaking of freight forwarders, how do you know which one of them is the best? The same rules for finding out which banks are good also apply to freight forwarders. How many foreign offices do they have, how much experience, and how promptly do they act? Other import-exporters can also tell you which freight forwarders are the best. If you already have a bank you might ask them for recommendations of freight forwarders.

In closing, I would like to quote Faucher once again: "There are three cardinal rules in international banking: process documents quickly, trace and report regularly, and pay drafts promptly."

12

Credit Systems: Manual and Computerized

To have an efficient and effective credit and collections department, the credit manager should organize the department's paperwork and procedures. This chapter describes two different types of credit and collection systems that the credit manager can use to arrive at these goals. These systems are based on past experience and actual operating programs of several different corporations. You, as the credit manager, because of the circumstances of your own business, may not be able to use these suggested systems exactly as described, but they can give you an idea of the possibilities.

What happens from the time your customer orders your product? Which persons must be seen and what paperwork is required? How do you assure that first and subsequent orders are processed as quickly and accurately as possible? How do you keep track of the essential information on all the customers and how is the information reviewed? The system that you choose for your company should be able to answer all these questions.

MANUAL CREDIT SYSTEM

Figure 12.1 illustrates a typical manual (noncomputerized) credit system. By following the numbers indicated on the chart, you can easily see how the system works.

First Order

Buyco, a new customer, places an order with your company's (Hero Manufacturing Company) sales representative (Step 1, Fig. 12.1). Since this represents a new account, your representative fills out a credit application for Buyco Company (Step 2). The credit application contains the following information:

> Name, address, and date started for the customer, Buyco
> Legal form of business (corporation, partnership, or proprietorship)
> Names of the officers, partners, or owner
> Three commercial references
> Name of the client's customer's bank
> Product wanted
> Dollar amount of order
> Expected terms

This completed credit application is then forwarded to the credit department. The credit department checks the Dun and Bradstreet Reference Book to find out whether the customer is listed, the customer's rating, and how long the business has existed (Step 3). If the company has a high composite credit appraisal rating and a satisfactory estimated financial strength rating, the order is approved up to the maximum credit allowable for that rating. If the order does not exceed the D & B credit limit, an approval letter is sent to the customer with a copy to your sales representative and the order is released for shipment. If the order exceeds the D & B rating, the composite rating is very low, estimated financial strength is poor, or there are inconsistencies in the reports, credit information is ordered and analyzed. The following steps are taken: (1) a full D & B report and Credit Interchange reports are ordered; (2) trade reference and banks are contacted; and (3) a financial statement is requested from the customer.

The information received is then analyzed. This analysis could range

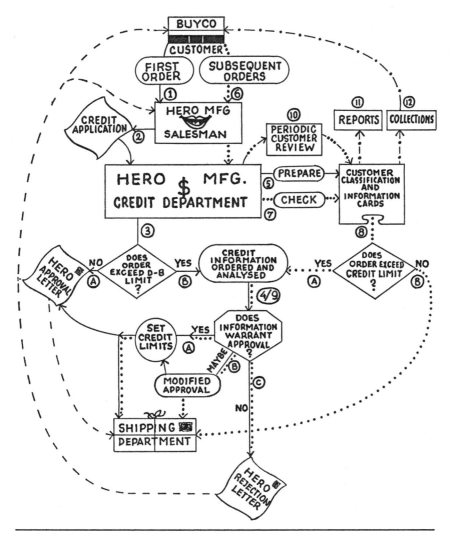

FIGURE 12.1
Manual Credit System

from a detailed review of the company's financial situation to a limited check of trade and bank references.

From the analysis, you should determine if the situation warrants approval (Step 4). If you determine that the application should be approved, a credit limit is set and an approval letter is sent to Buyco with a copy to your sales representative. Credit limits are set according to several criteria:

1. The kind of business. Is Buyco, the customer, a retailer, wholesaler, or manufacturer? Is the company a large regional company? Some companies find it economically feasible to establish a single upper limit for all retailers or all wholesalers. They may also have a two-thirds upper limit, one for large firms, and one for small- to medium-sized firms.
2. Consideration of the customer's needs.
3. Financial strength.
4. The past paying habits of the customer.

If the analysis shows that you can give the company (Buyco) some credit, but not the amount requested, you might want to propose a modified amount. If the customer accepts, you then set credit limits, send an approval letter, and release the order for shipping. If the information does not justify granting credit, you send a rejection letter to your customer (Buyco) with a copy to your salesperson.

If the order is accepted, the credit department should make a record of the new account and classify it for easy reference (Step 5). In the manual system, this is usually done with rolodex and other cards.

Customer Classification and Information Cards

We discussed in Chapter 3 the classification of customers into the four groups: automatic (or prime); semiautomatic (good); average (limited); and marginal. An automatic account is one of the larger companies in an industry. Since the automatic account always pays its bills and is in a strong financial position, it is generally given whatever it wants (a requirements limit). The semiautomatic is a highly-rated customer whose ability and willingness to pay are virtually unquestioned, but whose account is followed more closely than the automatic account. The average account, in which you may give approval according to the industry ratings, is one that might not be as strong as other larger companies. The average account usually requires some analysis by the credit manager. The marginal account is a definite risk. You can accept marginal accounts as long as its losses do not exceed its profits. If you classify all your customers according to these categories, it will be easier to make subsequent credit decisions. Some companies color code customer cards according to the kind of customer classification they fall into. If, for instance, the automatic account has a red colored card, anyone who is checking out an order will know to process it as fast as possible if the card they pull is red.

Customer information should be recorded on a desk volume kept by the credit manager and/or separate cards kept in a file or rolodex. On each card the following information is recorded:

Customer's name and address
Account number
Name of the product(s) the customer usually buys
Terms
Dun & Bradstreet rating
Date of the *D & B Reference Book* from which the rating was taken
Date the customer's file was last reviewed
Customer's credit limit
Who made the reviews and approved the credit limit

These cards are filed chronologically-alphabetically to insure customer review (discussed shortly).

Subsequent Orders

For subsequent orders the customer, Buyco, places an order with Hero Manufacturing salesman, and he gives the order directly to the credit department (Step 6).

The person in the credit department checks the name and address on the order with that appearing on the information cards discussed above (Step 7). This will immediately tell him the status and the credit limit of the customer. If it is an automatic account, the order is sent to shipping. For other classifications of customers, the credit person checks the accounts receivable ledger cards (discussed in Chapters 2 and 3) to see what the balance outstanding is. The credit person adds together the amount outstanding and in transit to the new order and determines if that amount exceeds the credit limit shown on the information cards.

If the order exceeds the set credit limit, credit information is requested (perhaps a financial statement). If the order does *not* exceed the credit limit, the order is approved and released for shipping (Step 8).

If analysis of the credit information indicates that an approval is possible, new credit limits are set and the order is released for shipping (Step 9). If the order is approved on a modified basis (on special credit terms such as COD or for a smaller amount), the order is approved and released for shipping. If the order is not approved, a rejection letter is sent to the customer, Buyco.

Periodic Customer Reviews

All customer's accounts should be reviewed periodically (Step 10) because credit ratings may change or present credit limits may be inadequate. The following is a recommended review period for the different classifications of accounts: (1) automatic accounts — once a year; (2) semiautomatic accounts — every eight months; (3) average accounts — every six to eight months; (4) marginal accounts — every three to four months.

For the review, the credit manager should look at the customer's file and especially the trade experience with the customer. Additionally, a current Dun and Bradstreet Information Report and other industry reports should be ordered and analyzed. If trade experience has been poor, financial statements should be looked at and perhaps a personal visit is called for. If, however, there is no dramatic change in industry ratings or payment performance, reviews are handled normally.

Reports to Management

We discussed management reports concerning the credit department in Chapter 4. Briefly, the following reports might be called for in Step 11:

1. Days sales outstanding report calculated according to the formula in Chapter 4.
2. Agings of accounts receivables, discussed in Chapter 4.
3. Special write-ups, sometimes required for annual reports (example, Chapter 4), or to describe particular circumstances of past-due accounts if the volume of these accounts gets past a certain company limit.
4. Periodic litigation reports if your company is involved in court proceedings against certain accounts.
5. Cash forecasts (briefly discussed in Chapter 6) on your department.

Most of the information on which these reports are based should be in your customer account folders, the information cards, accounts receivable ledgers, and the accounting functions of your credit department.

Collections

Figure 12.2 demonstrates how your collection letters (Chapter 7) and invoices should be sent to your customers in most cases (Step 12 in Fig. 12.1).

A.   All invoices should be filed chronologically according to due date. Three or four days before the due date, these invoices are transferred to another file.

B.   The almost-due invoices are filed in accordion files chronologically and alphabetically.

C.   If payments are not received 5 days after the due date (notice the time line on the right in Fig. 12.2), a duplicate invoice with a stamped reminder is mailed to the customer (Buyco).

D.   If after another 9 days (two weeks after the due date) there has been no payment, the first collection letter goes out. This can be a form letter.

E.   Two weeks later, four weeks after the due date, a second form collection letter is sent to the customer.

F.   Two weeks later (six weeks past due), a third collection letter — this time typewritten and signed by the credit manager — is sent.

G.   Two weeks later (eight weeks past due), a fourth letter is sent. This letter is also typewritten and signed and should be especially written for this case.

H.   One week later (nine weeks past due) either a telephone call or a personal visit would be in order. A promise to pay or a special arrangement should be worked out. If not, then go on to Step 1.

I.   One week later, ten weeks after the account was due, if you still do not have payment or a promise of payment, the fifth collection letter is sent. This letter should state that if payment or arrangements for payment are not made, the account will be sent to a collection agency.

J.   If at the end of twelve weeks there is still no payment forthcoming, the account should be referred to a collection agent.

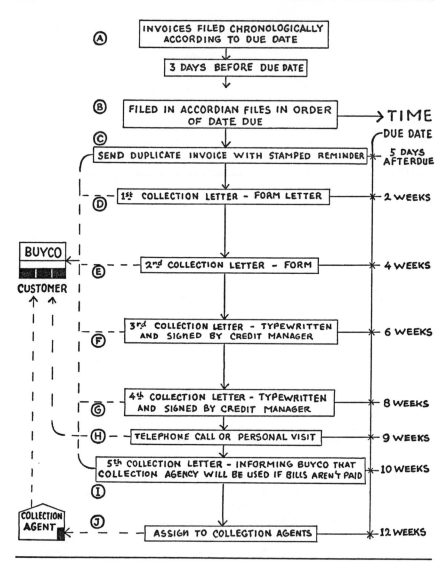

FIGURE 12.2
Collection Letter Procedure

The foregoing collection techniques may not work for your company but you should be able to come up with a good one styled to your own needs. A collection system that is easily followed and effective is a necessity for all companies.

COMPUTERIZED CREDIT SYSTEM

Every credit manager in the United States is aware of the impact of computerized systems, not only on credit and collections but also on business in general. Computers have become a part of everyone's daily life. You go to the bank and a teller enters your account on an on-line computer terminal. At the supermarket and department store, clerks punch a series of numbers in slick-looking buzzing cash registers. Some people have undoubtedly seen computer cash registers with optical "wand" readers. The clerk passes the wand over the optical code that is on the side of practically every consumer item and an LED (light emiting diode) number appears on the cash register.

Any operation that requires storage and manipulation of numbers and words can be handled more rapidly by a computer than by any manual system devised. There are enormous possibilities for increased speed and efficiency for those functions credit departments have traditionally carried out manually.

In order to develop a useful computerized credit system and thus maintain a position of importance and ever growing responsibility in a company, a credit manager must work with data-processing personnel from the beginning to see that all of the requirements of the credit department are met. It is better if the credit manager designs and programs the system personally. But, at the least, the credit manager must be knowledgeable about computer systems and how they work for the credit department. This section is designed as an introduction to the field. First, we will discuss what a computer system is made up of and what it will do for you. Second, we will talk about computer systems you can use for your company.

WHAT IS A COMPUTER?

Newcomers to computers often do not understand that a computer is not just a single enormous device. In fact, a computer consists of several distinct sections that can vary greatly in complexity. Not only does their speed vary but also the size of their memories, the number and speed of their input/output devices, the types of tasks that they are best suited to perform, and the number of peripheral devices and programs (software) that are available with them. A total computer is more than just an electronic brain. The brain must have a memory to store information, channels over which to transfer information to and from the outside world, and input/output devices that prepare data or record results. A computer without these features is like a person who can think but cannot remember and has no senses to provide information or muscles for the brain to direct.

A computer consists of three basic sections: the control section (central processing unit or CPU), the memory section, and the input/output section (see Fig. 12.3). The *control section* (CPU) processes the data. It gets the instructions from memory, decodes and executes them, performs arithmetic and logical functions, transfers data to and from the memory and the input/output devices, and provides timing and control signals. The *memory section* contains storage for instructions and data. The *input/output section* (I/O) handles the communications between the computer (CPU) and the outside world.

The memory section may use tapes, disk drives, or integrated circuits to store information. The CPU has some memory in it, but if you need

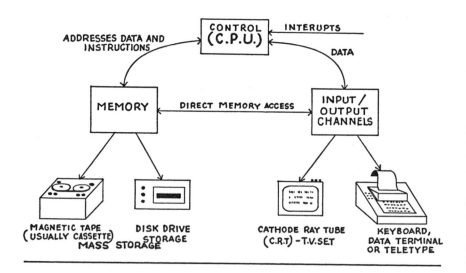

FIGURE 12.3
Basic Computer Design

more memory than can be provided in the CPU, which is almost always the case, you need to have peripheral devices such as disk drives or tapes to store the information. Information or sometimes whole programs or languages are stored on a disk or magnetic tape to be accessed by the computer when the information is needed. The computer may also store information on these devices to be used when it is performing a program.

The central processing unit (CPU) has memory besides the memory in any peripheral devices. These memories are the ones that have wired-in memory space required for arithmetical calculations, controlling functions, and language that is needed all the time and should not have to depend on external devices. The memory that is part of the CPU is a semiconductor memory and built into the hardware. This memory has both data and instructions stored on a permanent or semipermanent basis.

The memory section of the CPU contains other devices besides memory itself. The address decoder uses addresses to select particular memory locations. Other circuitry can provide control signals for the memories, allow the memory section and control section to communicate properly, and ensure that the memory section retains its contents. Special integrated circuits are used to preserve the contents of memories. Other integrated circuits are decoders, buffers, and latches. Therefore, the memory section of all computers contains several circuit boards, each containing a few thousand words of memory and some supporting circuitry.

When people talk about computers they sometimes describe them as having 8 K, 16 K, or 32 K of memory. K is the roman numeral for 1,000. When someone speaks of 32 K of memory they mean that the central processor has room for 32,000 bytes (each byte equals eight bits) of information. A bit is an on or off state at one memory cell location. The order in which a series of memory cells are on or off relates to a piece of information. So a bit is the basic unit of information in a computer.

Since the CPU must handle more than 1 bit at a time to store a complex message, bits are usually grouped into a fixed length. The smallest grouping of bits is a byte, which is 8 bits long. The most well-known grouping of bits, and the basic length that a CPU can understand, is called a word. Computer word lengths vary from 8 bits (a microcomputer) to 64 bit words (the biggest computer now made). Therefore, the best indicator of the size of a computer is how many bits in size its average word length is.

Word length is one measure of the power of a computer. A computer with a longer word length can do more work than one with a shorter word length, even if both computers operate at the same speed. A word length determines the amount of work done during each cycle. Large computers have long words. An IBM 360 has 32 bit words, a Univac 1110 has 36 bit words and a Control Data 660 has 64 bit words. Minicomputers have shorter words — 12 bits (Digital PDP-8) or 16 bits (Digital PDP-11 or Data General Nova). Microcomputers (the ones we talked about earlier as little computers) usually have 8-bit words. The biggest computers (with 32 plus-bit words) do more work in each cycle (can "crunch" more numbers), but this does not mean that they are more efficient for business purposes.

The input/output section of a computer is an interface between the computer and the outside world (including you). The computer is a digital electronic device that has its own internal clock and uses certain specified voltage levels to indicate bit states (on or off). Obviously, few external devices operate in the same way as the computer. The input/output section must convert the input data from the outside world to a form the computer can understand and convert the output data sent by the computer to a form the outside world can understand. This conversion may be a very complex task. Often the CPU will perform part of the conversion; some large computers have separate processors that handle input/output.

Connected to the input/output section is the peripheral equipment such as the *keyboard* (typewriter or teletype) and the *cathode ray* tube (CRT), which is a television screen. These peripheral input/output devices are for inputting information into the computer and for getting out information from the computer. These devices are hooked into the CPU's input/output boards, which interpret the information for the CPU as discussed in the last paragraph.

The input/output section of the computer (CPU) considers many characteristics of the transmitted signals to and from the peripherals in order to convert the signals into their proper input or output form. The input/output section of the CPU must consider several characteristics of the signals including signal level (voltage level), signal type (type of electric current), signal duration, timing, and signal format.

Computer Cost and Size

You may not be aware of it, but in the last five years, there has been a revolution going on. A revolution in computers. Most of us are aware of the big IBM 360 and other big computer systems that cost thousands of dollars per month to rent (few businesses, even rich ones, can afford to purchase one). But few people are aware of the new smaller computers (called microcomputers) that are coming down in price faster than calculators of a few years ago. It is now possible to buy the central processing unit (CPU) of a computer in kit form for only a few hundred dollars. The same processing power ten years ago would have cost tens of thousands of dollars.

The microcomputers (not much bigger than a bread box) are able to do almost all the number functions (accounting, calculating, storage) that a small business needs. And very few credit and collection departments need more computing power than the microcomputer can deliver.

You can rent one of these little computers complete with all the memory and input/output devices (keyboard and display) and software (instructions) you need for $300 per month from Administrative Systems, Inc., in Denver, Colorado. By the time this book is published, I am sure almost every major city will have a similar service. Compare that to the $2,000 plus per month that you have to pay for the more sophisticated IBM and Control Data Systems with basically the same functions. The main difference between large and small systems is the "language" they can use. Large systems can use COBOL and other sophisticated languages, whereas the small systems use BASIC, a simpler language. For most businesses this language difference does not matter. Is the additional sophistication worth $1,700 a month more?

Businesses across the country are also starting to realize that most of the time it is cheaper to have several smaller computers (like the micros we discussed) in each department than to have one large computer with a series of terminals. This is a trend that will undoubtedly accelerate as time goes on.

Microcomputers offer the advantage of allowing smaller businesses to have a computer they can afford. It is reasonable to assume that within the next ten years more than half of the businesses with sales over $2 million will have computers.

Small computers are not "number-crunchers" like the large computers. That is, small computers cannot do complicated mathematical calculations or mathematical models like the big computers. Small computers are too slow to do any major number-crunching. But a good many firms do not need such capability. The functions of business, mostly sorting, printing out reports and statements, simple mathematical calculations, and storage of information can be very easily performed by the microcomputers. Moreover, if you need additional storage capacity or additional terminals, you just add them on as you need them, making the cost even more favorable.

The only major disadvantage of the small computer is that presently there is not much software (instructions to the computer) available on the market. However, I am sure that this problem will be overcome within the next year. There is some software available now, enough for medium-sized or small companies, but not much available for special functions.

Based on individual needs, cost could vary from as little as $800 for the PET 200 to as much as $50,000 plus for the large scientific computers.

The Microcomputer Computerized System

Just as the microprocessor is a smaller brother of the large-scale computer, the small business system is a little brother to the large data processing system made by people like IBM and Burroughs. The small business microcomputer may be programmed to implement all of the functions performed by its larger brothers, but with significant savings in price. Some features, of course, like multiple simultaneous on-line users (several people using the computer at once) and foreground-background processing, are a bit impractical to implement on a microcomputer. This is because there are limitations on the speed of the hardware and the CPU/peripheral resources that are available. Yet jobs like calculating payroll for up to 1,000 employees, accounts receivable, and various credit and collection requirements for up to 2,000 accounts, and accounts payable for up to 2,000 venders are implemented easily. At the same time the computer can do inventory control for up to 2,000 items or general ledger for up to 650 accounts easily and inexpensively. All this can be done with one microcomputer. The small business microcomputer system is not limited to the above functions — it can perform virtually any record-keeping operation that you are now performing, and even some things that you would currently find almost impossible to do manually.

Typically, a small business microcomputer system consists of a central processing unit, a solid state "volatile" memory, some form of bulk program data storage like floppy discs or cassette tapes, a keyboard entry terminal such as a cathode ray tube (CRT) terminal or teletype, and a hard-copy output device such as a character printer, line printer, or teletype. We have already discussed these components and how they interrelate. Such a system, with 16K bytes of main memory and one-half million bytes of bulk memory, would be fully capable of handling the bookkeeping capacities noted and would carry a hardware price tag of from $5,500 to $10,000 (depending on the type of peripherals chosen). The input/output peripherals would adequately keep up with a single operator and the overall system throughput would satisfy most businesses with ten to two hundred employees (or $500 thousand to $5 million in annual revenue per year).

If the microcomputer was used only for the accounts receivable and other credit and collection programs, you could handle all the customers that would be generated by a company doing up to $20 million in sales.

When it is found that the work load cannot be handled by such a system (usually not because of the speed of the processor, but mainly due to the limitations of the system's input and output peripherals), a business need not scrap its present system and run to the open, often greedy, arms of the "big boys" with their $100,000 to $500,000 systems. It could simply add faster peripherals or additional complete microcomputer systems at $1,500 to $8,000 each. Thus, one system could handle accounts receivable, inventory control, and cost analysis. The two systems could talk to each other (so that data entries would automatically ripple through to the correct journals and ledgers) through a simple interface and some communication programs. Whether a single or multiple processor system is required, a small businessperson or a single credit and collections department would be better off financially using a microprocessor-based system instead of changing to a system made by the "big boys."

The small business microcomputer system, if purchased in a "turnkey" fashion (delivered with all the hardware and programming), should be very simple to operate. Normally, an office clerk would be assigned as the operator. The skills required to become proficient in the use of the system are a little more sophisticated than those required to operate a typewriter.

There are over one hundred small computer retail stories around the United States. These small computer stores not only sell computer hardware and peripherals, but they also service the machines, can point out classes you can take, and offer many technical knowledge services. In other words, the people at retail computer stores can tell you anything you want to know about the small systems.

Figure 12.4 is an illustration of what the keyboard-monitor and the central processing unit look like. Figure 12.5 is an illustration of what the basic small system looks like laid out. This schematic, box diagram

FIGURE 12.4
Keyboard Monitor and Central Processing Unit
Courtesy of ASI

shows an average size, small system with two disk drives, 32 K bytes of memory, television screen or CRT (called video terminal, see Fig. 12.4) and a hard-copy printer for printing out reports and letters. The diagram also shows the computer and BASIC language disc, PROM card, and connection boards. The boxes with dotted lines are "optional," but for our purposes, required equipment. The numbers in the boxes represent the price for the equipment in kit form (bottom left number) or assembled (bottom right number). This is for an MITS system (a brand name of one of the small computer systems). But there are several systems and some are better or cheaper.

The Bigger Computer System

There are several big computer systems for business and generally speaking these systems have been around for a number of years and have all the bugs worked out. Big systems can naturally do more work faster than small systems, use languages such as COBOL, FORTRAN, PL/I, or others that are more flexible, and have a lot more software already in use. Many people were trained in these languages so that they may seem more familiar. Small computers cannot handle these complex languages because they require too much memory space to be practical.

MITS DISK BASIC SYSTEM

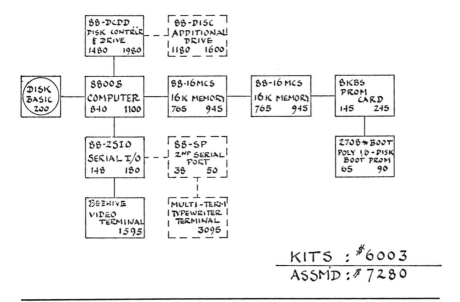

KITS : #6003
ASSMD : #7280

FIGURE 12.5
MITS Disk Basic System

One of the big accounts receivable and credit and collection systems is the Multiple Business Entity–Accounts Receivable Management System (MBE–ARMS) developed by Fortex Data, a Dun and Bradstreet company (See Figs. 12.6a and b). This system provides accounts receivable processing and supports related activities such as credit collection and sales analysis for one or more separate and diverse business organizations. Examples of multiple-related businesses that would use this system are businesses within a conglomerate, separate divisions, groups, or other corporate categories of a single entity. Account management, delinquency, customer statement billing, and system input and control information is provided separately for each business, location, region, or corporate division.

The features of the system include automated surveillance of receivable processing and support activities, flexibility of design, and control techniques.

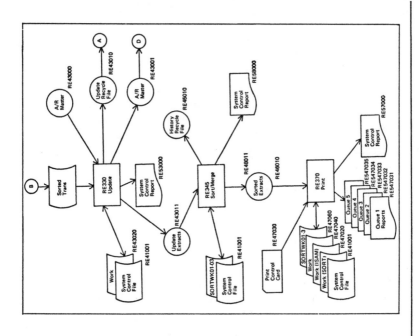

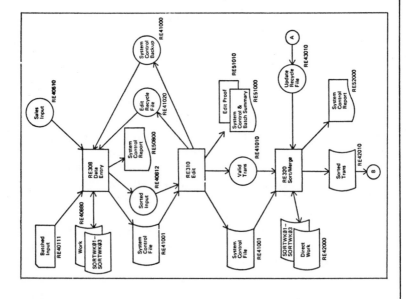

FIGURE 12.6(a)
MBE-ARMS System Flow Chart
Source: Dun & Bradstreet, Inc.

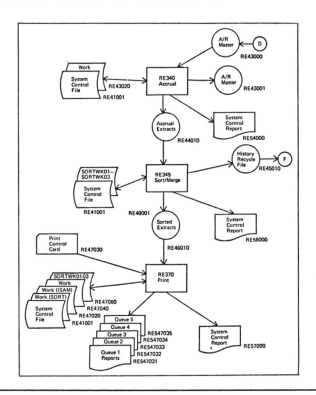

FIGURE 12.6(b)
MBE-ARMS System Flow Chart (continued)

Automated surveillance of receivables processing and support activities provide an automated solution to problems such as credit authorization and past-due collections. Features of this system are: (1) posting of activity to customer accounts on a real-time or daily basis with constant updating; (2) reporting a change in basic customer account data (causing a report to be produced along with a credit-collection worksheet when the customer becomes delinquent); (3) automatic preparation of past-due notices for delinquent accounts unless a deferral is ordered.

The system will apply finance charges; combine installment, balance forward, and open-item multiple accounts; do management reporting; and audit account balances. Each business can have separate write-off and discount policies and up to twenty-two billing cycles.

Control techniques include batch balancing, detail validation of all system input, and reports by type of transaction in dollar amounts and record count. Dollar amounts that cannot be posted are retained in the system in "suspense" for later auditing.

All customer account and business entity data is organized for each separate business organization in the system. Files can be accessed by sequential, index sequential, and direct methods. The customer segments of the data base provide detailed identification of the customer, account, balance and activity, delinquency, and sales history for the entire account as well as for each separate customer purchase obligation.

System reports include:

1. system control reports — show file activity and status
2. input/output reports — show which input batches are out of balance or contain certain errors
3. file maintenence and exception reports — indicate customer transactions that were rejected in the inputting process
4. suspense reports — transaction report in dollars where whole transaction could not be reported
5. dunning-billing reports — statements for each business entity, past-due notices, statements that require review or special handling prior to being sent to the customer, and collection worksheets showing the history of a delinquent account
6. accounting reports — for trial balances or aging of accounts receivable
7. conversion-addition reports — result from the addition of new accounts or changes in basic account data

Orders are received by the accounts receivable department in one of two forms: (1) keypunched and batched according to division to be entered into the computer or (2) written out in longhand. Orders are then batch-entered into the computer. *Batch entry* is when you take a lot of data at once (a batch) and enter it into the computer. The other method of data entry is *on-line* data entry when each entry is made separately at the time of the transaction.

USING A COMPUTER CREDIT AND COLLECTION SYSTEM

The last part of this chapter will be devoted to showing how a computer system operates on a day-to-day basis. I will illustrate some of the inputs and outputs that will normally be used and describe how the system functions as a whole.

In Appendix B of this book there is an illustration of a small computer credit and collections system designed and used by William L. Boggs. He explains in his own words how it works and some things that can be done with it. Reading his account should give you some additional understanding of these programs over and above what we have and will discuss in this chapter.

Figure 12.7 shows what a simple invoicing/accounts receivable program looks like and how the computer system works. It represents a beginning of the month initialization of invoicing and credit transactions during the month.

Inputting Credit Transactions

You sit down at the keyboard terminal looking at the blank television screen (which I shall call CRT from now on for cathode ray tube).

Your customer A-A Liquor just made a $151.30 payment on account and you want to update its account. Your company is a service business and customers are charged a monthly charge for use of your mailing machine. It is the first of the month.

To start the program you enter the invoicing and credit program name, for instance, INV. AND CREDIT, and you push the Run key on the keyboard.

The words DAY AND MONTH appear on the screen so you input the current date (2/25) on the keyboard. The CRT flashes the information seen in Figure 12.8.

In the upper left-hand corner of the screen you see the name of the customer, A-A LIQUOR, and his address. In the upper right, the display tells the monthly charge, PRE-BAL meaning previous balance, the total charges to date, and the PAYMENTS, which mean the total payments this month (zero in this case) and the balance due from the customer ($200.60).

In the bottom left of the CRT screen are the transaction codes, 1 for the previous balance if you need to add to or change the one recorded; 2 for payments; the numbers 3, 5, 6, and 7 represent extra services that your customer might request; and 4 is inputted if you want to stop the program. Following the transaction codes is a question mark and AMOUNT. The first question mark requests an input of what transaction code you want to use — payments, previous balance, extra services, or

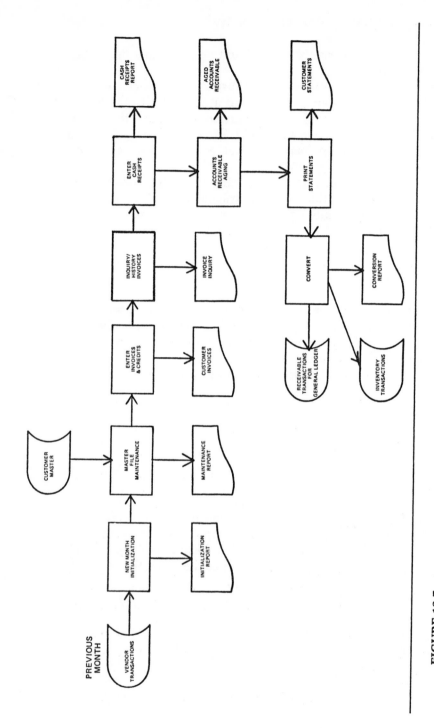

FIGURE 12.7
Invoicing/Accounts Receivable System Flow

```
ACCOUNT #   1
-----  --- ---
A-A LIQUOR                MONTHLY CHG:       $49.30
220 S. WESTERN AVE.       PRE-BAL:          $151.30
LOS ANGELES
                          ----- --- --- --- --- ---
                          TOTAL CHGS:       $200.60
                          PAYMENTS:           $0.00
                          ----- --- --- --- --- ---
                          BALANCE:          $200.60


TRANSACTION CODES:
1.  PRE-BAL        5.  INSTALLATION
2.  PAYMENT        6.  EXTRA WIRING
3.  I.D. CARD      7.  PRO-RATA RENT
4.  ABORT
?
AMOUNT ?
```

FIGURE 12.8
Inputting Credit Transactions — Step 1

---

abort. The AMOUNT? asks what amounts are applicable to the transaction code you want to enter.

Since you want to enter a payment of $151.30, you input "2" and "151.30" from the keyboard. The transaction code for payments is 2 and the amount of the payment is 151.30 dollars. When you input these numbers they will show up on the CRT screen (Fig. 12.9).

When you enter the payment, the display will automatically change and update the amount owed as seen in Figure 12.10. Notice that what used to be $0.00 for payments and $200.60 for BALANCE, now changes to $151.30 2/25 showing that a payment of $151.30 was made on today's date (2/25) with $49.30 BALANCE. The balance owed is automatically updated.

As you see from Figure 12.10, transition codes are sill at the bottom left. Assume that A-A Liquor orders extra wiring for the mailing machine that you are leasing to it. You want to put that information and how much it costs on its account. The extra wiring costs $100.

From the keyboard you enter "6" for the transaction code for extra

```
ACCOUNT #  1
-----------------
A-A LIQUOR                MONTHLY CHG:      $49.30
220 S. WESTERN AVE.       PRE-BAL:         $151.30
LOS ANGELES
                          -----------------------
                          TOTAL CHGS:      $200.60
                          PAYMENTS:          $0.00
                          -----------------------
                          BALANCE:         $200.60


TRANSACTION CODES:
1. PRE-BAL    5. INSTALLATION
2. PAYMENT    6. EXTRA WIRING
3. I.D. CARD  7. PRO-RATA RENT
4. ABORT
? 2
AMOUNT? 151.30
```

FIGURE 12.9
Inputting Credit Transactions — Step 2

```
ACCOUNT #  1
-----------------
A-A LIQUOR                MONTHLY CHG:      $49.30
220 S. WESTERN AVE.       PRE-BAL:         $151.30
LOS ANGELES
                          -----------------------
                          TOTAL CHGS:      $200.60
                          PAYMENTS:        $151.30      2/25
                          -----------------------
                          BALANCE:          $49.30


TRANSACTION CODES:
1. PRE-BAL    5. INSTALLATION
2. PAYMENT    6. EXTRA WIRING
3. I.D. CARD  7. PRO-RATA RENT
4. ABORT

AMOUNT?
```

FIGURE 12.10
Inputting Credit Transactions — Step 3

wiring and you enter "100.00" for the $100 that the service will cost. As you type in these numbers they appear on the screen (Fig. 12.11).

After you enter the numbers, the screen changes to update the customer's account (Fig. 12.12). EXTRA WIRING: $100.00 appears on the screen between PRE-BAL: $151.30 and TOTAL CHGS. The amount of TOTAL CHGS changes from $200.60 in the previous screen to $300.60 because the extra wiring charge is automatically added in. The BALANCE changes from 49.30 to $149.30.

The customer wants an I.D. card at $3.00, so you input "3" for the transaction code and "3.00" for the amount. The screen (Fig. 12.13), shows the new entry I.D. CARD: $3.00 and *updates* the balances.

A-A Liquor now wishes to make a payment of $152.30 to pay off the balance. You enter the transaction code "2" and the amount "152.30." The new account balance (Fig. 12.14) shows that the customer has made a total of $303.60 in payments during the month and now has a zero ($0.00) balance owing.

As you can see, the inputting is not that difficult and it gives you a

```
ACCOUNT #   1
- - -- -- -- -- --
A-A LIQUOR                MONTHLY CHG:      $49.30
220 S. WESTERN AVE.       PRE-BAL:         $151.30
LOS ANGELES
                          -- -- -- -- -- -- --
                          TOTAL CHGS:      $200.60
                          PAYMENTS:        $151.30       2/25
                          -- -- -- -- -- -- -- --
                          BALANCE:          $49.30


TRANSACTION CODES:
1. PRE-BAL     5. INSTALLATION
2. PAYMENT     6. EXTRA WIRING
3. I.D. CARD   7. PRO-RATA RENT
4. ABORT
? 6
AMOUNT? 100.00
```

FIGURE 12.11
Inputting Credit Transactions — Step 4

```
ACCOUNT #  1
--- - ----- -- ---
A A LIQUOR              MONTHLY CHG:      $49.30
220 S. WESTERN AVE.     PRE-BAL:         $151.30
LOS ANGELES
                        EXTRA WIRING:    $100.00
                        - -----------

                        TOTAL CHGS:      $300.60
                        PAYMENTS:        $151.30      2/25
                        -----------------

                        BALANCE:         $149.30



TRANSACTION CODES:
1. PRE-BAL      5. INSTALLATION
2. PAYMENT      6. EXTRA WIRING
3. I.D. CARD    7. PRO-RATA RENT
4. ABORT
?
AMOUNT?
```

FIGURE 12.12
Inputting Credit Transactions — Step 5

```
ACCOUNT #  1
------------
A-A LIQUOR              MONTHLY CHG:      $49.30
220 S. WESTERN AVE.    PRE-BAL:         $151.30
LOS ANGELES
                       I.D. CARD:         $3.00
                       EXTRA WIRING:    $100.00
                       --------------

                       TOTAL CHGS:      $303.60
                       PAYMENTS:        $151.30      2/25
                       --------------

                       BALANCE:         $152.30



TRANSACTION CODES:
1. PRE-BAL      5. INSTALLATION
2. PAYMENT      6. EXTRA WIRING
3. I.D. CARD    7. PRO-RATA RENT
4. ABORT
?
AMOUNT?
```

FIGURE 12.13
Inputting Credit Transactions — Step 6

```
ACCOUNT #  1
-- -- -- -- -- -- --
A-A LIQUOR                 MONTHLY CHG:     $49.30
220 S. WESTERN AVE.        PRE-BAL:        $151.30
LOS ANGELES
                           I.D. CARD:        $3.00
                           EXTRA WIRING:   $100.00
                                           ----------------
                           TOTAL CHGS:     $303.60
                           PAYMENTS:       $303.60        2/25
                                           ----------------
                           BALANCE:          $0.00


TRANSACTION CODES:
1. PRE-BAL     5. INSTALLATION
2. PAYMENT     6. EXTRA WIRING
3. I.D. CARD   7. PRO-RATA RENT
4. ABORT
?
```

FIGURE 12.14
Inputting Credit Transactions — Step 7

balance instantaneously. Of course, your company may have different transaction codes and they may not be printed out except in a book that the operator looks at. If you have product numbers, you would want to enter the product numbers for each entry.

The entries discussed here are for the *data base*, but there are other parts of the program for reports, sending out dunning letters either automatically or when the operator wants it done, aging accounts receivable, and so on. Basically, what the operator does is call the program and tell the computer what it wants done.

Other Credit and Collection Computer Applications

The collections program (Fig. 12.15) can print out letters and statements that go to your accounts. The computer program can be set up to print out statements automatically at the end of each period or overdue notices when the time allowed for payment is up. The program can also do this on request from the operator. The computer already has all the customer information including name, credit rating, and dollar transactions. With a letter program, it can print out standard form letters with

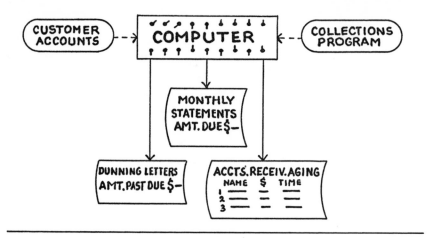

FIGURE 12.15
Collections System

the right amounts due and overdue and the customer's name and address. The program prints monthly statements addressed to your customers. The program produces aged trial balances to keep the department up to date on customer status. Dunning letters can be generated by the computer when the accounts are 30 days or 60 days overdue. If you look at Figure 12.2 of the collection letters procedure you can see how this manual system can be easily converted to a computer. The statement that is sent out 5 days after the due date and the first two form collection letters that are sent at 2 weeks and 4 weeks, respectively, after the due date, can be done by computer.

If you are processing an order for an existing account (Fig. 12.16) you can also use the computer advantageously. First, you manually add the order to the master card. If the account is an automatic account, which you can tell by looking at the master card, the order is approved. Master cards are filed alphabetically and have the following information: date order was written; divisional code; number of pieces; dollar amount appropriate for order; completion date; and classification of type of customer (which can be color coded).

If the account is not an automatic account, the master card is passed to the credit analysis department, or credit manager. The credit manager inputs the customer number or name into the computer and the CRT screen displays the following information (marked A in Fig. 12.16):

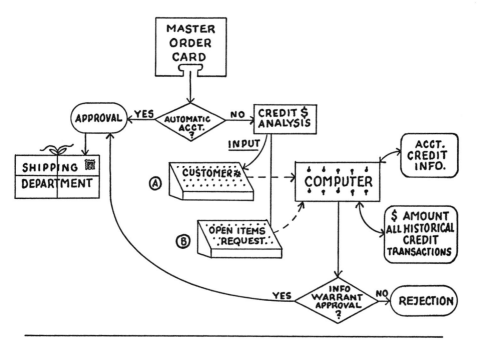

FIGURE 12.16
Order Processing Existing Account

Customer name and address
Account number
Dun and Bradstreet credit rating
Customer's credit limit
High credit and the date when it was reached
Amount and date of the most recent payment check
One year history of the accounts payments

If the credit manager needs more information on the customer the code for an "open items" display (marked B in Fig. 12.16) can be entered. The CRT will display additional identification data, the dollar amount of each singular transaction still open, a transaction code, and an aging.

If the information warrants approval of the order, it is approved and released for shipping. If the information does not warrant approval of the order, the order is rejected.

The computer will also generate reports for either you or top management (Fig. 12.17). For the credit department, the computer can generate reports of aged trial balances, hold order reports (showing which orders are not filled), and an aged summary trial balance showing all the account transactions. For management, the computer can generate reports of summary totals by type of transaction and summary totals by credit unit.

The computer is not restricted to the types of uses we have discussed in this chapter. You can use it to do automatic credit analysis and ratios to judge credit worthiness of customers. All the credit analysis information we discussed in Chapter 6 can be done by the computer instead of by the credit manager. Bill Boggs, who wrote the Appendix B program, suggests that you could even design a program to make complex credit decisions by using all the ratios and financial projection techniques and weighting the various ratios as to their predictive ability. All hooked together, the program could tell you if your customer has cash flow problems, inventory problems, receivable problems, growth problems, tax problems, and how he compares with the rest of the industry.

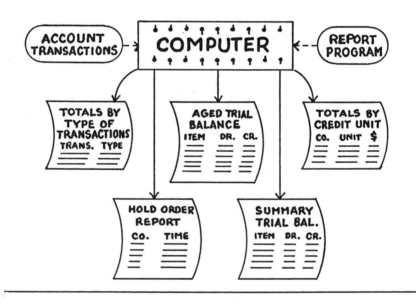

FIGURE 12.17
Computer Reports

APPENDIX A
Program for Credit and Collection Ratios

The following flow charts (Fig. A.1 through Fig. A.8) and program key strokes (Tables A.1 and A.2) for the Texas Instruments model SR-52 show a program that includes all the Dun and Bradstreet credit and collection ratios, except the funded-debts-to-net-working-capital ratio (excluded because of program length). This program, when put into a programmable calculator or (from the flow chart) a computer, will allow you to do all the necessary credit and collection ratios at a touch of the button. Using this program will cut your calculation time by about 30 minutes (if you just use a four-function calculator, you can cut up to 5 minutes using the program). And as every credit manager knows, saving 30 minutes per account can save days when you have several accounts.

When using the calculator program that I wrote, illustrated below, be sure and read the User Instructions very carefully. You input nine figures from the balance sheet and income statement of your customer; a tenth one, working capital, is automatically calculated. Care must be taken to

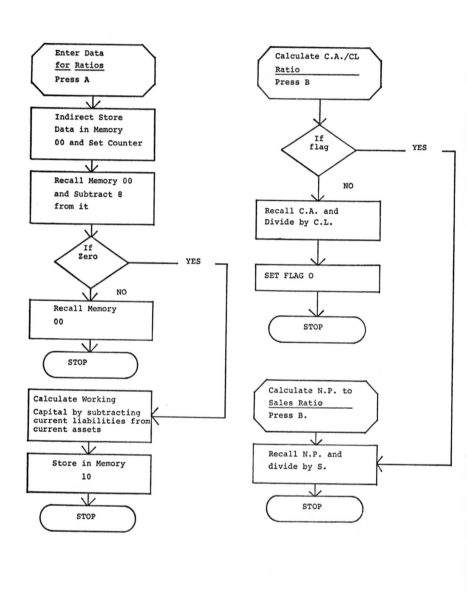

FIGURE A.1   FIGURE A.2

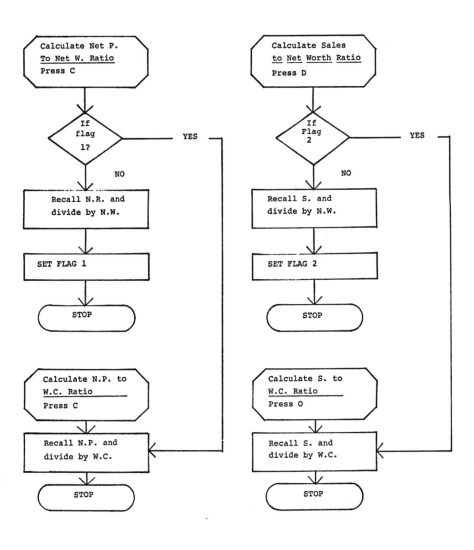

FIGURE A.3   **FIGURE A.4**

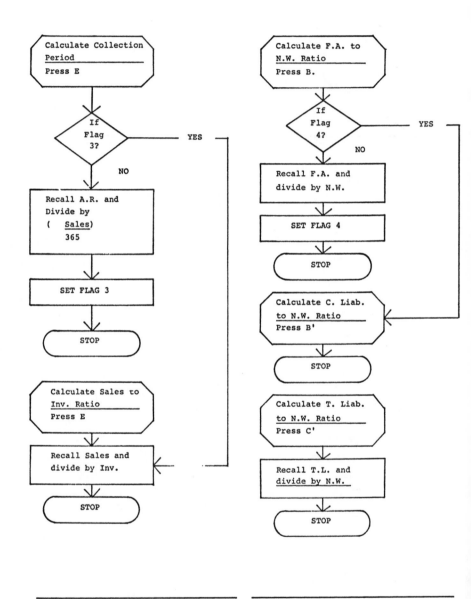

FIGURE A.5   FIGURE A.6

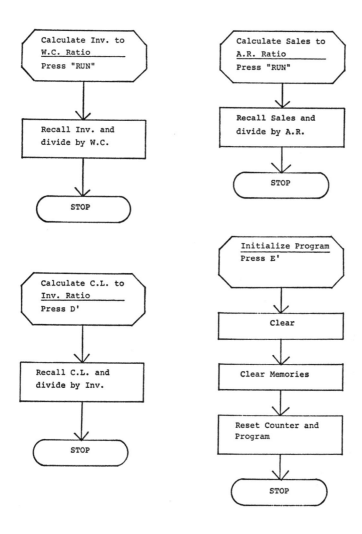

FIGURE A.7   **FIGURE A.8**

TABLE A.1
User Instructions for Credit and Collection Ratios

Step	Procedure	Enter	Press	Display
1	Initialized and Clear Memories	E′	E′	1
2	Input Data in this order:			
	Net Sales	$N.S.	A	2
	Net Profit After Tax	$.N.P.A.T.	A	3
	Accounts Receivable	$A.R.	A	4
	Inventory	$Inv.	A	5
	Total Current Assets	$C.A.	A	6
	Total Fixed Assets	$F.A.	A	7
	Total Current Liabilities	$C.L.	A	$Working Capital
	Total Liabilities	$T.L.	A	9
	Net Worth (Owner's Equity)	$O.W.	A	10
3	Calculate: Current Assets/ Current Liabilities		B	Times
	Net Profit/Sales		Bargain	%
4	Calculate: NetProfit/Net Worth		C	%
	Net Profit/Working Capital		C Again	%
5	Calculate: Sales/Net Worth		D	Times
	Sales/Working Capital		D Again	Times
6	Calculate: Collection Period		E	Days
	Sales/Inventory		E Again	
7	Calculate: FixedAssets/Net Worth		B′	%
	Current Liabilities/Net Worth		B′ Again	%
8	Calculate: Total Liabilities/ Net Worth		C′	%
	Working Inventory/Working Capital		RUN	%
9	Calculate: Current Liabilities/ Inventory		D′	%

TABLE A.1
User Instructions for Credit and Collection Ratios (contd)

	Sales/Account Receivables	RUN	Times
10	Initialize for new program	E'	
11	Steps 2 through 9 for new information	A- D'	

TABLE A.2
Credit and Collection Ratios — Keystrokes

Labels	Registers	Flags
	00 — INDIRECT MEMORY	
	01 — NET S.	
A = DATA	02 — N.P. AFTER TAX	0 — YES
B = CA/CL–NP/S	03 — ACCT. REC.	1 — YES
C = NP/NW–NP/WC	04 — INV.	2 — YES
D = S/NW–S/WC	05 — CUR. ASSETS	3 — YES
E = COL/PER–S/INV	06 — FIXED ASSETS	4 — YES
A' = NONE	07 — CUR. LIAB.	
B' = FA/NW–CL/NW	08 — TOTAL LIAB.	
C' = TL/NW–INV/WC	09 — NET WORTH	
D' = CL/INV–S/AR	10 — W.C. (CALCULATED)	
E' = INITIALIZE		

Loc.	Key	Loc.	Key
000–112	LBL*	005–117	0
	A		1
	IND*		SUM
	STO		0
	0		0

Loc.	Key	Loc.	Key
010–122	RCL		0
	0		HLT
	0	055–167	RCL
	+/−		0
	+		2
015–127	8		÷
	=		RCL
	if ZRO*	060–172	0
	0		1
	2		=
020–132	5		HLT/LBL*
	RCL	065–177	C
	0		If FLG*
	0		1
	HLT		0
025–137	RCL		8
	0	070–182	2
	5		RCL
	−		0
	RCL		2
030–142	0		÷
	7	075–187	RCL
	=		0
	STO		9
	1		=
035–147	0		St. FLG*
	HLT/LBL*	080–192	1
	B		HLT
	If FLG*	082	RCL
040–152	0		0
	0		2
	5	085–197	1
	5		RCL
	RCL		1
045–157	0		0
	5		=
	÷	090–202	HLT/LBL*
	RCL		D
	0		IF FLAG*
050–162	7		2
	=	095–207	1
	St. FLG*		0

Loc.	Key	Loc.	Key
	9		St. FLG*
	RCL		3
	0		HLT/RCL
100–2'2	1	030–142	0
	÷		1
	RCL		÷
	0		RCL
	9		0
105–217	=	135–147	4
	St. FLG*		=
	2		HLT/LBL*
	HLT.		B'*
109	RCL	040–152	IF FLG.*
110–222	0		4
	1		1
000–112	÷		6
	RCL	045–157	9
	1		RCL
	0		0
	=		6
117	HLT/		÷
005–117	LBL*		RCL
	E	050–162	0
	If FLG*		9
	3		=
	1		St. FLG⋆
010–122	4		4
	2	055–167	HLT
	RCL		RCL
	0		0
	3		7
015–127	÷		÷
	(	060–172	RCL
	RCL		0
	0		9
	1		=
020–132	÷		HLT/
	3	065–177	LBL*
	6		C'*
	5		RCL
	)		0
025–137	=		8

Loc.	Key		Loc.	Key
070–182	÷		090–202	÷
	RCL			RCL
	0			0
	9			4
	=			=
075–187	HLT		095–207	HLT
	RCL			RCL
	0			0
	4			1
	÷			÷
080–192	RCL		100–212	RCL
	1			0
	0			3
	=			=
	HLT		217	HLT
085–197	LBL*			LBL*
	0'*		105	E'*
	RCL			CLR
	0			CMS*
	7		222	RSET*

input the figures in the *exact* order the User Instructions explains. In all except the last two sets of ratio calculations (C' and D'), the first time you push the button you get one ratio and if you push the button again you get another ratio. In these last two sets you push the button for the first ratio but you have to push RUN on the calculator keyboard to get the second ratio of the pair.

Key E' is to initialize the computer and erase all the data that is already in memory. By using this key you can do one set of ratios, push E' and then input a new series of figures for another complete set of ratios. The A key is for all figure input (sales, profit, current assets, and so on).

The ratios on the program are the Dun and Bradstreet credit and collection ratios illustrated in Chapter 6 in the order they are used in the *Dun and Bradstreet Key Business Ratios Book* (except for the funded-debts-to-net-working-capital ratio, which is not included). The ratios are (in order):

Current ratio (current assets divided by current liabilities) (B)
Net profit to sales (B)

Net profit to net worth (C)
Net profit to working capital (C)
Sales to net worth (D)
Sales to net working capital (D)
Collection period (E)
Sales to inventory (E)
Fixed assets to net worth (B')
Current liabilities to net worth (B')
Total liabilities to net worth (C')
Inventory to working capital (RUN)
Current liabilities to inventory (D')
Sales to accounts receivable (RUN)

Special Note

The collection period ratio used in this program automatically calculates the collection period based on 365 days, or a one-year statement. If the statement you are using is for less than one year, then you should ignore the answer to the first ratio on the E button and calculate the ratio by hand. The ratio for collection period in days is: Accounts receivable net sales ÷ No. of days in the period.

APPENDIX B

Computer Credit and Collections

The following appendix contains a program listing in BASIC language for computerized credit and collections. This listing, for the program illustrated in Chapter 12, was developed by William Boggs. Following the listing is an explanation of a typical small computer credit and collections system written by Boggs illustrating a variety of things that can be done by the computer. The system he explains does not have a complete listing but hints at how the program can be done.

A discussion of a second program follows, quoted from *Kilobaud Magazine*, Issue No. 2, Vol. I, February 1977. This explanation was written by Lee Wilkinson to describe his method of printing out notices to his customers. He developed it for his small computer.

The information on small computer business applications is rather sparse now because the application of small computers has only been happening for the last couple of years, since 1975 for all intents and purposes. Hopefully, these program listings and explanations will allow you not only to get some immediate use and application if you have a small computer, but will give you a guide to further computer development for yourself and your company.

LIST FOR PROGRAM IN
CHAPTER TWELVE

```
LIST

10 OPEN"R",1,"TESTDAT"

15 INPUT"DAY AND MONTH";T3$

16 IF T3$="XXXX" THEN 1000

20 FOR U=1 TO 25:PRINT:NEXT

30 INPUT"ACCOUNT #";I

40 GET#1,I

50 FIELD#1,25 AS X$,25 AS Y$,15 AS Z$,5 AS A$, 5 AS B$,6 AS C$,

3 AS D$,7 AS E$,7 AS F$,7 AS G$,7 AS H$,7 AS I$,5 AS D2$

60 E1$=E$:F1$=F$:D1$=D$:G1$=G$:H1$=H$

65 D3$=D2$

70 E=VAL(E$):F=VAL(F$)

80 C=VAL(C$)

90 D=VAL(D$)

91 J=VAL(I$)

100 G=VAL(G$):H=VAL(H$)

110 B=0

120 T=0

130 B=(J+C+D+E+G+H)-F

140 PRINT"ACCOUNT # "I

145 CONSOLE 14,2

150 PRINT"----------"

160 Q$="$$#####.##"

170 T=J+G+H+C+E+D
```

```
180 PRINTX$,"MONTHLY CHG: ",USING Q$;C

190 PRINTY$,"PRE-BAL: ",USING Q$;F

200 PRINTZ$

210 IF D>0 THEN PRINT,,"I.D. CARD:",USINGQ$;D

220 IF G>0 THEN PRINT,,"INSTALLATION:",USINGQ$;G

230 IF H>0 THEN PRINT,,"EXTRA WIRING:",USING Q$;H

232 IF J>0 THEN PRINT,"MONTHLY CHG. (PRO-RATA):",USING Q$;J

240 PRINT,,,"---- -- ------"

250 PRINT,,"TOTAL CHGS:",USINGQ$;T

260 PRINT,,"PAYMENTS: ",USING Q$;F;:PRINT,D3$

270 PRINT,,,"  - ---- --  "

280 PRINT,,"BALANCE: ",USING Q$;B

290 IF B<0 THEN PRINT,,"* CREDIT BALANCE *"

300 PRINT:PRINT:PRINT

310 PRINT"TRANSACTION CODES:"PRINT"1. PRE-BAL","5. INSTALLATION":PRINT"
2. PAYMENT","6. EXTRA WIRING":PRINT"3. I.D. CARD","7. PRO-RATA RENT":PRI
NT"4. ABORT"

320 INPUTP$

330 IF P$="1" THEN INPUT"AMOUNT";E1$:E1$=STR$(VAL(E1$)+VAL(E$))

340 IF P$="2" THEN INPUT"AMOUNT"; F1$:F1$=STR$(VAL(F1$)+VAL(F$)):D3$=T3$

350 IF P$="3" THEN INPUT"AMOUNT";D1$:D1$=STR$(VAL(D1$)+VAL(D$))

360 IF P$="4" THEN 20

370 IF P$="5" THEN INPUT "AMOUNT";G1$:G1$=STR$(VAL(G1$)+VAL(G$))

380 IF P$="6" THEN INPUT"AMOUNT";H1$:H1$=STR$(VAL(H1$)+VAL(H$))

381 IF P$="7" THEN INPUT"AMOUNT";I1$

390 LSET X$=X$:LSET Y$=Y$:LSET Z$=Z$:LSET A$=A$:LSET B$=B$:LSET C$=C$:
LSET D$=D1$:LSET E$=E1$:LSET F$=F1$:LSET G$=G1$:LSET H$=H1$:LSET I$=I1$:
LSET D2$=D3$

400 PUT#1,I

410 G=0:H=0:E=0:F=0:T=0:C=0:D=0:R=0:J=0

420 FOR U=1 TO 15:PRINT:NEXT
```

```
430 IF M>1 THEN 20

435 CONSOLE 0,2

440 GOTO 60

1000 I=1

1010 GET#1,I

1020 FIELD#1,25 AS X$,25 AS Y$,15 AS Z$,5 AS A$,5 AS B$,6 AS C$,3 AS D$

7 AS E$,7 AS F$,7 AS G$,7 AS H$,7 AS I$,5 AS D2$

1030 C=VAL(C$):D=VAL(D$):E=VAL(E$):F=VAL(F$):G=VAL(G$):H=VAL(H$):

J=VAL(I$)

1040 B=(C+E+D+G+H+J)-F

1050 E1$=STR$(B)

1060 M1$="00.00"

1070 FIELD#1,25 AS X$,25 AS Y$,15 AS Z$,5 AS A$,5 AS B$,6 AS C$,3 AS D$

7AS E$,33 AS M$

1075 LSET X$=X$:LSET Y$=Y$:LSET Z$=Z$:LSET A$=A$:LSET B$=B$:LSET C$=C$:L

SET D$=M1$:LSET E$=E1$:LSET M$=M1$

1080 PUT #1,I

OK
```

COMPUTERIZED CREDIT/ORDER SYSTEM

The following is an elementary approach to an automated credit/order system. It is designed as a first step in the automation of a small business. This system is designed for operation by the currently employed office staff (not computer operators) with no previous computer training.

After the system has gained the confidence of management and office personnel, (it does not take long), other portions of office procedure can be added by simply purchasing additional programs. These additional programs may include inventory control, accounts receivable, accounts payable and general ledger.

The system we will describe was designed for a microcomputer, typically an Altair^{tm} 8800. The system requires one computer, one CRT terminal, one printer, and two disk storage units.

Suppose for a moment that this small computer system is installed in the offices of the Hero Manufacturing Company, as described in the text. The typical transactions from the time a new account is signed may proceed as follows.

The Hero System

The Hero Manufacturing Company salesperson lands a new account! The initial order, along with the application for credit, are sent to the Hero Credit Department. The department checks the D & B rating and the credit references, and determines the feasibility of extending credit. When credit is approved, the limit of credit is established and the new account is entered (input) into the computer — this is the Hero System.

The computer first asks for the transaction type, (Fig. B.1). In this case, we want to enter a new customer. So, we enter the number 4, (enter new

```
ENTER TRANSACTION TYPE:


1 - ENTER ORDER
2 - CHECK CUSTOMER CREDIT INFO
3 - CHANGE CUSTOMER CREDIT INFO
4 - ENTER NEW CUSTOMER
5 - CHECK CUSTOMER ORDER


*   ENTER TRANSACTION NUMBER . . . . . . . ? 4
```

FIGURE B.1

customer). The computer then asks a series of questions about the new customer. The questions are all plain English and completely nontechnical. Typical computer-to-operator conversation is shown in Figure B.2, (enter new account).

When you, the computer operator, have answered all the questions, the information is automatically stored on the magnetic disk for future reference, (this takes a split second). The computer then displays the transaction types again and waits for your next command. If you want to check the information just entered, use transaction type 2, (check customer credit info.), Figure B.3. You type the number 2 on the keyboard. The computer will then ask for the customer account number. Since our new customer, Buyco, is account number 19, enter the number 19. On the CRT, the computer will display all of the customer information previously input. This takes under a second.

```
NEW ACCOUNT NUMBER?  19
* COMPANY NAME . . . . . . . ? BUYCO INC.
* COMPANY ADDRESS . . . . . . . ? 22321 SHERMAN WAY
* CITY . . . . . . . ? VAN NUYS
* STATE . . . . . . . ? CA
* ZIP CODE . . . . . . . ? 91423
* TERMS . . . . . . . . ? C
* DATE LAST REVIEWED . . . . . . . ? 04/29/77
* REVIEWED BY . . . . . . . ? JM
* CREDIT LIMIT . . . . . . . ? 5600.00
* D & B RATING . . . . . . . ? A1
```

FIGURE B.2

Now that Buyco officially has a credit rating with Hero Manufacturing, it places an order. The transaction type to place an order is number 1, (enter order). The computer will then ask for the order date, usually today's date. Next, enter the part number being ordered. Then, enter the quantity, the salesman number, and the price per unit. To place an order in this manner takes under ten seconds! (Fig. B.4)

Now, the fringe benefits of the computerized system! After the order has been input, the computer automatically looks up the previous balance for Buyco, if any. The computer then looks up, on its magnetic disk, the credit limit previously established for Buyco. If the order we have just input *exceeds* Buyco's credit limit, an undeniable warning is displayed on the CRT and the order is rejected or "kicked out." If Buyco's order is within the preset credit limit, the order is stored on the magnetic disk and the shipping order is printed on the printer.

Now that Buyco's order has been accepted, the current account balance, order dates, and the *remaining* available credit are accessible in a fraction of a second by entering transaction type 2, (check customer info), and Buyco's account number, (Fig. B.5). Each time Buyco orders merchandise, their customer credit info is automatically updated, no file cards, no posting, no ledgers. Current account status is available for any of your accounts in this manner.

Going a step further, suppose we want to check or follow up an order for Buyco. Enter transaction type 5, (check customer order). The computer will ask for the customer account number. Remember, Buyco is

```
ENTER TRANSACTION TYPE:


1 - ENTER ORDER
2 - CHECK CUSTOMER CREDIT INFO
3 - CHANGE CUSTOMER CREDIT INFO
4 - ENTER NEW CUSTOMER
5 - CHECK CUSTOMER ORDER


*  ENTER TRANSACTION NUMBER . . . . . . . ? 2


*  ENTER CUSTOMER ACCOUNT NUMBER . . . . . . . ? 19


              * BUYCO INC.
              * 22321 SHERMAN WAY
              * VAN NUYS
              * CA, 91423            ACCOUNT # 19


==========================================================

TERMS . . . . . . .            C

LAST REVIEW . . . . . . .      04/29/77

REVIEWED BY . . . . . . .      JM

CREDIT LIMIT . . . . . . .     $  5600.00

D & B RATING . . . . . . .     A1

CURRENT BALANCE . . . . . . .  $     0.00

ORDER DATES . . . . . . .      : : : :

AVAILABLE CREDIT . . . . . . . $  5600.00
```

FIGURE B.3

account number 19. Enter number 19. The computer will then display, on the CRT, all order activity for Buyco, the part number ordered, the date ordered, the salesman number, the unit price, and the extended price, (quantity times units ordered). Buyco's current balance will be displayed as a total, (Fig. B.6).

If at any time it becomes necessasry to change Buyco's customer

```
ENTER TRANSACTION TYPE:


1 - ENTER ORDER
2 - CHECK CUSTOMER CREDIT INFO
3 - CHANGE CUSTOMER CREDIT INFO
4 - ENTER NEW CUSTOMER
5 - CHECK CUSTOMER ORDER


*  ENTER TRANSACTION NUMBER . . . . . . . . ? 1
*  ENTER CUSTOMER ACCOUNT NUMBER . . . . . . . ? 19


*  ORDER DATE . . . . . . . ? 04/29/77
*  PART NUMBER . . . . . . . ? 3312
*  QUANTITY . . . . . . . ? 45
*  SALESMAN . . . . . . . ? 02
*  PIECE PRICE . . . . . . . ? 1.98
```

FIGURE B.4

```
*  BUYCO INC.
*  22321 SHERMAN WAY
*  VAN NUYS
*  CA, 91423                    ACCOUNT # 19


=========================================================

TERMS . . . . . . .              C

LAST REVIEW . . . . . . .        04/29/77

REVIEWED BY . . . . . . .        JM

CREDIT LIMIT . . . . . . .       $  5600.00

D & B RATING . . . . . . .       A1

CURRENT BALANCE . . . . . . .    $    89.10

ORDER DATES . . . . . . .        04/29/77 : : : :

AVAILABLE CREDIT . . . . . . .   $  5510.90
```

FIGURE B.5

credit information, transaction type 3 would be used, followed by Buyco's account number and the appropriate revised information.

FOR THE (NOT SO DISTANT) FUTURE

To project out a computerized credit/order system, think in terms of the information necessary to conduct ordinary business on a manual basis.

1. New accounts must be logged.
2. Orders must be logged.
3. Order balances must be checked to not exceed credit limit.
4. Orders must be traceable for follow up.
5. Available credit should be easily verified.

```
    ENTER TRANSACTION TYPE:


    1 - ENTER ORDER
    2 - CHECK CUSTOMER CREDIT INFO
    3 - CHANGE CUSTOMER CREDIT INFO
    4 - ENTER NEW CUSTOMER
    5 - CHECK CUSTOMER ORDER


    *   ENTER TRANSACTION NUMBER . . . . . . . ? 5
    *   ENTER CUSTOMER ACCOUNT NUMBER . . . . . . . ? 19



    ACCOUNT # 19
    PART #     QUANTITY    SALESMAN    UNIT PR.    EXT. PR.
    ====================================================
    3312         45          02         1.98      $  89.10
    04/29/77
    --------------------                          --------
                                                  $  89.10
```

FIGURE B.6

Now, instead of logging information on ledger cards, in file folders or in accordion files, consider that under a computerized credit/order system, with proper programming, the following additional information

```
              * BUYCO INC.
              * 22321 SHERMAN WAY
              * VAN NUYS
              * CA, 91423              ACCOUNT # 19
=========================================================
```

TERMS   C

LAST REVIEW 04/29/77

REVIEWED BY . . . .   JM

CREDIT LIMIT . . . . $ 5600.00

D & B RATING A1

CURRENT BALANCE . . . . $ 6089.10

ORDER DATES . . . .   :04/29/77:04/30/77::

(* * * CREDIT LINE OVER EXTENDED * * *) $ -489.10

ENTER TRANSACTION TYPE:

1 - ENTER ORDER
2 - CHECK CUSTOMER CREDIT INFO
3 - CHANGE CUSTOMER CREDIT INFO
4 - ENTER NEW CUSTOMER
5 - CHECK CUSTOMER ORDER

*   ENTER TRANSACTION NUMBER . . . . ? 5
*   ENTER CUSTOMER ACCOUNT NUMBER . . . . ? 19

ACCOUNT # 19

PART #	QUANTITY	SALESMAN	UNIT PR.	EXT PR.
3312	45	02	1.98	$ 89.10
04/29/77				
3342	4	01	1500.	$6000.00
04/30/77				
				$6089.10

        * * WARNING - CREDIT LINE EXCEEDED * *

FIGURE B.7

---

about your customers and about your organization can be obtained without any additional entries and at *no additional labor expense:*

1. Salesmen commissions can be automatically maintained using the information existing in the customer order log.
2. Terms of accounts can be checked and changed (to increase immediate cash flow) from customer credit information.
3. Manufacturing requirements can be projected from information in the customer order log, (who's ordering what? and how many?).
4. Customer credit review can be scheduled from the "date last reviewed" section of the customer credit information.
5. Current credit policies may be modified according to number of "credit limit exceeded" occurrences.

COMPUTERIZED STATEMENT . . . THE ANSWER TO SLOW-PAYING CUSTOMERS

This program was written in MITS 8K BASIC for my Altair 8800 and allows me to keep my accounts receivable on cassette through the CSAVE feature.

Let me qualify my expertise in programming. When I purchased my Altair in November of 1975, I had never seen a computer operate. So I am a complete neophyte in software, but I enjoy the challenge of creating. My primary interest is in amateur radio computing, but, in order to justify the cost of the computer, I use it in my small business of photography.

Since I didn't have access to a floppy disc or a CRT, I wrote the program to accomplish the desired results as quickly as possible using my KSR-33 teletype. The inconvenience of having to up-date the data statements by retyping the *previous balance, payments made* and *balance due* each month, is offset by the ease of preparation. When preparing statements, I can now go watch television or play ham radio knowing that when I come back in an hour or so my statements will be prepared and ready for stuffing into window envelopes.

I soon became aware of another advantage of this method of sending statements — increased speed of collection. The first month we used the program, our accounts receivable return was 100%. *Customers indicated that they didn't want the computer company (the one "doing our billing") to think they were tardy with their payments!*

When the program is first called up it asks what function you wish to use: (1) list data statements; (2) search for a particular account number; (3) prepare the actual statements. On occasion, I have decided that I should change some of the data (e.g., closing an account) on a customer while the program is running. The program can search for the account number, list out the information and then continue running the statements from the name. You type control C if only the statement is desired. This function is handy if the customer comes in and wants to know his or her balance. The computer *can* easily prepare a statement on the spot.

Since my version of BASIC does not allow me to store variables, the data statement method of entry was chosen. The balance statements were input as string statements since I do not personally care for the floating decimal point style of deleting trailing zeros. The inclusion of the "bell," after the "statements finished" print out, alerts me that the program is over and that I should turn off the teletype in order to conserve the clutches.

The ideas used in this program could probably be condensed and simplified by a professional programmer; however, the program works for me and it may give you an idea how to start your own accounts receivable adaptation for your small business or other uses.[1]

[1]Program listing appears in an article by Lee Wilkinson, *Kilobaud Magazine*, Vol. I, Issue No. 2, February 1977, pp. 134–135.

Bibliography

BOOKS

Barzman, Sol. *Everyday Credit Checking: A Practical Guide.* New York: Thomas Y. Crowell Co., 1973.

Beckman, Theodore N. *Credit and Collections Management and Theory.* New York: McGraw Hill, 1962.

Chapin, Albert F., and Hassett, George E., Jr. *Credit and Collections Principles and Practice.* New York: McGraw Hill, 1960.

Harrington, J. A. *Specifics on Commercial Letters of Credit and Banker's Acceptance.* New Jersey: Scott Printing Corp., 1974.

Hayes, Rick Stephan. *Business Loans: A Guide to Money Sources and How to Approach Them Successfully.* Boston: CBI Publishing Company, Inc., 1977.

Miller, Donald E., and Relkin, Donald B. *Improving Credit Practice.* American Management Association, New York, 1971.

Redding, Harold T., and Knight, Guyon H. *The Dun and Bradstreet Handbook of Credit and Collections.* New York: Thomas Y. Crowell Co., 1974.

PAMPHLETS AND INDUSTRY PUBLICATIONS

Credit Managers Association of Southern California (affiliate of National Association of Credit Management):
NACIS Reports — Report forms for Credit Interchange Bureau and Collection Division.
The Computer System Center *Product Catalog,* Atlanta, Georgia.
Dun and Bradstreet publications: *Dun and Bradstreet Key Business Ratios, Dun and Bradstreet Reference Book, Dun and Bradstreet—A Chronology of Progress, Dun and Bradstreet Reference Book: How to use it to enhance business opportunities . . . speed important decisions, How to Use Your Dun and Bradstreet Service Most Effectively, The Pitfalls in Managing a Small Business* International Chamber of Commerce, *Uniform Customs and Practice for Documentary Credits,* 1976.

MAGAZINE ARTICLES

Anderlik, John A. "How Bankers Make Their Credit Decisions," *Credit and Financial Management.* August 1974, pp. 112–6.
Connolly, Hugh J. "So You Want to Increase Collections," *Credit and Financial Management.* September 1974, pp. 8–12.
Schiller, Glen. "How to Sharpen Your Credit and Collection Efforts," *Credit and Financial Management.* September 1974, pp. 19–23.
"Fair Credit Reporting Act," *Business Week.* December 7, 1974, p. 97.
"The Telephone as a Collection Tool," *Credit and Financial Management.* January 1975, p. 27.
"More About NACIS," *Credit and Financial Management.* April 1975, p. 14.
"Fair Credit Billing Act," *Merchandising Week.* October 20, 1975, p. 3

Index